AQA GCSE GERMAN
Higher

Mariela Affum
Heather Murphy
David Riddell

OXFORD
UNIVERSITY PRESS

OXFORD
UNIVERSITY PRESS

Great Clarendon Street, Oxford, OX2 6DP, United Kingdom

Oxford University Press is a department of the University of Oxford.
It furthers the University's objective of excellence in research, scholarship,
and education by publishing worldwide. Oxford is a registered trade mark
of Oxford University Press in the UK and in
certain other countries.

© Oxford University Press 2024

The moral rights of the authors have been asserted

First published in 2024

All rights reserved. No part of this publication may be reproduced, stored
in a retrieval system, or transmitted, in any form or by any means, without
the prior permission in writing of Oxford University Press, or as expressly
permitted by law, by licence or under terms agreed with the appropriate
reprographics rights organization. Enquiries concerning reproduction
outside the scope of the above should be sent to the Rights Department,
Oxford University Press, at the address above.

You must not circulate this work in any other form and you must impose
this same condition on any acquirer

British Library Cataloguing in Publication Data
Data available

978-1-38-204589-6

978-1-38-204590-2 (ebook)

10 9 8 7 6 5 4 3 2 1

The manufacturing process conforms to the environmental regulations of
the country of origin.

Printed in Great Britain by Bell and Bain Ltd., Glasgow

Acknowledgements
The publisher and authors would like to thank the following for permission to use photographs and other copyright material:

Cover artwork by Sua Balac

Artworks by Javier Joaquin, Martyn Cain, Andrew Painter and Sua Balac

Photos: **p14**: BearFotos / Shutterstock; **p14**: TunedIn by Westend61 / Shutterstock; **p16 (background)**: Maria Zvonkova / Shutterstock; **p17 (a)**: muse studio / Shutterstock; **p17 (b)**: bernatets photo / Shutterstock; **p17 (c)**: Ground Picture / Shutterstock; **p17 (d)**: Prostock-studio / Shutterstock; **p17 (e)**: Rawpixel.com / Shutterstock; **p18 (l)**: Westend61 on Offset / Shutterstock; **p18 (r)**: Ground Picture / Shutterstock; **p19**: pixelheadphoto digitalskillet / Shutterstock; **p20 (r)**: SeventyFour / Shutterstock; **p20 (background)**: Gorbash Varvara / Shutterstock; **p20 (l)**: Lopolo / Shutterstock; **p22 (a-f)**: Lena Berezkina / Shutterstock; **p22 (1)**: PeopleImages.com - Yuri A / Shutterstock; **p22 (2)**: Monkey Business Images / Shutterstock; **p22 (3)**: Lopolo / Shutterstock; **p22 (4)**: Zamrznuti tonovi / Shutterstock; **p22 (5)**: Rachata Teyparsit / Shutterstock; **p22 (6)**: Wavebreak Media / Shutterstock; **p24 (tl)**: Nuva Frames / Shutterstock; **p24 (tr)**: VH-studio / Shutterstock; **p24 (bl)**: New Africa / Shutterstock; **p24 (br)**: William Perugini / Shutterstock; **p24 (background)**: 1527529412 / Shutterstock; **p26 (tl)**: Monkey Business Images / Shutterstock; **p26 (tr)**: ya_blue_ko / Shutterstock; **p26 (br)**: Irina Strelnikova / Shutterstock; **p27**: © FAO 2010 Food-based dietary guidelines - Austria; **p28**: Alexander_Safonov / Shutterstock; **p28 (background)**: Nik Merkulov / Shutterstock; **p29 (tr)**: New Africa / Shutterstock; **p29 (bl)**: Drazen_ / Getty; **p30 (l)**: Pixel-Shot / Shutterstock; **p30 (r)**: Monkey Business Images / Shutterstock; **p32 (tl)**: Perfect Angle Images / Shutterstock; **p32 (ml)**: HuHu / Shutterstock; **p32 (mr)**: Benvenuto Cellini / Shutterstock; **p32 (br)**: FixiPixi_Design_Studio / Shutterstock; **p32 (background)**: Daria Kubrak / Shutterstock; **p34**: Monkey Business Images / Shutterstock; **p37 (l)**: Juice Flair / Shutterstock; **p37 (r)**: Monkey Business Images / Shutterstock; **p38**: BearFotos / Shutterstock; **p39**: kckate16 / Shutterstock; **p40 (tl)**: Daniel Hozs / Shutterstock; **p40 (tr)**: VH-studio / Shutterstock; **p40 (bl)**: Jazzmany / Shutterstock; **p40 (br)**: NeonShot / Shutterstock; **p42 (t)**: katatonia82 / Shutterstock; **p42 (b)**: Vitalii Vitleo / Shutterstock; **p42 (banner)**: Andrey_Popov / Shutterstock; **p42-p43 (background)**: BTC Studio / Shutterstock; **p43 (l)**: Binder Medienagentur / Shutterstock; **p43 (m)**: Eileen Kumpf / Shutterstock; **p43 (r)**: Klaus Brauner / Shutterstock; **p55 (t)**: LStockStudio / Shutterstock; **p55 (b)**: Monkey Business Images / Shutterstock; **p57 (background)**: sobakapavlova / Shutterstock; **p58**: Monkey Business Images / Shutterstock; **p59**: Tatjana Baibakova / Shutterstock; **p60 (t)**: POP-THAILAND / Shutterstock; **p60 (m)**: SeventyFour / Shutterstock; **p60 (b)**: bbernard / Shutterstock; **p60 (banner)**: mapman / Shutterstock; **p61 (a)**: BRO.vector / Shutterstock; **p61 (b)**: vectorlab2D / Shutterstock; **p61 (c)**: Nicoleta Ionescu / Shutterstock; **p62**: zabanski / Shutterstock; **p63 (l)**: Anton Watman / Shutterstock; **p63 (r)**: evafrey / Shutterstock; **p63 (m)**: Veres Production / Shutterstock; **p64 (l)**: PeopleImages.com - Yuri A / Shutterstock; **p64 (r)**: Rawpixel.com / Shutterstock; **p65**: Nejron Photo / Shutterstock; **p66 (a)**: Strahil Dimitrov / Shutterstock; **p66 (b)**: Rich Carey / Shutterstock; **p66 (c)**: Jag_cz / Shutterstock; **p66 (d)**: Inga Gedrovicha / Shutterstock; **p66 (e)**: Photo Volcano / Shutterstock; **p66 (f)**: PRIYA DARSHAN / Shutterstock; **p66 (g)**: areporter / Shutterstock; **p68 (t)**: Krakenimages.com / Shutterstock; **p68 (m)**: SpeedKingz / Shutterstock; **p68 (b)**: Max Topchii / Shutterstock; **p70 (t)**: United Archives GmbH / Alamy Stock Photo; **p70 (tm)**: Usa-Pyon / Shutterstock; **p70 (bm)**: chingyunsong / Shutterstock; **p70 (b)**: Denis Makarenko / Shutterstock; **p72 (l)**: Krakenimages.com / Shutterstock; **p72 (m)**: Asia Images Group / Shutterstock; **p72 (r)**: DisobeyArt / Shutterstock; **p72 (icons)**: a Sk / Shutterstock; **p72 (background)**: Jan Engel / Shutterstock; **p73**: Romas_Photo / Shutterstock; **p74**: Boris Stroujko / Shutterstock; **p74 (background)**: Lenka_X / Shutterstock; **p76**: FooTToo / Shutterstock; **p77**: Kinek00 / Shutterstock; **p78**: Marquess789 / Shutterstock; **p79**: Sunshine Seeds / Shutterstock; **p80 (l)**: TonelloPhotography / Shutterstock; **p80 (r)**: Eugene Robert Richee / Contributor / Getty; **p82**: 360b / Shutterstock; **p83**: Featureflash Photo Agency / Shutterstock; **p84**: berlinpictures16 / Shutterstock; **p85**: Toru Hanai / Stringer / Getty; **p86**: Stanislav Kachyna / Shutterstock; **p87**: KOTOIMAGES / Shutterstock; **p88 (br)**: Antoine Flament / Contributor / Getty; **p88 (tr)**: Abdul Razak Latif / Shutterstock; **p88 (bl)**: Peter Bischoff / Stringer / Getty; **p88 (tl)**: Alex Davidson / Stringer / Getty; **p88-p89 (background)**: alevtina / Shutterstock; **p89 (banner)**: Wirestock Creators / Shutterstock; **p89 (t)**: Andreas Rentz / Staff / Getty; **p89 (b)**: lev radin / Shutterstock; **p101 (t)**: Sergey Novikov / Shutterstock; **p101 (b)**: IVASHstudio / Shutterstock; **p104**: Monkey Business Images / Shutterstock; **p105**: digitalskillet / Shutterstock; **p106 (banner)**: BublikHaus / Shutterstock; **p108 (a)**: AlessandroBiascioli / Shutterstock; **p108 (b)**: dotshock / Shutterstock; **p108 (c)**: stock35 / Shutterstock; **p108 (d)**: Folenial / Shutterstock; **p108 (e)**: VH-studio / Shutterstock; **p108 (f)**: karelnoppe / Shutterstock; **p108 (g)**: Mo Photography Berlin / Shutterstock; **p108 (h)**: svsumin / Shutterstock; **p108 (i)**: Firn / Shutterstock; **p108 (j)**: orinocoArt / Shutterstock; **p108 (k)**: Cavan-Images / Shutterstock; **p108 (l)**: Sorbis / Shutterstock; **p109 (tl)**: Artur Wagner / Shutterstock; **p109 (tm)**: anweber / Shutterstock; **p109 (tr)**: FooTToo / Shutterstock; **p109 (bl)**: anweber / Shutterstock; **p109 (bm)**: imageBROKER.com / Shutterstock; **p109 (br)**: Sam Coultrip / Shutterstock; **p110 (tl)**: Imgorthand / Getty; **p110 (tr)**: Stephen Lux / Getty; **p110 (bl)**: Ian Francis / Shutterstock; **p110 (br)**: Ron Karpel / Shutterstock; **p112 (t)**: ddisq / Shutterstock; **p112 (b)**: Dallas and John Heaton / Getty; **p113**: DavideAngelini / Shutterstock; **p114**: moreimages / Shutterstock; **p115**: PhotoRoman / Shutterstock; **p116 (a)**: photoRia / Shutterstock; **p116 (b)**: MikeDotta / Shutterstock; **p116 (c)**: trabantos / Shutterstock; **p116 (d)**: LStockStudio / Shutterstock; **p118 (l)**: Dejan Dundjerski / Shutterstock; **p118 (r)**: Ground Picture / Shutterstock; **p120 (r)**: Monkey Business Images / Shutterstock; **p120 (l)**: Billion Photos / Shutterstock; **p121**: BublikHaus / Shutterstock; **p124 (l)**: Andrey_Popov / Shutterstock; **p124 (r)**: VAKS-Stock Agency / Shutterstock; **p126 (tl)**: Russ Heinl / Shutterstock; **p126 (tm)**: MOHAMED ABDULRAHEEM / Shutterstock; **p126(tr)**: Morakot Kawinchan / Shutterstock; **p126 (bl)**: Rawpixel.com / Shutterstock; **p126 (bm)**: Alessandro28 / Shutterstock; **p126 (br)**: smereka / Shutterstock; **p127**: Maskot / Getty; **p128 (l)**: Westend61 / Getty; **p128 (tr)**: petrmalinak / Shutterstock; **p128 (br)**: smereka / Shutterstock; **p130 (t)**: Monkey Business Images / Shutterstock; **p130 (m)**: zhukovvvlad / Shutterstock; **p130 (b)**: Dimedrol68 / Shutterstock; **p131**: Boris Stroujko / Shutterstock; **p132**: Jazzmany / Shutterstock; **p133 (l)**: Edrich / Shutterstock; **p133 (r)**: 123RF; **p134 (banner)**: Funtap / Shutterstock; **p147 (t)**: Blue Images / Getty; **p147 (b)**: CandyBox Images / Shutterstock; **p148**: WarmWorld / Shutterstock; **p150**: GaudiLab / Shutterstock; **p151**: Rasto SK / Shutterstock; **p134 (a)**: Pashu Ta Studio / Shutterstock; **p134 (b)**: Dmitry Eagle Orlov / Shutterstock; **p134 (c)**: New Africa / Shutterstock; **p134 (d)**: adamwilbert / Shutterstock; **p134 (e)**: I. Noyan Yilmaz / Shutterstock; **p135**: Everett Collection / Shutterstock; **p155 (t)**: Lucky Business / Shutterstock; **p155 (b)**: Ground Picture / Shutterstock; **p158**: icemanphotos / Shutterstock; **p159**: Brian A Jackson / Shutterstock;

This textbook has been approved by AQA for use with our qualification. This means that we have checked that it broadly covers the specification and we are satisfied with the overall quality. Full details of our approval process can be found on our website.

We approve textbooks because we know how important it is for teachers and students to have the right resources to support their teaching and learning. However, the publisher is ultimately responsible for the editorial control and quality of this book.

Please note that when teaching the AQA GCSE German course, you must refer to AQA's specification as your definitive source of information. While this book has been written to match the specification, it cannot provide complete coverage of every aspect of the course.

A wide range of other useful resources can be found on the relevant subject pages of our website: aqa.org.uk

Contents

Introduction	7–9
Useful language	10–11
Sound-spelling links	12–13

Theme 1 People and lifestyle — 14

Introduction: Identity and relationships with others	14
Introduction: Healthy living and lifestyle	15
Introduction: Education and work	16

Unit 1 – Identity and relationships with others — 18

Spread title	Verb focus	Grammar focus	Pronunciation focus	Page
1.1F Familie und Freunde	The present tense of weak and strong verbs; The present tense of *haben* and *sein*			18
1.1H Meine Leute und ich	Verbs used with *zu* plus infinitive	The gender of nouns	*-e* as final letter	20
1.2F Lebensweisen und Lebensbeziehungen	Reflexive verbs; Separable verbs	Reflexive pronouns	*-ig* at the end of a word	22
1.2H Wichtige Beziehungen	Reflexive verbs (revision)	Plural nouns		24

Unit 2 – Healthy living and lifestyle — 26

Spread title	Verb focus	Grammar focus	Pronunciation focus	Page
2.1F Wir essen gern!	The perfect tense with *haben*	Using *ein* and *kein*	*ei* and *ie*	26
2.1H Ein gesundes Leben	Using *seit* with the present tense	Articles and cases (nominative and accusative)		28
2.2F Glück und Gesundheit	The perfect tense with *haben* and *sein*	Possessive adjectives	*pf*	30
2.2H Pass gut auf dich!	The imperfect tense of *sein*	Using *sondern* to say 'but'	*sp* at the start of words	32

Unit 3 – Education and work — 34

Spread title	Verb focus	Grammar focus	Pronunciation focus	Page
3.1F Eine gute Ausbildung	The imperfect tense of *sein* and *haben*	The verb as second idea	*sch*	34
3.1H Nun heißt's lernen!	The imperfect tense of weak and strong verbs	Direct and indirect object pronouns		36

drei 3

Contents

3.2F Jetzt geht's an die Arbeit!	The perfect and imperfect tenses	Coordinating and subordinating conjunctions	*u* and *ü*	38
3.2H Ein schönes Stück Arbeit	Relative clauses in the nominative and accusative cases	Relative clauses in the nominative and accusative cases	*zw*	40

Kultur: Sport macht Spaß	42
Grammar practice	44
Vocabulary	48

Test and revise	Listening	52
	Speaking	54
	Reading	56
	Writing	58

Theme 2 Popular culture — 60

Introduction: Free time activities	60
Introduction: Customs, festivals and celebrations	62
Introduction: Celebrity culture	63

Unit 4 – Free time activities

Spread title	Verb focus	Grammar focus	Pronunciation focus	Page
4.1F Sportstars der Zukunft	The future tense with *werden*	Using *gern* and *lieber*	*w*	64
4.1H Extremsportarten für alle	The present tense of *wissen*	Using *bei/am* + infinitives as nouns		66
4.2F Auf geht's zum Konzert!	*mögen* and *wollen*	Question words	*o* and *ö*	68
4.2H Filme, die man sehen muss	Using *ich möchte* to say what you would like	Using the demonstrative adjective *dies-*		70

Unit 5 – Customs, festivals and celebrations

Spread title	Verb focus	Grammar focus	Pronunciation focus	Page
5.1F Alles Gute zum Geburtstag!	The modal verbs *dürfen, können, mögen* and *wollen*	Word order: time, manner, place	Long and short vowels	72
5.1H Weihnachtszeit in Deutschland	Revising modal verbs	Revising subordinate clauses		74
5.2F Schöne und seltsame Traditionen	The modal verbs *sollen* and *müssen*	The negatives *nicht* and *nie*	Two-vowel combinations (diphthongs)	76

vier

Contents

5.2H Wenn ich reich wäre …	Conditional clauses	The genitive case for possession		78

Unit 6 – Celebrity culture				34
Spread title	Verb focus	Grammar focus	Pronunciation focus	Page
6.1F Alt und cool	Revising the perfect tense	Adjective endings in the nominative and accusative cases		80
6.1H Berühmt und beliebt?	Different ways to use *werden*	Adjectival nouns after *viel*, *etwas*, *nichts* and *alles*	*w* and *v*	82
6.2F Superstars	Modal verbs in the imperfect tense (singular forms)	Checking adjective endings		84
6.2H Es ist nicht alles Gold was glänzt	Modal verbs in the imperfect tense (all forms)	Dative reflexive pronouns		86

Kultur: Mehrsprachig und berühmt	88
Grammar practice	90
Vocabulary	94

Test and revise	Listening	98
	Speaking	100
	Reading	102
	Writing	104

Theme 3 Communication and the world around us	106
Introduction: Travel and tourism	106
Introduction: Media and technology	107
Introduction: The environment an d where people live	108

Unit 7 – Travel and tourism, including places of interest				
Spread title	Verb focus	Grammar focus	Pronunciation focus	Page
7.1F Was machst du gern in Urlaub?	Revising the perfect and imperfect tenses	Indefinite pronouns (*jemand* and *niemand*)	*b*, *d* and *g*	110
7.1H Was hast du in den Ferien gemacht?	Using *es gibt* and *es gab*	Plural indirect object pronouns	*er*	112
7.2F Was kann man hier machen?	Using verbal nouns	Singular indirect object pronouns	Hard and soft *ch*	114
7.2H Reiseziele, die wir lieben	Avoiding using the passive	Revising relative pronouns		116

fünf

Contents

Unit 8 – Media and technology

Spread title	Verb focus	Grammar focus	Pronunciation focus	Page
8.1F Soziale Medien – toll oder?	Revising the perfect tense of separable and reflexive verbs	Using *als* and so … *wie*	*s* before a vowel	118
8.1H Eine Welt ohne Medien? Unmöglich!		Revising dative reflexive pronouns; Using superlative adjectives		120
8.2F Wir streamen Sendungen		Prepositions followed by the accusative case; Prepositions followed by the dative case	The letter *e*	122
8.2H Hier kommt die Zukunft	Revising past, present and future tenses	Prepositions followed by the dative or accusative		124

Unit 9 – The environment and where people live

Spread title	Verb focus	Grammar focus	Pronunciation focus	Page
9.1F Was sollte man machen?	Revising modal verbs	Indefinite adjectives	*st* and *sp* at	126
9.1H Unsere Umwelt	Using *ohne / statt … zu …*	Using 'it'/'them' and 'what' with prepositions	*tio*	128
9.2F Wie ist deine Gegend?	Using the correct tense	Revising adjective endings	*au* and *äu*	130
9.2H Wie kann man die Gegend verbessern?	The imperative	Using the genitive after some prepositions		132

Kultur: Erfinder, Erforscher und Entdecker		134
Grammar practice		136
Vocabulary		140
Test and revise	Listening	144
	Speaking	146
	Reading	148
	Writing	150
Test and revise: All themes	Listening	152
	Speaking	154
	Reading	156
	Writing	158
Reference	Grammar	160
	Verb tables	178
	Glossary	181

Introducing AQA GCSE German

| Learning vocabulary | Sound–spelling links | Translation skills | Writing | Reading & reading aloud |

| Dictation | Speaking | Culture | Grammar knowledge | Listening |

Understanding how the specification works

The AQA GCSE German specification is divided into three main subject areas, called Themes. This book is divided up in the same way, with colour-coding to help you know where you are.

Theme 1 People and lifestyle

Theme 2 Popular culture

Theme 3 Communication and the world around us

Each Theme is divided into three Topics, making a total of nine Topics to study during the course. The exam is divided up according to the four Language Skills: Listening, Speaking, Reading and Writing. Each one of these has its own separate exam, in the form of an end-of-course paper.

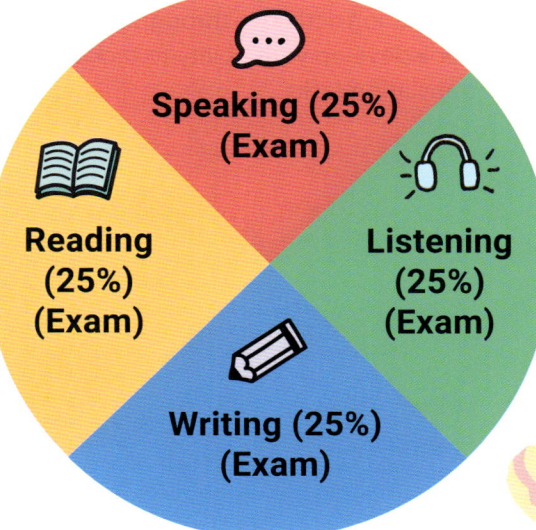

sieben 7

Introduction

Useful language
The section on pages 10-11 provides useful key vocabulary and phrases which are commonly used in real-life everyday situations.

 Phonics and sound-spelling links

- The section on pages 12-13 groups together all the sounds included in the *Aussprache* boxes and provides tips on how to pronounce widely used words and phrases *to* speak German confidently and clearly. Your knowledge of how spelling represents sounds will be tested through **dictation and a read-aloud task in the exam.**
- The Aussprache boxes cover all the common sounds in the German language and the sound-spelling links included in the specification, and include pronunciation tips.

> **Aussprache**
>
> **The *sp* sound t the start of words**
>
> *sp* at the start of German words such as **sp***ielen* and **Sp***ort* sounds like 'shp'.

Themes and topics
Each Theme is divided into three topics. Each Theme starts with two introductory double-page spreads introducing key themes, core vocabulary and structures that you may have covered at Key Stage 3. These pages provide an opportunity to recap and practise important language and/or lay the foundations for further learning.

The three topics are then each covered over four double-page spreads, two at Higher level and two at Foundation level. Each spread introduces specification vocabulary and features a verb focus and a grammar focus. All the key skills required in the specification are also covered, including phonics and cultural knowledge.

Learning vocabulary
Vocabulary support is provided in various ways throughout the book and on Kerboodle:

- Vocabulary lists – the introductory double-page spreads at the start of each Theme include lists of key words and phrases practised in the texts and on the page. Vocabulary from each of the core spreads and the culture pages is listed in the vocabulary pages at the end of each Theme. Items highlighted in grey are words that are useful but do not appear in the specification. It is important that you learn the specification vocabulary.
- Vocabulary tasks – these help to build the vocabulary required in each topic of the specification.
- Interactive activities – the vocabulary builder on Kerboodle provides activities with instant feedback.*
- Glossary – the glossary at the back of the book combines the vocabulary from the Themes' vocabulary pages.

Features

Reading
The Student Book contains plenty of German reading material on the themes and topics included within the specification. The activities that follow the reading passages help develop your comprehension skills so that you can access unfamiliar texts in the future.

Listening
Activities with a listening icon next to them help you to improve listening comprehension skills. The audio can be accessed through Kerboodle.

Speaking
The speaking activities are designed to build your confidence in speaking German and to practise using the vocabulary you've learned in the unit or theme. There are also practice role plays and photo card activities throughout the book.

Writing
The writing icon indicates an activity that will help you to use the language you've learned to build sentences and paragraphs of written German.

Translation
Translation activities throughout the book develop your ability to tackle translation tasks.

Introduction

Language support in speaking and writing

Examples of language to be used or language structure boxes are provided for some speaking and writing tasks. These can be used as models to build your own sentences.

Ich finde die Schule	toll / langweilig / interessant / cool / furchtbar.		
Der Schultag ist			
Mein Lieblingsfach ist	Deutsch / Sport / Mathe / Physik,	weil	ich Lesen liebe. ich gute Noten bekomme. die Stunden so interessant sind.
Gestern hatte ich	Englisch / Kunst / Geschichte.	Das war	toll / interessant / lustig.

7 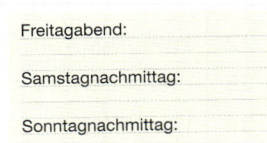 Working in groups of three or four, make arrangements to meet over the weekend.
- Hast du am Freitagabend Zeit?
- Ja, ich habe Zeit. / Nein, ich habe keine Zeit.
- Möchtest du in die Disco gehen?
- Ja, wann treffen wir uns? / Nein, danke.

Freitagabend:

Samstagnachmittag:

Sonntagnachmittag:

Building grammar knowledge

- Understanding grammar is key to understanding German and building your own phrases. AQA GCSE German helps you to consolidate and deepen your grammar knowledge in a logical way with no assumption of prior learning.
- Grammar boxes outline key grammar points, with accompanying activities on the same page to put theory into practice.

> **Grammatik**
>
> **Using the accusative case**
> You use the accusative case after *in* when you are going into or towards a place:

- Additional grammar practice is also provided in two double-page spreads at the end of each Theme.
- Interactive activities on Kerboodle provide further consolidation with instant feedback.*
- There is a grammar section at the back of the Student Book to refer to whenever you need to.

Verbs

Specific emphasis is given to the formation of verbs and tenses, and how they are used.

> **Verben**
>
> **Using weak (regular) verbs in the present tense**
> Many verbs in German follow a regular pattern in the present tense. The stem (the infinitive minus *-en*) remains

🌐 Culture

- Culture boxes throughout the book highlight aspects of culture from the German-speaking world relevant to each topic.

> **Kultur**
>
> The Berlinale is the international film festival which takes place every year in

- There is a Culture double-page spread at the end of each Theme showcasing aspects of history, literature and contemporary culture from the German-speaking world.

Language tips

These boxes give extra support and information about what to look out for or how to do a particular activity.

> **Tipp** ❗
>
> Remember that you will get to listen to each extract twice. Don't panic about getting the

Test and Revise

There are regular revision and practice opportunities throughout the book in the four test and revise sections (one test per theme and a cross-theme test at the end of the book). Each test offers exam-style activities in the four skill areas.

Kerboodle

Kerboodle for AQA GCSE German includes resources focused on developing key grammar, vocabulary, phonics, and all the language learning and exam skills required at GCSE. These resources include auto-marked interactive activities and tests, worksheets, listening activities with downloadable transcripts, practice questions and assessments, and comprehensive teacher support.

Interactive activities can be completed on tablets or mobile devices.

Kerboodle Books

Kerboodle Books are digital versions of the Student books which can be accessed on a range of devices and tablets.

Activities and audio can be launched directly from the page and individual users have their own digital notebook for use within their Kerboodle Book, where they can use various tools and annotate pages to create their own personalised copy.

*These resources are not part of the AQA approval process.

neun

Useful language

Numbers

Numbers are very logical in German, and it's best to revise them in three stages.

- **Stage 1:** the numbers 1–12, which you should just learn if you haven't done so already.

1	*eins*	4	*vier*	7	*sieben*	10	*zehn*
2	*zwei*	5	*fünf*	8	*acht*	11	*elf*
3	*drei*	6	*sechs*	9	*neun*	12	*zwölf*

- **Stage 2:** Once you have mastered these basics, the rest is easy and is done by **combining** what you already know. So 13 = 3+10 > *dreizehn*. The other numbers up to 19 follow this pattern:

14	*vierzehn*	16	*sechzehn*	18	*achtzehn*
15	*fünfzehn*	17	*siebzehn*	19	*neunzehn*

Though note that with *sechzehn*, the *s* from *sechs* and with *siebzehn*, the *en* from *sieben* have been dropped.

The combining process continues throughout the formation of German numbers. Remember the nursery rhyme about 'four and twenty blackbirds', as this will remind you that the combining happens the opposite way round from in English. The units and tens are joined by **und** and numbers are written as **one word**.

21	*ein**und**zwanzig*	26	*sechs**und**zwanzig*
22	*zwei**und**zwanzig*	27	*sieben**und**zwanzig*
23	*drei**und**zwanzig*	28	*acht**und**zwanzig*
24	*vier**und**zwanzig*	29	*neun**und**zwanzig*
25	*fünf**und**zwanzig*		

- **Stage 3:** After this, you only need to know the tens numbers to make any number you need up to 100, and beyond. For example, *einundzwanzig* (21), *vierhundertneunundneuzig* (499). The 'ein' often gets dropped after 100 and 1000 e.g. 121 can be *einhunderteinundzwanzig* or just *hunderteinundzwanzig*.

30	*dreißig*	60	*sechzig*	90	*neunzig*
40	*vierzig*	70	*siebzig*	100	*hundert*
50	*fünfzig*	80	*achtzig*		

Days and dates

- Remember the days of the week:

Montag	Monday	*Freitag*	Friday
Dienstag	Tuesday	*Samstag*	Saturday
Mittwoch	Wednesday	*Sonntag*	Sunday
Donnerstag	Thursday		

- And the months of the year:

Januar	January	*August*	August
Februar	February	*September*	September
März	March	*Oktober*	October
April	April	*November*	November
Mai	May	*Dezember*	December
Juni	June		
Juli	July		

- Days and months are all masculine nouns and are always written with a capital letter.
- To say dates, you need also to adapt the basic numbers to say 2nd / 6th / 28th etc. The way to do this is, for numbers up to and including 19 to add *-te* to the end of the number (*der elfte Januar / der sechste Juni*) and for numbers from 20 onwards add *-ste* to the end of the number (*der achtundzwanzigste September, der dreißigste März*). When we write a date in German with digits, we add a full stop, eg. *der 4. März*.
- Note that there are a couple of important exceptions *erste* (first), *dritte* (third) and *siebte* (seventh).
- To say **on a particular day**, for example to say your birthday, you need to use *am* (on the) and add an *-n* to the end of the number: *Ich habe am vierten März Geburtstag.*

10 zehn

Useful language

Time

To say what time it is, start with *Es ist …*

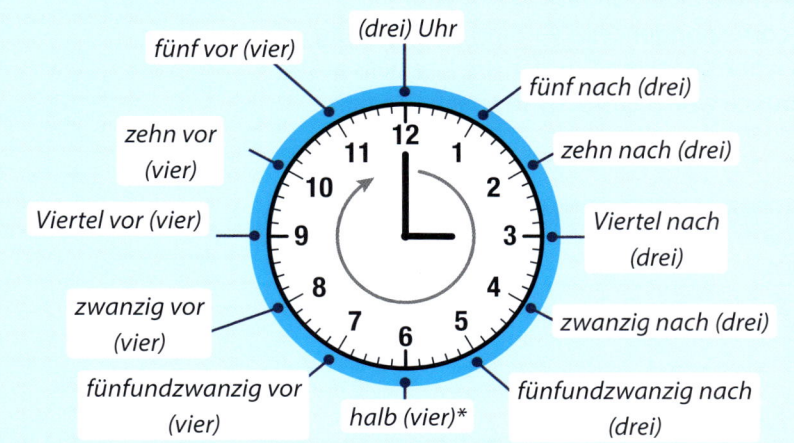

*Es ist **halb vier*** means 'it's half three', not 'it's half four' – the *halb* indicates **half to the hour**, not half past.

To say at what time something happens, you use *um* followed by the above.

Um *halb neun gehe ich in die Schule.*   I go to school at half past eight.

Intensifiers

besonders	especially
echt	truly, really
ein bisschen	a little
ganz	completely
gar nicht	not at all
mega (e.g. mega wichtig)	super (e.g. super important)
nicht so	not very
sehr	very
voll	totally
völlig	completely
ziemlich	quite
bestimmt	certainly, definitely
zu	too

Conjunctions

Coordinating (word order remains the same)

und	and
aber	but
denn	because
oder	or

Subordinating (main verb is sent to the end of the clause)

weil	because
da	because, since
obwohl	although
wenn	if

Adverbs of frequency

nie	never
selten	rarely
ab und zu	now and then
manchmal	sometimes
oft	often
immer	always
normalerweise	normally
meistens	mostly

Interrogatives

Was?	What?
Wann?	When?
Wie?	How?
Wer?	Who?
Wo?	Where?
Wohin?	Where to?
Woher?	Where from?
Warum?	Why?

Greetings and ages

Hallo!	Hello!	Gut, danke.	Good, thank you.
Guten Tag!	Good day!	Tschüss!	Bye!
Guten Morgen!	Good morning!	Auf Wiedersehen!	Goodbye!
Guten Abend!	Good evening!	Bis bald!	Bye! Til later!
Grüß Gott!	Good day! (southern Germany and Austria)	Wie alt bist du?	How old are you?
		Ich bin … Jahre alt.	I'm … years old.
Wie geht's?	How are you?		

elf

Sound–spelling links

The new GCSE Exams involve a reading aloud task and a dictation task to test your knowledge and understanding of sound-symbol correspondences. Learning how spelling represents sounds and using clear pronunciation when speaking German are key skills at GCSE. It is important that you know how to pronounce words correctly to speak German confidently.

Sound	Example	Page
s and ß	hei**ß**t, gro**ß**, ha**s**t, Mau**s**	19
-e as final letter	Haar**e**, Jahr**e**, Klass**e**, Spiel**e**	21, 123
-ig at the end of a word	langweil**ig**, witz**ig**	23
ei and ie	k**ei**n, **Ei**, Fl**ei**sch St**ie**fvater, schw**ie**rig, B**ie**r	27
pf	A**pf**el, Rheinland-**Pf**alz, em**pf**ehlen	31
sp at the start of words	**Sp**ort, **sp**ielen, **Sp**anien	33, 127
sch	**Sch**ule, Deut**sch**, Franz**ö**si**sch**	35
u and ü	Sch**u**le, B**u**ch Sch**ü**ler, B**ü**ro, Gl**ü**ck	39
zw	**zw**ei, in**zw**ischen, **zw**ölf	40
w	**w**er, **w**ird, **w**erden	65, 83
o and ö	w**o**llen, K**o**nzert m**ö**gen	69
long and short a	Sp**a**ß St**a**dt	73
long and short e	R**e**gen T**e**nnis	73, 123
long and short i	Sp**i**elen W**i**nd	73
long and short o	gefl**o**gen t**o**ll	73
long and short u	g**u**t Wohn**u**ng	73
Two-vowel combinations (diphthongs)	**Eu**le, B**eu**le gl**au**ben, **au**a	77
w and v	**w**underbar, **w**ill, **w**irklich **v**iele, **V**orbild, **v**erdienen, **V**ater	83
b, d and g at the start and end of words	**b**is, **g**ern, **d**as gi**b**, Monta**g**, Aben**d**	111
er	B**er**lin, v**er**bringen Brud**er** **er**ster	112
Hard and soft ch	dana**ch**, ko**ch**en spre**ch**en, Mil**ch**	114

Sound-spelling links

s before a vowel	**S**ommer, **s**ozial, **S**onne le**s**en, Kä**s**e, bö**s**e	119
st and *sp* at the start and middle of words	**St**adt, **sp**ielen Haupt**st**adt, Fußball**sp**iel	127
tio	Organisa**tio**n, funk**tio**nieren, Informa**tio**nen	129
au and *äu*	B**au**m B**äu**me	131

Aussprache

Umlauts

Umlauts – two dots over a vowel – change the sound of the vowel. The word roughly translates as around (*um*) sound (*Laut*).

ä is pronounced in a similar way to the English 'e' as in 'get' and 'set': der K**ä**se, die M**ä**nner

ö is is similar to the English 'er' in 'her': m**ö**chten, k**ö**nnen.

ü, as in gr**ü**n or d**ü**rfen, is similar to the English 'ew' sound as in 'chew'.

äu, as in B**äu**me or Geb**äu**de, is similar to the English 'oi' in 'boiling'.

Aussprache

ie and *ei*

The *ie* and *ei* sounds in German are often confused.
ie sounds like the English 'e': B**ie**r, v**ie**l, sp**ie**len
ei sounds like the English 'i': Fr**ei**heit, m**ein**, **Ei**er

Aussprache

s and *ß*

The letter *ß* is unique to the German alphabet.

It is always pronounced as an English 's', such as in seal or self.

Remember how German spelling behaves for this sound:

ss after a short vowel: das Schl**oss**

ß after a long vowel and the letter combination *ei*: gr**oß**, w**eiß**

Tip box

Reading aloud in German poses challenges when you come across new words, or sometimes words just come out wrong when you read them off the page!

- Try to read and understand the sentence before you start.
- Work with a partner and seek their advice once you have finished.
- Practise reading aloud regularly.
- Record yourself and listen to it with a critical ear!

Tip box

Intonation

To sound as fluent as possible in German, it is important to think not just about *what* you say, but also *how* you say it. You also need to think about 'stress' (where the emphasis is placed within words); 'rhythm' (the beat and flow of the language in sentences) and 'pitch' (varying the tone of your language). Listen to as much authentic German as possible and imitate as best as you can!

dreizehn

Theme 1
People and lifestyle

Identity and relationships with others

1 📖 You receive an introductory email from your new Austrian friend. Answer the questions in English.

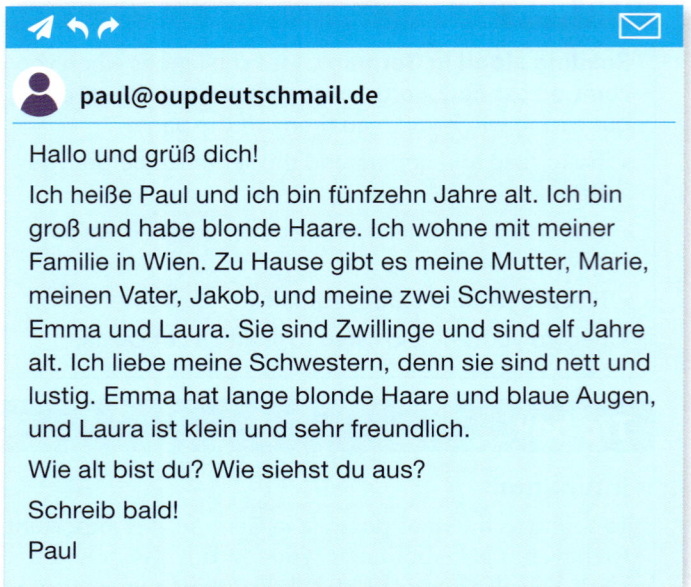

paul@oupdeutschmail.de

Hallo und grüß dich!

Ich heiße Paul und ich bin fünfzehn Jahre alt. Ich bin groß und habe blonde Haare. Ich wohne mit meiner Familie in Wien. Zu Hause gibt es meine Mutter, Marie, meinen Vater, Jakob, und meine zwei Schwestern, Emma und Laura. Sie sind Zwillinge und sind elf Jahre alt. Ich liebe meine Schwestern, denn sie sind nett und lustig. Emma hat lange blonde Haare und blaue Augen, und Laura ist klein und sehr freundlich.

Wie alt bist du? Wie siehst du aus?

Schreib bald!

Paul

a What does Paul look like? (two details)
b Who is Marie?
c How old are Paul's sisters?
d What does Paul like about his sisters? (two details)
e What does Emma look like? (two details)
f How does Paul describe Laura? (two details)

groß	tall
Haare (pl)	hair
Zwillinge (pl)	twins
nett	nice
lustig	funny
lang	long
Augen (pl)	eyes
klein	small

2 📖 Your German friend, Liesel, sends you this photo and description. Can you name each person in the photo?

Ich spiele gern Fußball mit meinen Freunden. Hier spiele ich mit meiner besten Freundin, Annika. Sie hat braune Haare und trägt eine Brille. Elias ist links und hat kurze braune Haare. David ist groß und sportlich.

spielen	to play
tragen	to wear
eine Brille	glasses
links	on the left

14 vierzehn

People and lifestyle   Theme 1

3 **Listen to six people (a–f) speaking about important relationships in their lives. Write down what the relationship is and then add two further pieces of information about the person they are describing.**

a Max
b Frieda
c Mehmet
d Leon
e Aysa
f Georg

der Sohn	son	der Onkel	uncle
die Tochter	daughter	Stief-	step-
der Mann	man, husband	verheiratet	married
die Frau	woman, wife	geschieden	divorced
die Schwester	sister	ruhig	calm, quiet
der Bruder	brother	alt	old
der Opa	grandpa	älter als	older than
die Oma	grandma	jung	young
die Tante	aunt	jünger als	younger than

4 **Listen to six people (a–f) talking about family members and friends. Choose the correct word to complete each statement.**

a He has a lot in common with his ___ .
   1 brother   2 stepbrother   3 stepfather

b She doesn't get on well with her ___ .
   1 stepfather   2 grandfather   3 father

c She thinks her friend is ___ .
   1 funny   2 helpful   3 difficult

d He often finds his son ___ .
   1 annoying   2 lazy   3 impatient

e He admires his wife's ___ .
   1 calmness   2 patience   3 humour

f His ___ is always happy.
   1 girlfriend   2 uncle   3 friend

gemeinsam	in common
auskommen mit	to get on with
hilfsbereit	helpful
lieb	kind
die Beziehung	relationship
geduldig	patient
witzig	funny, witty

Healthy living and lifestyle

5 **Read the comments on an online forum about healthy lifestyles, then match each English statement below to the correct person.**

a I like exercise classes.
b I avoid drinking fizzy drinks.
c I love sweet foods.
d My fitness matters to me.
e I exercise regularly with one of my parents.

Selim Ich denke, ich lebe gesund. Ich trinke viel Wasser und keine Cola und ich gehe oft schwimmen.

Sarah Fußball ist meine Lieblingsaktivität. Es ist wichtig für mich, dass ich fit bleibe. Ich esse also viel Obst und Gemüse.

Laura Vielleicht esse ich zu gern Kuchen und Kekse. Das schmeckt so gut! Aber ich gehe jede Woche ins Fitness-Studio und mache gern Tanzstunden.

Melissa Zu Hause essen wir gesund. Ich gehe jeden Tag mit meiner Mutter joggen und ich spiele Basketball.

fünfzehn 15

Theme 1 — People and lifestyle

Education and work

6 🎧 Listen to the young people (a–f) talking about school subjects. Which subject (1–6) does each person mention?

7 🎧 Listen again and note **one** comment each person (a–f) makes about the subject.

Deutsch	German	Erdkunde	geography
Mathe	maths	die Welt	world
Noten (pl)	marks, grades	das Klima	climate
Musik	music	Kunst	art
das Klavier	piano	malen	to paint
die Geige	violin	Sport	sport, PE

8 📖 Read the messages between Eren and Alex, then answer the questions in English.

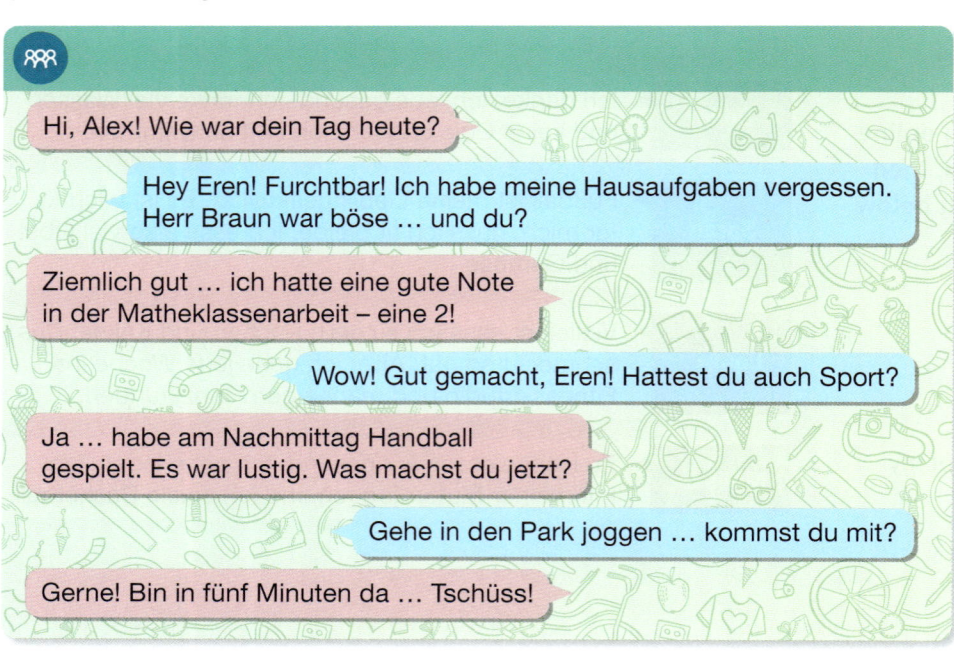

a How was Alex's day in school?
b Why?
c Why was Eren happy?
d What did Eren do in the afternoon?
e What do they plan to do now?

People and lifestyle — **Theme 1**

9 Listen to these young people (a–e) talking about their future plans. Choose the best job (1–5) for each person.

1

2

3

4

5

sich interessieren für	to be interested in
die Gesundheit	health
der Chef	boss
die Zukunft	future
der Roman	novel
die Natur	nature
im Freien	in the open air, outdoors

10 Now match these German jobs to the photos (1–5) from activity 9.

a Bauer / Bäuerin
b Autor / Autorin
c Kellner / Kellnerin
d Lehrer / Lehrerin
e Arzt / Ärztin

11 Read the comments about different jobs. Make a note of the job that each person mentions, as well as one positive aspect and one negative aspect.

Ella
Ich will nie Lehrerin werden. Das ist so eine harte Arbeit. Der Tag ist lang und ermüdend, auch wenn man schöne lange Ferien hat.

Manfred
Polizist ist ein guter Beruf für mich. Es kann gefährlich sein und ist nicht gut bezahlt, aber der Kontakt zu Menschen ist ein Vorteil.

Lisa
Meine Schwester ist Schauspielerin. Sie findet ihre Arbeit spannend und gut bezahlt, aber es ist schwierig, bekannt zu werden.

Rowan
Als Arzt oder Ärztin verdient man gut und macht eine wichtige Arbeit, denn man hilft anderen Menschen. Auf der anderen Seite ist das Studium sehr lang und man hat sehr lange Arbeitszeiten.

ermüdend	tiring
gefährlich	dangerous
Menschen (pl)	people
der Vorteil	advantage
spannend	exciting
schwierig	difficult
bekannt	famous
verdienen	to earn
Arbeitszeiten (pl)	working hours

siebzehn 17

1.1F Familie und Freunde

OBJECTIVES
- Talking about yourself, family and friends
- The present tense of *haben* and *sein*
- The present tense of weak and strong verbs
- Pronunciation: *s* and *ß*

1 📖 Match the German and English words for different family members.

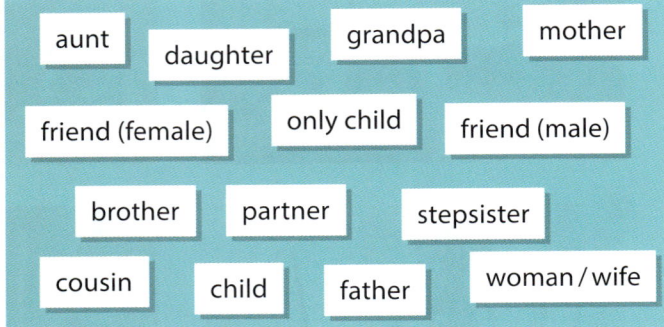

2 ⭐ Using the nouns from activity 1, make three lists: one for masculine nouns (*der / ein*), one for feminine nouns (*die / eine*) and one for neuter nouns (*das / ein*).

3 📖 Read what Leon and Kaya say about their family and friends, then decide whether the statements in English are true (T) or false (F).

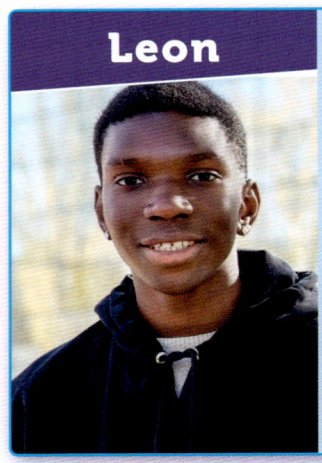

Leon: Mein Name ist Leon und ich bin sechzehn Jahre alt. Ich bin Einzelkind. Meine Eltern sind geschieden, und meine Mutter hat einen Partner, der Georg heißt. Ich habe auch einen Opa, aber ich sehe ihn nicht sehr oft. Mein bester Freund, Theo, ist auch sechzehn. Ich spiele manchmal mit ihm Tennis.

Kaya: Ich heiße Kaya und ich bin siebzehn. Ich wohne mit meinen Eltern und meinen drei Schwestern. Meine Oma wohnt auch bei uns. Ich habe eine nette Freundin, die Sofia heißt. Sie ist älter als ich. Ich spreche jeden Tag mit Sofia und ich fahre mit ihr zusammen im Bus zur Schule.

a Leon has no siblings.
b Leon's parents are divorced.
c Leon's father is called Georg.
d Leon often sees his grandfather.
e Theo and Leon are the same age.
f Kaya is younger than Leon.
g Kaya has four siblings.
h One of Kaya's grandparents lives with the family.
i Kaya is older than Sofia.
j Kaya and Sofia cycle to school.

4 📖 Read Leon and Kaya's texts again and note down the following phrases.

a not very often
b also
c sometimes
d with us / at our house
e older than

Kultur

There are over 8 million families in Germany, of which 5.5 million have married parents, around 2 million have a single parent, 900,000 have unmarried parents and around 8,000 have parents in a same-sex relationship.

Over 50% of families have just one child, 36% have two, 9% have three and only 2% have four children.

achtzehn

Identity and relationships with others 1.1F

5 🎧 **Listen to Lea, Ben and Hanna. Answer the questions in English.**
  a What siblings does Lea have?
  b Who is Oskar?
  c How old is Lea?
  d How old is Ben?
  e Who is Maya?
  f How old is Maya?
  g What does Ben like to do with friends?
  h Who does Hanna live with?
  i How does Hanna's aunt help her?
  j What does Hanna enjoy in her free time?

6 ✏️ **Choose the correct form of the verb to complete each sentence. They are all strong verbs!**
  a Ich **fahre / fährst / fährt** mit meiner Freundin zur Schule.
  b Mein bester Freund **spreche / sprichst / spricht** Deutsch.
  c Wie **fahre / fährst / fährt** du in die Stadt?
  d Meine Schwester **isst / esse / essen** kein Fleisch.
  e Was **trage / trägt / trägst** du heute?
  f Mein Freund **gebe / gibst / gibt** mir ein Buch.

7 ✏️ **Working with a partner, take turns to ask and answer the following questions.**
  • Wie ist deine Familie?
  • Hast du Geschwister?
  • Wie alt ist er / sie? / Wie alt sind sie?
  • Was machst du mit Freunden?
  • Wer ist dein bester Freund / deine beste Freundin?

8 ✏️ **Now write a paragraph (50 words) about yourself and the people who matter to you. Use your answers for activity 7 and the texts in activity 3 to help you.**

9 ✏️ **Copy and complete the following sentences with the correct form of the verb in brackets.**
  a Ich ___ einen Bruder. *(haben)*
  b Mein Bruder ___ sehr sportlich. *(sein)*
  c ___ du Geschwister? *(haben)*
  d Wir ___ zwei Katzen. Sie heißen Fritz und Franki und sie ___ niedlich. *(haben, sein)*
  e ___ du älter als deine Schwester? *(sein)*
  f Ich ___ Einzelkind. *(sein)*

Aussprache

s and ß
The letter ß is the equivalent of a double 's', and is pronounced like the 's' in *hast* or *Maus*:
hei**ß**t, gro**ß**

Verben

The present tense of weak and strong verbs

Weak verbs are regular in the way they are formed. The stem (e.g. *spielen* → *spiel-*, *wohnen* → *wohn-*) does not change:

ich spiel**e**	ich wohn**e**
du spiel**st**	du wohn**st**
er / sie / es spiel**t**	er / sie / es wohn**t**

Some strong verbs change their stem vowel in the second and third person singular (*du* and *er / sie* forms) in the present tense. The verb endings do not change:

fahren	*sprechen*
ich fahre	ich spreche
du f**ä**hrst	du spr**i**chst
er / sie / es f**ä**hrt	er / sie / es spr**i**cht

Plural forms are regular.
Here are a few more examples:
geben: ich gebe but *du gibst, er / sie / es gibt*
essen: ich esse but *du isst, er / sie / es isst*
tragen: ich trage but *du trägst, er / sie / es trägt*

Verben

The present tense of *haben* and *sein*

The verbs *haben* (to have) and *sein* (to be) are very important strong verbs to learn and don't follow the usual pattern. You must learn these by heart!

	haben (to have)	*sein* (to be)
ich	habe	bin
du	hast	bist
er / sie / es	hat	ist
wir	haben	sind
ihr	habt	seid
sie / Sie	haben	sind

neunzehn **19**

1.1H Meine Leute und ich

OBJECTIVES
- Describing appearance, interests and personality
- Working out the gender of nouns
- Verbs used with *zu* plus infinitive
- Pronunciation: *-e* as final letter

1 Read what Lukas and Mathilda say about themselves, then answer the questions in English.

Mathilda

Hi. Ich heiße Mathilda, bin sechzehn Jahre alt und wohne auf dem Land in der Schweiz. Ich wohne mit meiner Familie zusammen, das heißt mit meinen Eltern, meiner Schwester und meinem jüngeren Bruder, Liam. Ich bin freundlich, hilfsbereit und sportlich. Ich versuche, jeden Tag etwas Sport zu treiben und Zeit draußen zu verbringen. Das ist mir wichtig. Ich hoffe, in den Ferien Klettern zu lernen.

Lukas

Hallo. Hier ist Lukas. Ich bin ziemlich klein, habe braune Augen und im Moment blaue Haare. Ich denke, das sieht cool aus. Ich bin witzig und ich mag Mode. Ich verbringe viel Zeit mit Freunden, und wir genießen es, am Wochenende etwas zusammen zu machen. Wir hoffen, am Samstag in zwei Wochen in ein Konzert zu gehen.

a Where does Mathilda live? (two details)
b How does Mathilda describe herself? (three details)
c Apart from sport, what does she try to do every day?
d What does she hope to do in the holidays?
e How does Lukas describe his appearance? (three details)
f What does Lukas like to do at weekends?
g When does he hope to go to a concert?

2 Copy and complete the table with the nouns that appear in the texts in activity 1. Look up those that you cannot work out from the text.

masculine	feminine	neuter	plural
der Bruder	die Schweiz	das Land	die Eltern

Grammatik

Working out the gender of nouns

German nouns are masculine, feminine or neuter. You will need to learn the gender of new nouns you encounter, but there are some general rules:

masculine
Male people, e.g. *Mann, Vater*
Days of the week, months, seasons
Nouns ending in *-er, -ling, -or*

feminine
Female people, e.g. *Frau, Mutter* (but *Mädchen*, girl, is neuter)
Nouns ending in *-in, -heit, -keit, -schaft, -ung, -tion*
Many (but not all) nouns ending in *-e*

neuter
Letters of the alphabet
Most nouns beginning with *Ge-*
Nouns made from the infinitive of verbs, e.g. *Schwimmen, Lesen*
Diminutives ending in *-chen* and *-lein*

Identity and relationships with others 1.1H

3 Put the words in these sentences into the correct order, adding a comma if one is needed. The first word of each sentence is in bold.

a Musik   versuche   hören   **Ich**   die   zu

b Deutsch   lernen   zu   beginnen   **Wir**

c hofft   Bruder   ins   gehen   zu   **Mein**   Kino

d beginnt   arbeiten   **Die**   Klasse   zu

e Freundin   nett   **Meine**   sein   immer   zu   versucht

4 Five young people are describing friends and family members. Listen to each description and match a photo to each name. One of the photos is not described.

Max   Leni   Emma   Deedra   Jakob

5 Listen again to the descriptions in activity 4. Note a detail about each person that is *not* about their appearance.

6 Work with a partner. Take turns to describe a friend or family member. The other person notes down the description. Include the following information:
- Name and age
- Appearance
- Character / personality
- Likes and dislikes

Verben

Verbs used with *zu* + infinitive

Some verbs are used with *zu* plus the infinitive of another verb. There are some examples in the texts from activity 1:

hoffen zu – to hope to

versuchen zu – to try to / try doing

Note that *zu* + infinitive goes at the end of the sentence:

Ich versuche zu schlafen.
I'm trying to sleep.

If there are additional words in the sentence, a comma is needed to divide the clauses:

Ich versuche, jeden Tag Sport zu treiben.
I try to do sport every day.

7 With your partner, take turns to read the following sentences aloud. Then listen to compare and check.

a Ich bin sechzehn Jahre alt.
b Er ist jünger als sie.
c Sie hat blonde Haare.

Aussprache

-e as final letter

Remember that -e is sounded as its own syllable when it appears at the end of a word: *Haare, Jahre*.

8 Choose two people you know and write a description of each of them. Write at least 90 words.

Er/Sie/Diese Person heißt …			
E/Sie	ist	vierzehn fünfzehn …	Jahre alt.
	hat	lange / kurze … braune / rote …	Haare.
		blaue / braune	Augen.
	ist	sehr / ziemlich	groß / klein … sportlich / cool …
	genießt es, … zu tun		

einundzwanzig 21

1.2F Lebensweisen und Lebensbeziehungen

OBJECTIVES
- Talking about family life and social lives
- Reflexive pronouns
- Reflexive verbs
- Pronunciation: *-ig* at the end of a word

1 📖 Read the texts and match the people's names to the pictures (1–6).

Jan: Ich wohne mit meiner Mutter und meinem Vater. Sie sind schon lange verheiratet und sind meistens glücklich. **Ich verstehe mich gut mit meinen beiden Eltern**.

Emre: Ich bin verlobt und wohne mit meiner Verlobten, Susi, zusammen. Wir hoffen, nächstes Jahr zu heiraten. Ich liebe Susi sehr und **ich freue mich auf die Hochzeit**.

Erika: Ich wohne mit meiner Mutter und ihrer Partnerin zusammen. Sie haben eine Lebenspartnerschaft. Das heißt auch eine zivile Partnerschaft.

Magda: Ich bin ledig und wohne allein. Mein Leben ist aber nie langweilig, und ich habe viele Freunde und Freundinnen. **Wir amüsieren uns gut** und gehen oft aus.

Elma: Ich bin neunzehn Jahre alt und wohne nicht mehr bei meiner Familie, sondern mit drei Freund*innen. Wir haben eine Wohnung in der Stadt. **Wir kennen uns seit langem und verstehen uns gut**.

Osman: Meine Eltern sind getrennt, und ich wohne mit meinem Vater und meinem jüngeren Bruder. Meine Mutter wohnt nicht weit von uns, und **wir sehen uns jedes Wochenende**.

1  **2**  **3**

4  **5**  **6**

Verben

Reflexive verbs

Reflexive verbs have an extra part called the reflexive pronoun:

*Ich wasche **mich**.* – I wash (**myself**).

These often relate the action to the subject of the sentence:

*Er amüsiert **sich**.* – He enjoys **himself**.

On the right is a full example of the reflexive verb *sich waschen* – to wash (yourself).

	verb	reflexive pronoun
ich	wasche	mich
du	wäschst	dich
er / sie / es	wäscht	sich
wir	waschen	uns
ihr	wascht	euch
sie / Sie	waschen	sich

Identity and relationships with others — 1.2F

2 Match the sentences in bold in activity 1 to the translations below. Each sentence contains a reflexive verb.

a I'm looking forward to the wedding.
b We see each other every weekend.
c I get on well with both my parents.
d We enjoy ourselves a lot.
e We've known each other for a long time and get on well.

Grammatik

Reflexive pronouns

Reflexive pronouns are words such as 'myself', 'herself', 'yourself'. For German reflexive verbs you must always use the reflexive pronoun, although it may not be needed in an English translation, e.g.:

Ich dusche mich – I shower (**myself**) / I have a shower
Ich freue mich auf … – I look forward to …

3 Complete the sentences by adding the correct reflexive pronoun in each gap. Use the *Verben* box on page 22 to help you.

a Ich verstehe ___ gut mit meiner Tante.
b Er wäscht ___ schnell.
c Sie sehen ___ am Sonntag.
d Die Freunde kennen ___ gut.
e Kennt ihr ___ schon?
f Verstehst du ___ mit deinen Eltern?
g Meine Familie und ich verstehen ___ gut.

4 Listen to six people talking about relationships. For each, note whether the relationship is positive (P) or negative (N).

5 Choose the right word to complete the sentences in German. Then listen and check.

a Ich **verstehen / verstehe / verstehst** mich nicht gut mit meinem Bruder.
b Ich habe **ein / eine / einen** gute Beziehung zu meiner Mutter.
c Ich streite **sich / dich / mich** oft mit meinem Vater.
d **Ich / Wir / Sie** streiten uns fast jeden Tag.
e Ich **helfe / hilfst / helfen** ihr gern, wenn sie Probleme hat.

Kultur

Recent figures show that 17.3 million people in Germany live alone. That is over 20% of the population. Figures in Austria and Switzerland are slightly lower at about 17%.

Regensburg in Bavaria has the highest percentage share of single-person households (56%), while Germany's capital, Berlin, is in twentieth place with 49%. Single living affects mainly older people, who may have lost a lifelong partner, or young people who are studying in a city away from home.

6 Working in pairs, take turns to ask and answer the following questions. Advice on how to answer is supplied in brackets.

- Mit wem wohnst du? *(Say who you live with.)*
- Mit wem verstehst du dich gut? Warum? *(Say who you get on well with at home and why.)*
- Mit wem verstehst du dich nicht gut? Warum? *(Say who you don't get on with and why.)*
- Wie ist dein bester Freund / deine beste Freundin? *(Describe your best friend.)*
- Was machst du gern mit Freunden? *(Say what you like to do with friends.)*

Aussprache

-ig at the end of a word

-ig at the end of a word (such as *langweilig* or *witzig*) can be pronounced either like *ich* or like the 'ick' in 'tick' or 'lick'.

7 Now write down your answers to the questions in activity 6. Try to write 50–60 words.

Ich wohne mit		meiner Mutter
Ich verstehe mich (nicht) gut mit		meinem Vater meinen Großeltern …
Mein bester Freund Meine beste Freundin	ist	freundlich / sportlich …
Wir		gehen / spielen gern … amüsieren uns gut.

8 Translate the following sentences into German.

a I live with my parents and my sister.
b I get on well with my father.
c My best friend is very funny.
d I do not get on with my mother.
e I think she is too strict.

dreiundzwanzig 23

1.2H Wichtige Beziehungen

OBJECTIVES
- Talking about relationships with others
- Plural nouns
- Separable verbs

1 📖 Read the posts on relationships with others, then answer the questions in English. Write J for Johanna, A for Ayla, K for Kai and M for Matteo.

Johanna

Ich bin Einzelkind und wohne mit meiner Mutter zusammen. Unsere Beziehung ist nicht schlecht, und **wir verstehen uns normalerweise gut. Mutti kümmert sich immer um mich**, und das finde ich lieb. Meine Eltern sind geschieden, und mein Vater hat eine neue Frau und ein neues Leben. **Wir sehen uns nicht oft**.

Ayla

Meine Familie und Freunde sind alle sehr wichtig für mich. Ich komme gut mit meinen Eltern aus. **Wir streiten uns selten** und dann nur über Kleinigkeiten, wie zum Beispiel meine Kleider oder meine Haarfarbe. Ich habe einige gute Freunde, und wir gehen oft aus. Wir gehen tanzen, einkaufen oder ins Kino.

Who …
a sees films with friends?
b feels their parents have no time for them?
c gets on well with their sibling?
d relies on friends to sort out difficulties?
e rarely argues with their parents?
f has parents who are divorced?
g has no siblings?
h has a strict parent?

Kai

Mein Bruder und ich sind enge Freunde mit vielen gemeinsamen Interessen. Wir kommen gut miteinander aus. Wir sind beide aktiv und treiben oft zusammen Sport, um uns zu entspannen. Wir wohnen bei unseren Eltern. Wir haben eine schwierige Beziehung zu unserem Vater, weil er streng ist und uns keine Freiheit erlaubt.

Matteo

Meine Freunde sind mir viel wichtiger als meine Familie. **Meine Eltern beschäftigen sich immer mit der Arbeit. Sie interessieren sich kaum für meine Schwester und mich**. Ich habe aber eine tolle Freundesgruppe, und **wir amüsieren uns gut zusammen. Wir treffen uns oft** nach der Schule und gehen Kaffee trinken. Da sprechen wir über alles und helfen einander, wenn jemand Probleme hat.

Kultur

The German-British Freundship award

The British Chamber of Commerce in Germany (BCCG) and the British Embassy in Berlin created this friendship award to honour the relationship between Germany and Great Britain. The first recipient was football manager Jürgen Klopp in 2021.

2 🔀 Translate the bold sections in the texts from activity 1 into English. (They all include reflexive verbs.)

3 🎧 Listen to these people talking about important relationships. For each person, note down which of the statements are true. There are six true statements overall.

Robert
a has been married for 14 years.
b thinks arguing is not unusual.
c thinks marriage is a good thing.

Sofia
d is nineteen years old.
e is engaged.
f will get married next year.

Nico
g has a male partner.
h thinks Jonas is good-looking.
i hopes they will move in together soon.

Gudrun
j is no longer married.
k lives with her daughters.
l misses having a social life.

Identity and relationships with others 1.2H

4 Copy and complete the sentences with both parts of the separable verbs shown.

a Ich ___ heute mit meinen Freundinnen ___ . *(ausgehen)*
b ___ du gut mit deinen Eltern ___? *(auskommen)*
c Meine Schwester ___ schön ___ . *(aussehen)*
d Der Lehrer ___ spät ___ . *(ankommen)*
e Meine Freundin ___ mich ___ . *(anrufen)*
f Wir ___ morgen ___ . *(zurückkommen)*

5 Translate the sentences into German. Take care with the separable prefixes!

a I get on well with my friends.
b We are going out at the weekend.
c I am coming back late.
d He arrives tomorrow.
e They never call us.

6 Working with a partner, take turns to ask and answer these questions. The words in bold show options – choose the most appropriate question to ask your partner.

> Mit wem hast du eine gute Beziehung? Warum?

> Mit wem kommst du nicht gut aus? Warum?

> Kommst du gut mit **deinem Bruder** / **deiner Schwester** / **deinen Freunden** aus?

> Beschreib **eine Person in deiner Familie oder einen Freund** / **eine Freundin**.

> Was machst du mit **deinen Freunden** / **deiner Familie**?

Verben

Separable verbs

These verbs have two parts: the main verb and the separable prefix, e.g *ausgehen*. The separable prefix often has a meaning of its own:

gehen = to go; *aus* = out, out of; *ausgehen* = to go out

When you use these verbs in the present tense in a main clause, the prefix separates from the rest and moves to the end of the clause or sentence:

ausgehen → *Ich gehe oft aus.*
I often go out.

The verb *auskommen* (to get on with) is another example of a separable verb. Here the prefix does not have a literal translation:

Ich komme gut mit meinen Eltern aus.
I get on well with my parents.

7 Translate the passage below into German.

> ✉ elisa@oupdeutschmail.de
>
> I live with my father and my stepmother. I also have two stepsisters. I get on well with my stepmother. She is kind. My father works a lot and we don't often see each other.
>
> My friends are important to me. We go out at weekends.

Grammatik

Plural nouns

German nouns form plurals in different ways, so always learn the plural form each time you learn a new noun. Here are some of the ways plurals are formed (a dictionary will give you the way to form the plural in brackets):

	singular	plural
no change	der Partner (-)	die Partner
add -e	der Freund (-e)	die Freunde
add -n	die Schwester (-n)	die Schwestern
add -en	die Person (-en)	die Personen
add umlaut	der Bruder (ü)	die Brüder
add umlaut + -er or -e	der Sohn (Söhne)	die Söhne

8 How many plurals can you find on these two pages? The target is 9!

funfundzwanzig 25

2.1F Wir essen gern!

OBJECTIVES
- Talking about food and a healthy lifestyle
- Using *ein* and *kein*
- The perfect tense with *haben*
- Pronunciation: *ei* and *ie*

1 📖 Read Marie's post about what she likes to eat, then answer the questions in English.

Marie

Hallo. Ich bin die Marie aus Österreich. Ich versuche, gesund zu essen, und ich benutze die österreichische Ernährungspyramide. Da kann ich nützliche Infos über eine gesunde Ernährung lesen.

Diese Woche habe ich genug Wasser getrunken, mindestens 1,5 Liter pro Tag, und ich habe jeden Tag fünf Portionen Obst und Gemüse gegessen. Das finde ich nicht schwierig, denn ich mag frisches Essen.

Käse und Joghurt sind auch wichtig für eine gesunde Ernährung, und diese Lebensmittel habe ich am Wochenende zum Frühstück gegessen. Abends haben wir dreimal Fisch und zweimal Fleisch mit Reis oder Kartoffeln gegessen. Zweimal haben wir Eier mit Brot und Salat gegessen. Ich habe keine Wurst oder Pommes gegessen und keine Cola getrunken.

a Why does Marie find the Austrian food pyramid useful?
b How much water has she drunk each day this week?
c What is her opinion about eating fruit and vegetables?
d Which dairy products does she mention?
e When has she eaten these foods?
f How many times did she eat meat this week?
g What did she eat with the meat?
h What did she eat with salad?
i What did she not eat and drink? (two things)

2 🎯 Complete these sentences with the correct past participle. There is a mix of regular and irregular forms.

a Mein Vater hat die Eier ___. (kochen)
b Ich habe einen Apfel ___. (essen)
c Er hat gestern keinen Tee ___. (trinken)
d Hast du einen Salat ___? (machen)

3 🎯 Now complete the sentences with the correct form of *haben* and a past participle.

a Wir ___ die Ernährungspyramide ___. (sehen)
b Svenja und Felix ___ Fußball ___. (spielen)
c Ich ___ am Wochenende Sport ___. (treiben)
d Du ___ nicht gut ___. (schlafen)

Verben

The perfect tense with *haben*

When using the perfect tense to talk about the past, you use an auxiliary verb (usually *haben*) plus a past participle:

*Wir **haben** Obst **gekauft**.* – We bought fruit.

Usually the past participle is formed by adding *ge-* and *-t* to the stem of the verb:

kaufen ⟶ *kauf* ⟶ **ge**kauf**t**

Some verbs, however, have an irregular past participle which usually ends in *-en* rather than *-t*. Here are some examples – can you spot any in activity 1?

essen ⟶ *gegessen*   *trinken* ⟶ *getrunken*
sehen ⟶ *gesehen*   *schlafen* ⟶ *geschlafen*

Some also have a vowel change in the stem:

treiben ⟶ *get**rie**ben*

It's a good idea to learn these as you go along.

26 sechsundzwanzig

Healthy living and lifestyle 2.1F

4  Listen to Karim, Clara, Luis and Amelie talking about what they eat and drink. Copy and complete the table.

Name	Karim
Eating / Drinking today	meat ...
Ate / Drank yesterday	...

Kultur

Austrian food pyramid

The Austrian government has produced guidelines for a healthy diet. Here are the first four steps:

1. 1.5 litres of fluid a day, preferably water or herbal teas.
2. Five servings of vegetables or fruit every day.
3. Four servings of potatoes, rice, grains or pasta every day.
4. Three servings of milk / dairy products every day.

5 Choose the correct form of *ein* or *kein* to complete each sentence. The gender of the noun is given in brackets.

a Er hat **ein / eine / einen** Salat (m) gegessen.
b Ich habe **einen / eine / ein** Tee (m) getrunken.
c Meine Schwester isst **keinen / keine / kein** Fleisch (n).
d Wir essen **kein / keine / keinen** Kartoffeln (f, pl).
e Mein Stiefvater hat **kein / keinen / keine** Fastfood (n) gegessen.
f Sie trinkt **eine / ein / einen** Tasse (f) Kaffee.

6 Working with a partner, take turns to practise reading these sentences aloud.
- Ich esse Hähnchen mit Gemüse.
- Ich habe zum Frühstück ein Ei gegessen.
- Ich habe keine Wurst gegessen.
- Das finde ich nicht schwierig.

Aussprache

ei and ie

ei in German is pronounced like the English 'i', e.g. *Ei, Fleisch*. The *ie* sound is pronounced like the English 'e', e.g. *Bier, schwierig*.

7 Work in a group of three. Person A asks the questions, Person B answers and Person C makes a note in German of the answers. Check your answers at the end of each round, then swap roles.
- Was isst du, was gesund ist?
- Was isst du gern? Warum?
- Was trinkst du gern?
- Was hast du gestern getrunken?
- Was hast du heute Morgen gegessen?

Grammatik

Using *ein* and *kein*

The endings for *ein* ('a') and *kein* ('not a'/'not any'/'no') change according to gender and case. They follow the same pattern:

	nominative	accusative
masculine	ein / kein	einen / keinen
feminine	eine / keine	eine / keine
neuter	ein / kein	ein / kein
plural	keine	keine

In the accusative case – where the noun is the direct object of the sentence – the masculine form adds *-en*. The other forms do not change. You can find out more about the nominative and accusative cases on page 29.

Here are some examples you heard in activity 4:

*Ich habe **einen** Apfel gegessen.*
*Ich habe **eine** Pizza gegessen.*
*Ich habe **ein** Glas Wasser getrunken.*

To say you didn't eat an apple, you would change *einen* to *keinen*:

*Ich habe **keinen** Apfel gegessen.*

How would you say you didn't eat a / any pizza or that you didn't drink a glass of water?

8 Write an email to a German-speaking friend about what you like to eat and drink. Aim to write about 50 words. Mention:
- your favourite food and why you like it
- what you don't like to eat and why
- your usual breakfast
- what you ate / drank yesterday.

siebenundzwanzig **27**

2.1H Ein gesundes Leben

OBJECTIVES
- Talking about a healthy lifestyle
- Articles and cases (nominative and accusative)
- Using *seit* with the present tense

1 📖 Read Werner's post about making improvements to his lifestyle. Answer the questions in English.

Hallo, alle zusammen! Ich will heute erklären, wie Sport mein Leben verbessert hat. Hoffentlich hilft das anderen Jugendlichen, die einen besseren Lebensstil suchen.

Vor einem Jahr war ich nicht sehr aktiv. Ich bin Computerfanatiker und habe die ganze Zeit nur im Internet gesurft und Online-Spiele gespielt. Interessant, aber nicht so gesund …

Eines Tages habe ich ein YouTube-Video über Freiwasserschwimmen gesehen. Das war faszinierend, und ich wollte sofort diese Sportart ausprobieren! Ich habe in der Nähe einen Schwimmclub gefunden und bin jetzt ein Mitglied. Das erste Mal im Meer war es ein Schock! Das Wasser war kalt, aber das Gefühl war wunderbar.

Seit vier Monaten schwimme ich jeden Tag und habe viele neue Freunde gefunden. Durch Freiwasserschwimmen bin ich seit April oft an der frischen Luft, fühle mich gesund und glücklich und habe viel mehr Energie.

a What does Werner hope to do by writing this post? (two details)
b How does he describe himself a year ago? (two details)
c What effect did the YouTube video have on Werner?
d What was his first experience of open water swimming like? (two details)
e Apart from new friendships, what other advantages does Werner mention? (two details)

der Lebensstil	lifestyle
Freiwasserschwimmen	open water swimming

Verben

Using *seit* with the present tense

Seit indicates how long something has been happening and can be translated as 'for', e.g. for two weeks/for five years, and as 'since', e.g. since April.

Look at these examples:

Seit vier Monaten schwimme ich jeden Tag.
For four months I've been swimming every day.

Ich bin seit April oft an der frischen Luft.
Since April I've often been out in the fresh air.

You might have noticed that the present tense is used with *seit* in German (*I swim*), whereas in English we use a past tense (*I've been swimming*). The German logic is that the activity is still happening now.

Note also the question form *seit wann …?* meaning 'how long …?' (literally 'since when …?'):

Seit wann wohnst du hier?
How long have you lived here?

Wir kennen uns seit sechs Monaten.
We've known each other for six months.

2 🎯 Practise using *seit* by writing these sentences in the correct order. The first word is shown in bold.

a seit / **Ich** / einem Jahr / spiele / Tennis / .
b wohnen / sechs Monaten / **Wir** / in Jena / seit / .
c sind / drei Wochen / **Sie** / seit / verlobt / .
d wann / er / verheiratet / ist / **Seit** / ?
e seit / meine beste Freundin / fünf Jahren / **Ich** / kenne / .
f **Er** / seit / des Schwimmclubs / Juni / ist / Mitglied / .

3 🔀 Translate the sentences from activity 2 into English.

Healthy living and lifestyle — 2.1H

4 🎧 **Listen to this podcast interview with two young Swiss people, who are discussing healthy eating. Answer the questions in English.**

a What is the first question asked by the interviewer?
b When did Clara change her way of eating?
c Why did she make this change?
d What does Elias eat at home?
e When does he eat fast food?
f What does he say about water?
g Why didn't Elias have time to eat breakfast?
h What did he eat before school?
i What did Clara eat for breakfast?
j When did she eat an apple?

5 💬🎧 **Working with a partner, take turns to read these sentences aloud. Help each other to get the pronunciation correct. Then listen to the audio to compare and check.**

- Ich esse nicht gern Bananen.
- Seit wann spielst du Fußball?
- Hast du einen Kaffee getrunken?
- Es ist wichtig, genug Wasser zu trinken.
- Rauchen ist schlecht für die Gesundheit.

6 💬 **Work with a partner to ask and answer questions about this photo.**

- Sag etwas über das Foto.
- Was isst du zum Frühstück?
- Was trinkst du gern?
- Was ist dein Lieblingsessen?
- Was hast du gestern Abend gegessen?

Kultur

Grießbrei is a popular German breakfast dish. It's rather like porridge, but made with milk, semolina, and sugar. Vanilla or cinnamon are often added for flavour. *Grießbrei* can be served with fresh fruit such as cherries, blueberries or strawberries.

Grammatik

Articles and cases (nominative and accusative)

Articles for the nominative case – used for the subject of the sentence – are as follows:

	definite article (the)	indefinite article (a)
masculine	der	ein
feminine	die	eine
neuter	das	ein
plural	die	-

In the accusative case – used for the direct object of the sentence – the masculine singular forms change:

der → den, ein → einen

Subject (nominative)	Verb	Object (accusative)
Der Mann	isst	einen Apfel.

In this sentence the man is the subject (doing the eating), and is therefore in the nominative case, whereas the apple is the object (being eaten), and is therefore in the accusative.

Feminine and neuter articles are the same in both the nominative and accusative cases.

7 **Translate these sentences into German. Some tips are included in brackets.**

a I never eat fast food. *(nie)*
b She has been ill for two weeks. *(seit + present tense)*
c We don't buy cake and chocolate. *(kein + accusative case)*
d For breakfast I eat an apple. *(accusative case)*
e How long have you been playing handball? *(seit + present tense)*

neunundzwanzig 29

2.2F Glück und Gesundheit

OBJECTIVES
- Talking about health and happiness
- Possessive adjectives
- The perfect tense with *haben* and *sein*
- Pronunciation: *pf*

1 📖 Read what Kaan and Mila think about their lifestyles, then complete the statements in English.

Kaan

Ich denke, mein Lebensstil ist genau richtig. Ich bin aktiv und mag Sport, aber ich habe auch andere Interessen, wenn ich mich nur entspannen will. Letzte Woche habe ich zum Beispiel viel Schularbeit gehabt und musste stundenlang lernen. Deshalb habe ich an einem Abend in der Woche Musik gehört und mein Buch gelesen – ich habe meinen ganzen Schulstress vergessen. Am Freitag habe ich meine Freunde zu mir eingeladen. Wir haben einen Film gesehen, Pizza gegessen und über unsere Woche gesprochen. Es ist gut, Probleme zu teilen, denn das hilft, sie zu lösen.

Mila

Meine Ernährung ist gut, aber andere Aspekte von meinem Lebensstil sind gar nicht gut. Ich möchte mehr Zeit draußen verbringen und mehr Bewegung haben. Leider habe ich keine Zeit. Ich bin oft müde und habe wenig Energie.
In letzter Zeit habe ich nicht genug geschlafen, denn ich habe so viele Hausaufgaben gehabt. Ich bin dann spät aufgestanden und habe morgens oft nichts gegessen, denn unsere Schule beginnt um 8 Uhr. Wir sitzen jeden Tag fast sieben Stunden im Klassenzimmer und das ist auch nicht gesund.

a Kaan thinks his lifestyle is ___.
b Kaan ___ sport.
c Kaan sometimes just wants to ___.
d ___ and ___ helped Kaan forget his stress.
e Kaan thinks it's helpful to ___.

f Mila would like to ___ and ___.
g She is often ___.
h Recently she has ___.
i She has not had breakfast because ___.
j She thinks it's unhealthy to ___.

2 🔀 Find all the sentences using the perfect tense in activity 1 and write down their English translations.

3 🎯 Copy the verbs in the box into two lists, one for those which take *haben* to form the perfect tense, one for those which take *sein*. Your target is two lists of six!

essen   tanzen   beginnen   fahren
lachen   geben   fliegen
laufen
werden   gehen   denken   kommen

Verben

The perfect tense with *haben* and *sein*

When you want to speak or write about an event which happened / has happened in the past, you need to use the perfect tense. This has two parts: the auxiliary verb and the past participle.

Usually the auxiliary verb is the present tense of *haben*, but in some instances – usually verbs denoting movement from one place to another, or a state or change of state – it is the present tense of *sein*. Verbs which take *sein* as an auxiliary include: *gehen, kommen, fahren, fallen, sein, bleiben, werden*:

Ich bin gegangen. – I went.
Wir sind geblieben. – We stayed.

When you look up a verb in the dictionary, it will tell you if the auxiliary is *sein* (e.g. *aux sein*).

dreißig

Healthy living and lifestyle — 2.2F

4 Referring to the past participle, decide whether each sentence should take *haben* or *sein* as the auxiliary verb, then write down the correct form to complete the sentence. Use the *Verben* box on page 30 to help you.

  a Ich __ zwei Äpfel gegessen.
  b Er __ in die Schule gegangen.
  c __ du nach London gefahren?
  d Du __ heute Basketball gespielt?

5 Complete these sentences in the perfect tense, adding the correct auxiliary verb and past participle for the verb given in brackets.

  a Ich __ in die Stadt __ . *(laufen)*
  b Mein Freund __ einen Kuchen __ . *(kaufen)*
  c Er __ eine Cola __ . *(trinken)*
  d Du __ spät nach Hause __ . *(kommen)*

6 Listen to this doctor's podcast about young people and health, then decide whether the following statements are true (T) or false (F).

  a Many young people don't take their health seriously enough.
  b A lot of young people are afraid of becoming ill.
  c Looking after yourself when young is important.
  d The doctor gives six basic rules about healthy lifestyles.
  e Rule Three concerns healthy eating.
  f Rule Four concerns sleep routines.
  g The last rule is about leisure time.

7 Translate these sentences into English. They all contain possessive adjectives Use the *Grammatik* box to help you.

  a Gestern habe ich mein Buch gelesen.
  b Ich habe meinen Schulstress vergessen.
  c Am Freitag habe ich meine Freunde zu mir eingeladen.
  d Wir haben über unsere Woche gesprochen.
  e Junge Leute müssen ihre Gesundheit ernst nehmen.

Aussprache

pf

pf is pronounced just as it looks – 'p' and 'f' run together: A**pf**el, Rheinland-**Pf**alz, em**pf**ehlen

Kultur

The German website Stress**Treff** is a source of sound advice on dealing with stressful moments. Tips include balancing stress with calming activities, such as a daily walk, reading or a short power nap (*ein Tagschlaf*).

Grammatik

Possessive adjectives

Possessive adjectives are words like 'my', 'your' and 'his / her / their', which indicate to whom something belongs. Can you find any examples in activity 1?

Possessive adjectives change according to the gender and case of the noun they describe. They follow the same pattern as *ein* and *kein*, with masculine -n endings changing to -en in the accusative case. Here is *mein* (my) as an example:

	nominative	accusative
masculine	mein	meinen
feminine	meine	meine
neuter	mein	mein
plural	meine	meine

Other possessive adjectives are *dein* (your – familiar singular), *sein* (his, its), *ihr* (her), *unser* (our), *euer* (your – familiar plural), *Ihr* (your – formal) and *ihr* (their).

8 You are writing about your lifestyle. Write about 90 words in German, mentioning the following:

  • whether you have a healthy lifestyle and why / why not
  • examples of healthy lifestyle choices you make
  • causes of stress in your life
  • something you have done recently to be healthy / relax.

9 Once you have written your answer to activity 8, read it aloud to a partner, who should note down the key details. Check they have understood, then swap roles.

einunddreißig 31

2.2H Pass gut auf dich auf!

OBJECTIVES
- Discussing lifestyle choices
- Using *sondern* to say 'but'
- The imperfect tense of *sein*
- Pronunciation: *sp* at the start of words

1 📖 Read this section of an online article about making positive lifestyle changes, then answer the questions in English.

Wie kann ich meinen Lebensstil verbessern?

Schon kleine Schritte in Richtung zu einem gesunden Lebensstil können eine große Wirkung haben. Es ist wichtig, dass die Änderung zu einer gesunden, aktiven Lebensweise langfristig ist. Wir informieren Sie hier, wie genau und warum das funktioniert.

Regelmäßiger Sport und genug Bewegung halten uns fit und gesund. Experten empfehlen pro Woche mindestens 150 Minuten Bewegung bei leichter Intensität und 75 Minuten bei mittlerer Intensität.

Das klingt zuerst nicht viel, doch leider bewegen sich viele Menschen weniger als diese 150 Minuten pro Woche. Zwei einfache Methoden, dieses Ziel zu erreichen:
- mehr Bewegung im Alltag, z. B. zu Fuß gehen, Rad fahren, Treppensteigen …
- zwei- bis dreimal pro Woche Krafttraining.

Regelmäßige Bewegung bringt auch für die mentale Gesundheit viele Vorteile. Sportarten, die gut für Anfänger sind, sind Spazierengehen, Wandern, Joggen und Schwimmen.

a According to the article, what can have a great effect?
b What does the article say is important about any changes in habits?
c What is the significance of 150 minutes? (two details)
d How can people exercise more in everyday life? (two details)
e What other advantage comes with regular exercise?
f What types of activity might beginners try? (two details)

Schritte (pl)	steps
mittlerer	medium
das Treppensteigen	climbing stairs
das Krafttraining	strength training
Anfänger (pl)	beginners

2 🎧 Listen to Alex talking about how his lifestyle has changed in recent years. Answer the questions in English.

a What was Alex like when he was younger? (three details)
b What did he spend a lot of time doing?
c When did he take up basketball?
d How has sport changed his life? (two details)
e What encouraged him to get involved in the sport? (two details)
f What advantages does Alex mention? (two details)

Kultur

Let's Go! Graz

The Austrian city of Graz recently held a *Grazer Sportjahr* to encourage people of all ages to exercise in and around the city. One of the straplines was 'Faulheit fasten!' (have a break from laziness). It is estimated that, in the last year, over 300,000 people climbed the famous Schloßberg.

Healthy living and lifestyle 2.2H

3 Complete these sentences (from Alex's statements in activity 2) using the imperfect tense with *sein*. Then listen again to check.

a Als ich jünger ___ , ___ ich nicht fit, sondern sehr ungesund.
b Ich ___ ein bisschen faul.
c Meine beiden besten Freunde ___ schon Mitglieder der Basketballmannschaft.
d Sie (*they*) ___ dreimal pro Woche in den Trainingsstunden.
e Ich ___ eifersüchtig!

4 Translate your completed sentences into English.

5 Complete these sentences using *aber* or *sondern*, then translate them into English.

a Mein Bruder ist sportlich, ___ nicht sehr groß.
b Der Film war nicht interessant, ___ langweilig.
c Mein Bruder ist toll, ___ sehr faul.
d Sie ist nicht meine Cousine, ___ meine Tante.
e Ich habe einen Bruder, ___ keine Schwester.
f Das Wetter ist sonnig, ___ nicht sehr warm.
g Kaffee schmeckt nicht lecker, ___ schrecklich.

6 Working in pairs, take turns to ask and answer the following questions. Advice on how to answer is supplied in brackets.

- Hast du einen gesunden Lebensstil? Warum (nicht)? *(Say whether you have a healthy lifestyle or not, giving reasons.)*
- Wie war dein Lebensstil, als du jünger warst? *(Say what your lifestyle was like when you were younger.)*
- Wie findest du Sport? Warum? *(Say what you think of sport and why.)*
- Was hast du in letzter Zeit für deine Fitness gemacht? *(Mention something you have done recently to keep fit.)*
- Was machst du am Abend? *(Say something you do in the evenings.)*

Verben

The imperfect tense of *sein*

The imperfect tense is useful to say what was happening or to describe things in the past.

You heard some examples in activity 2, e.g.:
Als ich jünger war, war ich nicht fit.

This is how *sein* looks in full in the imperfect:

ich war	I was
du warst	you (familiar singular) were
er / sie / es war	he / she / it was
wir waren	we were
ihr wart	you (familiar plural) were
Sie waren	you (formal) were
sie waren	they were

Grammatik

Using *sondern* to say 'but'

You will almost always use *aber* to say 'but' in German, BUT in specific circumstances, *sondern* is used instead. Use *sondern* if:

- the subject of the two clauses is the same
- the first clause is negative
- the statement in one clause contradicts the statement in the other.

Check this by imagining that *sondern* means 'but on the contrary':
*Ich war **nicht** fit, **sondern** lebte sehr ungesund.*
I wasn't fit, but (on the contrary) lived very unhealthily.
Use *sondern* auch to mean 'not only, but also'.
*Mein Leben ist **nicht nur** gesund, **sondern auch** glücklich.*
My life isn't only healthy, but also happy.

Aussprache

The *sp* sound at the start of words

The *sp* sound at the start of words such as *Sport*, *spielen* and *Spanien* sounds like 'shp'.

7 Now write down your answers to the speaking activity, adding further details and explaining some of your ideas in longer sentences. Make sure that you answer in the right tense! Aim to write about 90 words.

dreiunddreißig 33

3.1F Eine gute Ausbildung

OBJECTIVES
- Comparing school experiences
- The verb as second idea
- The imperfect tense of *sein* and *haben*
- Pronunciation: *sch*

1 📖 Read what Julia says about her previous and current schools. What does she say about:
   a the number of students at her current school?
   b the school day on Mondays, Wednesdays and Thursdays? (two details)
   c how Tuesdays and Fridays are different? (two details)
   d the size of her previous school?
   e the school day at her previous school? (two details)
   f breaks at her previous school? (two details)
   g homework at her previous school?

2 🎯 Copy and complete each sentence with the correct form of *sein* or *haben* in the imperfect tense.
   a Ich ___ in der Kantine.
   b Wir ___ Hausaufgaben.
   c Wie ___ dein Schultag?
   d Ich ___ gute Noten.
   e Er ___ jünger als ich.
   f ___ du gestern in der Schule?
   g Am Wochenende ___ wir in der Stadt.
   h Ich ___ keine Stunden am Nachmittag.
   i Er ___ eine Mathestunde.
   j Was ___ dein Lieblingsfach?

3 🔀 Translate the second paragraph of Julia's text from activity 1 into English.

4 🎧 Listen to Malik describing his school timetable (shown on the right) from the previous year. Write down the missing subjects a–h.

Julia

Ich besuche eine Hauptschule. Die Schule hat etwa 400 Schüler und Schülerinnen. Drei Tage die Woche haben wir von 8:15–15:00 Uhr Unterricht und essen um 12:45 Uhr Mittag. Aber dienstags und freitags essen wir um 13:30 Uhr und danach gehen wir nach Hause.

Als ich jünger war, war ich in der Grundschule. Meine Grundschule war klein. Der Unterricht war von 7:30 Uhr bis 13:00 Uhr, aber nachmittags waren wir nicht in der Schule. Wir hatten eine kleine Pause zwischen den Stunden und zwei längere Pausen. Ich hatte auch keine Hausaufgaben!

Verben

The imperfect tense of *sein* and *haben*

You can use the imperfect tense to describe how things were in the past:
Als ich jünger war, … – When I **was** younger, …
Ich hatte keine Hausaufgaben. – I **had** no homework.
The imperfect tense of *sein* (to be) and *haben* (to have) are very useful.

	sein	*haben*
ich	war	hatte
du	warst	hattest
er/sie/es	war	hatte
wir	waren	hatten
ihr	wart	hattet
sie/Sie	waren	hatten

Stunde	Montag	Dienstag	Mittwoch	Donnerstag	Freitag
1	a ___	c ___	Biologie	Mathe	Wirtschaft
2	Englisch		d ___	f ___	Englisch
3	Deutsch	Englisch	Geschichte	Deutsch	Physik
4	b ___	Mathe	Mathe	g ___	Deutsch
5		Biologie	Mathe	Geschichte	Erdkunde
	Mittagspause				
6	Geschichte		Wirtschaft	Religion	
7	Französisch		e ___	h ___	
8					

Education and work 3.1F

5 Put the words in these sentences into the correct order. The first idea in each sentence is shown in bold.

a Hausaufgaben / viele / **Heute** / ich / habe / .
b mein / **Dieses Jahr** / Lieblingsfach / Englisch / ist / .
c einen guten Tag / in der Schule / **Gestern** / ich / hatte / .
d eine Doppelstunde / wir / Kunst / haben / **Nach der Mittagspause** / .
e Mathestunde / ich / **Am Freitag** / keine / habe / .

6 💬 Working with a partner, take turns to ask and answer the following questions. Use the table below to help you.

- Wie ist deine Schule?
- Was ist dein Lieblingsfach? Warum?
- Welches Fach magst du nicht? Warum?
- Wie findest du die Lehrer und Lehrerinnen?
- Wie war dein Schultag gestern?

Grammatik

The verb as second idea

Note where the **verb** appears in these sentences:

*Dienstags **essen** wir um 13:30 Uhr.*
On Tuesdays we eat at 1:30 pm.

*Nach der Mittagspause **ist** die Schule zu Ende.*
School is finished after the lunch break.

When a word or phrase is added to the beginning of a sentence, the verb goes before the subject so that it remains the **second idea**.

First idea	Second idea		
Ich	**habe**	viele Fächer.	I have / am learning a lot of subjects.
Dieses Jahr	**habe**	ich viele Fächer.	This year I have / am learning a lot of subjects.

Remember that an idea can be more than one word!

Meine Schule	ist	eine Gesamtschule / ein Gymnasium / ein Internat. sehr / nicht sehr / nicht / zu groß.		
	hat	… Schüler / Schülerinnen.		
Ich lerne (gern / nicht gern)	Englisch / Mathe / Biologie / Deutsch / Französisch / …			
Ich mag nicht				
Mein Lieblingsfach ist …		denn	es ist / ich finde es	einfach / nützlich / interessant.
			ich bekomme	gute Noten / nicht viele Hausaufgaben.
Die Lehrer / Die Lehrerinnen	sind	nicht / sehr / meistens / zu / immer	gut / freundlich / nett / hilfsbereit / gemein / böse / streng.	
Gestern in der Schule	hatte ich	einen guten / schlechten Tag. eine Doppelstunde Mathe / Englisch …		

7 🔀 Translate these sentences into German.

a My school is too big.
b He hates the uniform because it's blue.
c The first lesson yesterday was history.
d Today I had a good day at school.

Aussprache

sch

The sound *sch* in words such as *Schule*, *Deutsch* and *Französisch* is pronounced like the English 'sh'.

8 ✏️ Write about 50 words in German about your school life. Mention:

- what you think of school
- your favourite subject and why you like it
- what you don't like and why
- your opinion on homework
- what your school day was like yesterday.

fünfunddreißig 35

3.1H Nun heißt's lernen!

OBJECTIVES
- Talking about school routine and rules
- Direct and indirect object pronouns
- The imperfect tense of weak and strong verbs

1. 📖 Read this extract from the rules of a *Hauptschule*. Which of the statements (a–f) are true (T) and which are false (F)?

> **Schulhausregeln**
>
> 1 Du sollst pünktlich um 8:00 Uhr zur Schule kommen. Der Unterricht beginnt um 8:15 Uhr.
> 2 Essen und Kaugummikauen sind während des Unterrichts nicht erlaubt. Während des Unterrichts darfst du Wasser trinken. Energydrinks sind auf dem gesamten Schulgelände verboten.
> 3 Du darfst das Schulgelände während der Pause nicht verlassen.
> 4 Handys sind in allen Unterrichtsstunden, in Klassenarbeiten und in Prüfungen strengstens verboten.
> 5 Das Aufnehmen von Fotos und Videos ist auf dem gesamten Schulgelände und im Schulgebäude nicht erlaubt.

a Lessons start promptly at 8 a.m.
b You can drink energy drinks in lessons.
c You must stay on the school premises during break.
d Mobile phones are allowed in lessons.
e Taking photos is forbidden on school premises.

| *das Kaugummikauen* | chewing gum chewing |
| *das Schulgelände* | school grounds / premises |

2. 📖 Read about the first half of Max's terrible day and answer the questions below in English.

> Gestern war ein furchtbarer Tag. Nichts war in Ordnung!
>
> Zuerst schlief ich zu lange und fuhr schnell mit dem Fahrrad zur Schule. Das war schlimm! Es regnete und es gab so viel Verkehr. Deshalb kam ich fünfzehn Minuten zu spät in die erste Stunde, und mein Mathelehrer war sehr böse auf mich. Ich fand das gemein.

a What was the first thing that went wrong for Max?
b Why was his cycle ride to school not great? (two details)
c What was his first lesson?
d Why was Max's teacher cross with him?
e What did Max think of this?

3. 🎯 Can you find any examples of irregular/strong forms of the imperfect tense in the text for activity 2?

4. 🎧 Now listen to the second half of Max's day and complete the statements in German (the infinitive forms are in brackets). Then translate the sentences into English.

a In der zweiten Stunde ___ Max eine Klassenarbeit in Englisch. (*schreiben*)
b Er ___ das sehr schwierig. (*finden*)
c Max ___ keine Ideen. (*haben*).
d In der Pause ___ er ein Butterbrot und ___ mit Freunden. (*essen, sprechen*)
e Er ___ seine Note für seine letzte Klassenarbeit. (*bekommen*)

| *die Note* | mark, grade |

Verben

The imperfect tense of weak and strong verbs

To form the imperfect tense of weak verbs, e.g. *spielen*, take the stem *spiel-*, then add the following endings:

ich	spiel**te**	wir	spiel**ten**
du	spiel**test**	ihr	spiel**tet**
er / sie / es	spiel**te**	sie / Sie	spiel**ten**

Irregular verbs have set stems to which the following endings are added (the example here is for *fahren* – to go / travel):

ich	fuhr	wir	fuhr**en**
du	fuhr**st**	ihr	fuhr**t**
er / sie / es	fuhr	sie / Sie	fuhr**en**

Some common stems are as follows:

essen – to eat	aß
sprechen – to speak	sprach
schreiben – to write	schrieb
bekommen – to get, receive	bekam
finden – to find	fand
geben – to give	gab

Education and work — 3.1H

5 Translate the statements into German, using the imperfect tense. Use the *Verben* box on page 36 to help you.

a I played handball.
b They ate during the break.
c We found the lesson boring.
d I got my mark for Maths.

Kultur

The usual way for assessing schoolwork in Germany is the 1–6 point system shown below:

1 *sehr gut* — very good
2 *gut* — good
3 *befriedigend* — fair
4 *ausreichend* — satisfactory
5 *mangelhaft* — poor
6 *ungenügend* — inadequate / unsatisfactory

6 Find the direct object pronoun in each sentence. Then translate the sentences into English, underlining the pronoun.

a Herr Schmidt, ich verstehe Sie nicht.
b Ach! Meine Deutschbücher! Ich habe sie vergessen!
c Der Lehrer mag uns nicht.
d Ich sehe euch in der Pause.

7 Find the indirect object pronoun in each sentence. Then translate the sentences into English, underlining the pronoun.

a Sie erklärt mir das Problem.
b Gib ihm das Buch!
c Ich schicke dir eine E-Mail.
d Ich gab ihnen die Adresse.

Grammatik

Direct and indirect object pronouns

Pronouns replace nouns in a sentence. Direct object pronouns replace a direct object in the accusative case, e.g. 'I read **the book**'. Indirect object pronouns replace an indirect object in the dative case, e.g. 'I read **you** the book'. These pronouns in German are as follows:

accusative	dative
mich	mir
dich	dir
ihn / sie / es	ihm / ihr / ihm
uns	uns
euch	euch
sie / Sie	ihnen / Ihnen

*Der Lehrer sieht **dich**.*
The teacher sees **you**.

*Das ist **mir** wichtig.*
It's important **to me**.

If you want to check whether a pronoun should be in the dative case, see if you can add 'to' or 'for' without changing the meaning, e.g. 'I read (to) you the book'.

8 Working with a partner, take turns to ask and respond to the questions based on the two photos.

- Was siehst du auf dem Foto A?
- Was siehst du auf dem Foto B?
- Wie findest du Erdkunde? Warum?
- Wie findest du Naturwissenschaften? Warum?
- Was hast du gestern in der Schule gemacht?

9 Write an article of around 90 words in German about your school. Mention:

- the name / size / location
- the school day
- some school rules
- a good day at school recently.

3.2F Jetzt geht's an die Arbeit!

OBJECTIVES
- Talking about jobs
- The perfect and imperfect tenses
- Coordinating and subordinating conjunctions
- Pronunciation: *u* and *ü*

1 📖 Read these job advertisements and answer the questions in English.

1 Busfahrer/in – Höchberg – Willkommensbonus von €1500

2 Zusteller*in für Briefe und Pakete (m/w/d) DEUTSCHE POST AG KAMP-LINTFORT MEHR INFOS Zum Job

3 Lehrer (m/w/d) 15537 Grünheide (Mark) Gymnasium, Oberschule Fächer: Deutsch, Geschichte Vollzeit

4 Kellner [m/w/d] für unser Anton & Anni Café am Flughafen Frankfurt Vollzeit

5 Gärtner ab April (w/m/d) IFA Graal-Müritz Hotel & Spa 18181 Seeheilbad Graal-Müritz Vollzeit

6 Online Journalist Wirtschaft [m/w/d] Jetzt bewerben IPPEN.MEDIA

der/die Zusteller/in   delivery person

a When does the gardening job start?
b In what sort of place will the gardener be working?
c Where is the café job based?
d Which organisation will the delivery person be working for?
e What will he/she be delivering?
f If you are interested in economics, which job might suit you?
g What is attractive about the bus driving job?
h What sort of teacher is being sought? (two details)

Kultur

It is now increasingly usual for job adverts in German-speaking countries to contain (m/w/d) or (w/m/d) in brackets.

This stands for *männlich/weiblich/divers* (male/female/non-binary) and indicates that the job is open to all applicants and that the appointment process is gender neutral.

For job titles that traditionally have a male or female variant spelling, we can separate the noun endings with a slash or an asterisk to avoid indicating any assumptions about the gender of the person: *Busfahrer/in; Zusteller*in*.

2 🎧 Listen to these young people talking about what they would like to do in the future. Copy and complete the table.

	wants to be …	Negative aspect	Positive aspect
Izel	a	b	c
Eren	d	hard work	e
Ben	f	g	h
Nina	i	difficult to succeed	j

Education and work 3.2F

3 Rewrite the sentences using the conjunction given in brackets. Take care with word order!

  a Ich möchte in einem Krankenhaus arbeiten. Es ist möglich. (*wenn*)
  b Er will Jura studieren. Er ist faul. (*aber*)
  c Ich möchte Arzt werden. Meine Noten sind gut. (*wenn*)
  d Ich will Informatiker werden. Ich finde Technologie interessant. (*denn*)
  e Schauspieler ist die perfekte Arbeit für mich. Ich liebe Theater. (*weil*)

4 Now try writing the sentences a, c and e in activity 3, starting with the conjunction each time, e.g. *Wenn es möglich ist …*

5 Working with a partner, take turns to ask and answer questions about this photo.
  - Sag etwas über das Foto.
  - Möchtest du in einem Büro arbeiten? Warum (nicht)?
  - Was ist die ideale Arbeit für dich? Warum?
  - Hast du einen Nebenjob?
  - Wie hast du in letzter Zeit Geld verdient?

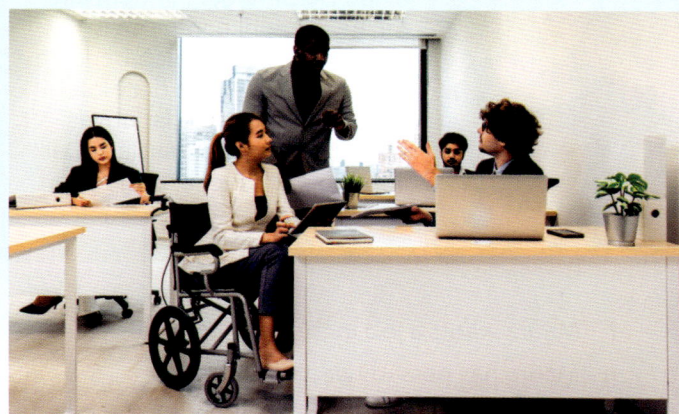

6 Translate the sentences into German. Use the *Verben* box to help you.

  a I worked in an office.
  b She earned a lot of money.
  c He was a waiter in a restaurant.
  d I had nice colleagues.
  e We worked every day.
  f It was interesting.

7 Write about jobs (90 words). Mention:
  - what sort of person you are
  - the job you would like to have and why
  - a job you have had and what you thought of it.

Grammatik

Coordinating and subordinating conjunctions

The conjunctions *und* (and), *aber* (but) and *denn* (because, since, as) join together sentences and clauses without changing the word order of the second part. These are **coordinating** conjunctions:

Ich will Designer werden. Ich bin kreativ. → *Ich will Designer werden, denn ich bin kreativ.*
I want to become a designer because I am creative.

The conjunctions *weil* (because) and *wenn* (if) send the verb in the second clause to the end. These are called **subordinating** conjunctions:

Ich will Designer werden. Ich bin kreativ. → *Ich will Designer werden, weil ich kreativ bin.*
I want to become a designer because I am creative.

Note the position of the verbs when a sentence starts with *weil* or *wenn*:

Weil ich kreativ bin, will ich Designer werden.
Because I am creative, I want to become a designer.

Aussprache

u and ü

The German *u* sound can be long or short, like the 'oo' in 'school' or 'book': *Juli* (July), *Bus* (bus).

The *ü* sound can also be long or short – make a higher 'oo' sound from the front of your mouth, pursing your lips as though whistling: *Schüler* (students), *Büro* (office), *Glück* (luck)

Verben

The perfect and imperfect tenses

You have learned two tenses to talk about the past in German.

The two-part perfect tense:
Ich habe vier Stunden gearbeitet.
I worked for four hours.
Ich habe einen Job gefunden.
I found a job.

The one-part imperfect tense:
Ich hatte einen Nebenjob in einem Geschäft.
I had a part-time job in a shop.
Meine Kollegen waren sehr freundlich.
My colleagues were very friendly.

neununddreißig

3.2H Ein schönes Stück Arbeit

OBJECTIVES
- Talking about work and future plans
- Clauses with *um … zu …*
- Relative clauses in the nominative and accusative cases
- Pronunciation: *zw*

1 📖 Read what each young person says about future plans. Decide if the statements are true (T) or false (F).

inzwischen	in the meantime
Sprachkenntnisse	language skills

MELISA

Ich möchte gern in der Zukunft Ärztin werden. Mein Vater, **der** Arzt ist, glaubt, dass ich das schaffe. Das Studium dauert sehr lange – sechs Jahre – aber das ist natürlich nötig. Für mich ist das Geld, **das** man verdient, nicht so wichtig wie Zufriedenheit am Arbeitsplatz.

MAURA

Ich habe keine Lust zu studieren. Ich interessiere mich für Autos und will nächstes Jahr Autofahren lernen, wenn ich alt genug bin. Danach möchte ich vielleicht Busfahrerin oder Taxifahrerin werden. Inzwischen will ich einen Job finden, um Geld zu verdienen, weil ich mir mein eigenes Auto kaufen will.

PHILIPP

Mein Traum ist es, Polizist zu sein. Ich will diesen Sommer mit 16 Jahren die Schule verlassen. Dann mache ich bei der Polizei eine Ausbildung, **die** zwei Jahre dauert. Um Polizist zu sein, muss man fit und zwischen 1,65 und 1,95 Meter groß sein.

BEN

Die besten Fächer, **die** ich in der Schule lerne, sind Fremdsprachen, und ich möchte einen Beruf haben, in dem ich meine Sprachkenntnisse in Englisch und Spanisch benutze. Eine Arbeitsstelle in der Hotel- oder Reiseindustrie ist etwas, was mich sehr interessiert. Der Job, **den** ich suche, darf nicht langweilig sein!

a Melisa wants to have the same career as her father.
b Melisa's main aim is to earn a high salary.
c Philipp doesn't want to stay at school for the Abitur.
d It's important for Philipp to be fit.
e Maura wants to go to university.
f Maura wants a job in the open air.
g Maura has passed her driving test.
h Ben's favourite subject is geography.
i Ben is learning French in school.
j Ben would like to work in tourism.

Kultur

Policing in Germany is the responsibility of the individual *Länder* (states). The government also has a federal police force tasked with domestic security. The *Bundesgrenzschutz* (*BGS*) (Federal Border Guard) deals with illegal immigration, smuggling, trafficking and organised crime activities.

Aussprache

zw

zw in German sounds like the English 'ts' and 'v' put together: **zw**ei, in**zw**ischen, **zw**ölf

Education and work 3.2H

2 Choose the correct relative pronoun to complete each sentence.

  a Das ist eine Arbeitsstelle, ___ interessant ist.
  b Der Lehrer, ___ Mathe unterrichtet, ist freundlich.
  c Das Geld, ___ ich verdiene, ist sehr wichtig für mich.
  d Ich arbeite mit Kollegen, ___ hilfsbereit sind.
  e Gibt es einen Beruf, ___ du haben willst?

3 Frau Müller is interviewing Mirko. Listen to the job interview and answer the questions in English.

  a What is Frau Müller's first question?
  b What is Mirko looking for in his career?
  c What are his interests? (two details)
  d What does he say about his personal qualities? (two details)
  e What has he done to perfect his IT skills?
  f What previous work experience does he have? (two details)

4 Translate the following into German using *um … zu …* Use the *Verben* box to help you.

  a in order to become an artist
  b in order to find a job
  c in order to be rich
  d in order to work in a hotel

5 Working with a partner, take turns to ask and answer the following questions about working life.
  - Welchen Beruf willst du in der Zukunft haben?
  - Warum ist diese Arbeit für dich richtig?
  - Was für Arbeit hast du schon gemacht?

6 Write down your answers for activity 5, adding further details (90 words). In your response try to use:
  - an example of a relative clause
  - an *um … zu …* structure.

Grammatik

Relative clauses in the nominative and accusative cases

Relative pronouns (who, whom, which, that) vary according to gender and case. Look at the **bold, highlighted examples** in activity 1. In the following example, the 'who' refers to a masculine noun (*Vater*) and is the subject of the relative clause, and is therefore in the nominative case:

Mein Vater, **der** *Arzt ist …* – My father, **who** is a doctor …

The relative pronoun in the next example is masculine again, but is the object of the relative clause, so is in the accusative case. The verb goes at the end of the relative clause and a comma separates it from the rest of the sentence:

Der Job, **den** *ich suche …* – The job which I am looking for …

Relative pronouns for the nominative and accusative cases are the same as the definite articles.

	masculine	feminine	neuter	plural
nominative	der	die	das	die
accusative	den	die	das	die

Verben

Clauses with *um … zu …*

To say 'in order to do something', put *um* at the start of the clause and *zu* before the infinitive at the end:

Ich will einen Job finden, **um** *Geld* **zu** *verdienen.*
I want to find a job to earn money.

If the *um … zu …* clause starts the sentence, invert the verb in the next clause:

Um *Geld* **zu** *verdienen,* **will** *ich einen Job finden.*
In order to earn money, I want to find a job.

Can you find an example in activity 1?

In der Zukunft	möchte ich will ich	Artz/Ärztin Lehrer/Lehrerin Autor/Autorin …	werden.
Mein Traum ist es,			zu sein.
Das ist ein Beruf,	der	wichtig interessant …	ist.
Der Job,	den ich suche, muss		sein.
Für mich ist es richtig,	denn	ich bin …	
	ich interessiere mich für …	
Ich habe schon als	Kellner/ Kellnerin …	gearbeitet.	

Theme 1

Kultur
Sport macht Spaß

1 Read the article about Alexandra Popp. Answer the questions in English.

Nationalspielerin des Jahres: Alexandra Popp

Alexandra Popp – auch Alex oder Poppi genannt – ist 32 Jahre alt und in Witten geboren. Sie ist eine deutsche Profifußballspielerin, eine der bekanntesten und erfolgreichsten Spielerinnen der Bundesliga-Mannschaft der Frauen. Seit 2019 ist sie Kapitänin der Mannschaft. Popp spielt im Mittelfeld / Sturm.

Früher besuchte sie die Eliteschule des Fußballs, die Gesamtschule Berger Feld in Gelsenkirchen, und war damals das einzige Mädchen an der Schule!

Nach dem Abitur machte sie ein Praktikum als Physiotherapeutin und danach eine Ausbildung als Zootierpflegerin im Duisburger Zoo, aber ihr Traum war immer, Profifußball zu spielen.

Ihre Fans wissen nicht viel über ihr Privatleben, das privat bleibt.

a Why is Popp famous in German football?
b Where was she educated?
c What was unusual about her education?
d Which other careers did she consider?
e In what way is she not a typical celebrity?

erfolgreich	successful
die Mannschaft	team
das Mittelfeld	midfield
der Sturm	attack
damals	at that time
einzig	only
die Ausbildung	training
der/die Zootierpfleger/in	zoo keeper

2 🎧 Listen to the report on ice hockey in the German-speaking world. Complete the gaps (a–g) in the text.

Diese Sportart ist in Deutschland, Österreich und der **a** ___ sehr beliebt.
Die heutige Version des Spiels hat sich aus sehr alten traditionellen Sportarten mit Stock und Ball entwickelt – hurling aus Irland, bandy aus **b** ___ und shinty aus **c** ___.
Die ersten Kunsteisbahnen waren in London und in New York. Frankfurt am Main wurde **d** ___ die dritte Stadt der Welt, die eine Eisbahn baute.
Das erste registrierte Eishockeyspiel wurde **e** ___ auf dem **f** ___ Halensee gespielt. Damals spielte man mit einem Ball, aber heute benutzt man einen Puck.
Die Nationalmannschaft der Männer debütierte 1910 in Deutschland, während die Frauen- und Juniorenteams **g** ___ und 1976 ihr Debüt gaben.

Kultur

The most popular sports in Austria are football, tennis, skiing, golf, gymnastics and ice / stick sports like ice hockey.

In Germany, football, golf and ice hockey top the popularity list, followed by basketball, motor racing, handball, and then by tennis, skiing, cycling and boxing.

Football is the number one sport in Switzerland. Next come ice hockey, winter sports like skiing, skating and snowboarding, then basketball, tennis, motorsport, rugby union and cycling.

sich entwickeln	to develop / evolve
Kunsteisbahnen (pl)	artificial ice rinks
debütieren	to debut / make a first appearance

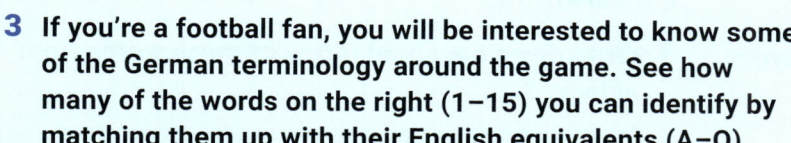

Theme 1

3 If you're a football fan, you will be interested to know some of the German terminology around the game. See how many of the words on the right (1–15) you can identify by matching them up with their English equivalents (A–O).

Kultur

Germany is one of the most successful nations in international football. The men's team have won the World Cup four times. In 1954, 1974 and 1990 this was as West Germany (the country was divided into East and West until 1991 – see p. 82 for more information), whereas in 2014 it won as Germany.

The women's team won the World Cup in 2003 and 2007.

German terms			English terms	
1	Mittelkreis	A	penalty area
2	Abpfiff	B	corner kick
3	Kopfball	C	centre circle
4	Stürmer	D	centre line
5	Spielfeld	E	extra time
6	Mannschaft	F	final whistle
7	Seitenlinie	G	goal area
8	Strafraum	H	header
9	Torraum	I	touchline
10	Eckstoß	J	throw in
11	Verlängerung	K	striker
12	Einwurf	L	free kick
13	Freistoß	M	team
14	Mittellinie	N	midfielder
15	Mittelfeldspieler	O	pitch

4 Read the article below on the popularity of open water swimming in Germany. Copy and complete the sentences in English.

a Open-water swimming has become _____. (two details)

b The DSV website gives information about the sport and about _____. (two details)

c The positive aspects of this sport are that _____. (two details)

Freiwasserschwimmen in Deutschland

Freiwasserschwimmen ist ein Sport, der in den letzten Jahren sehr beliebt geworden ist. Der DSV (Deutscher Schwimm-Verband) hat eine Webseite mit Informationen über den Sport, die Ausrüstung und über Schwimmwettbewerbe.

Die Webseite beschreibt das Freiwasserschwimmen als eine Extremsportart, die im Einklang mit der Natur ist und einen sanften, umweltfreundlichen Tourismus fördert.

Es gibt wunderbare Orte in Deutschland, wo man Freiwasserschwimmen ausprobieren kann. Beispiele sind:

1 der Vulkankratersee Pulvermaar in Rheinland-Pfalz

2 das Strandbad West in Überlingen (ein Badestrand mit eigener Insel und Blick auf die Alpen)

3 der Geroldsauer Wasserfall bei Baden-Baden (Baden-Württemberg) im Schwarzwald.

Schwimmwettbewerbe (pl) — swimming competitions

5 Match the photos (a–c) to the three locations (1–3) mentioned in the article in activity 4.

a

b

c

6 The following are unusual sports from the German-speaking world. Research one of them, answering the questions below.

Wattolümpiade   Hornussen

Steinstossen

- Where is it played?
- When did it start?
- What are the rules?

dreiundvierzig

Theme 1 — Grammar practice

Present tense of weak and strong verbs

1 Copy and complete the sentences with the correct form of the verb given in brackets.

  a Ich ___ keine Schwestern. (*haben*)
  b Wir ___ oft wandern. (*gehen*)
  c Er ___ gern Basketball. (*spielen*)
  d Was ___ du zum Frühstück? (*essen*)
  e Das Kind ___ fünf Jahre alt. (*sein*)
  f Mein Vater ___ mit dem Auto in die Stadt. (*fahren*)
  g Die Lehrerin ___ uns viele Hausaufgaben. (*geben*)
  h Ich ___ nicht gern. (*schwimmen*)
  i Die Schüler ___ pünktlich in die Stunde. (*kommen*)
  j ___ du genug Wasser? (*trinken*)

Gender of nouns

2 Group these nouns according to whether they are masculine, feminine or neuter. Which of the nouns has a predictable gender? Which did you have to look up?

> Freundin   Onkel   Familie   Tag
> Haar   Frau   Person   Konzert
> Stunde   Wochenende   Kind   Freiheit
> Zucker   Essen   Wasser   Salat
> Lebensstil   Café   Mann   Partner

Grammatik

It's best to learn the gender of any new nouns you come across, plus the plural form, but there are some guidelines that can help you to work them out. For instance, nouns that describe people are usually male or female gender according to the person, e.g. *der Lehrer / die Lehrerin*. Exceptions are *das Mädchen* (girl) and *das Fräulein* (young woman) because these are diminutive forms. Other words ending in *-chen* and *-lein* are neuter for the same reason, e.g. *das Hündchen* = puppy. *Die Person* can refer to a person of any gender.

Plural nouns

3 Write down the plural forms of these words from activity 2.

> Freundin   Onkel   Familie   Tag
> Person   Stunde   Kind
> Café   Mann   Partner

Verbs with *zu* + infinitive

4 Translate these sentences into German.

  a I hope to get good marks.
  b They decide (*beschließen*) to eat healthily.
  c We begin to learn German.
  d He plans to be a doctor.
  e She tries to run every day.

Verben

Some verbs are used with *zu* plus the infinitive of another verb. The infinitive goes at the end of the sentence:
Ich hoffe, eine Arbeit zu finden. – I hope to find a job.

Direct and indirect object pronouns

5 Put the words in these sentences into the correct order.

  a ihm / **Sie** / bringt / es / .
  b **Hast** / ihr / gegeben / das Buch / du / ?
  c es / ihnen / **Können** / Sie / schicken / ?
  d erklärt / **Meine** / Schwester / hat / es / mir / .

Grammatik

When you have both a direct object pronoun and an indirect object pronoun in the same sentence, the direct object pronoun always comes first, e.g.:
Gib es mir! – Give it to me!

Think of the acronym PAD: Pronoun Accusative Dative

N.B. When you are using two nouns or a pronoun and a noun, the indirect object comes first instead, e.g.: *Gib mir den Apfel! Gib dem Mann das Geld!* Give me the apple! Give the man the money!

People and lifestyle — Theme 1

Reflexive verbs and pronouns

6 Copy and complete the sentences with the correct forms of the reflexive verb and pronoun given in brackets.

a Ich ___ ___ nicht gut mit meinem Bruder. (*sich verstehen*)
b Er ___ ___ nicht genug. (*sich bewegen*)
c Meine Freunde ___ ___ auf der Feier. (*sich amüsieren*)
d Die Kinder ___ ___ nicht oft. (*sich streiten*)
e ___ du ___ auf die Party? (*sich freuen*)
f Wir ___ ___ sehr gut. (*sich kennen*)

Verben

Reflexive verbs have an extra part called the reflexive pronoun, which reflects the action onto the subject:

sich duschen to have a shower

ich dusche **mich**   wir duschen **uns**
du duschst **dich**   ihr duscht **euch**
er/sie/es duscht **sich**   sie/Sie duschen **sich**

Reflexive pronouns in German can usually be translated as 'yourself', 'myself', etc.

Reflexive verbs (translation)

7 Translate the sentences in activity 6 into English.

Separable verbs

8 Rewrite these sentences, putting the words in the correct order. The first word is shown in bold.

a an / **Die** / fängt / Stunde / in zwei Minuten / .
b mit deinen Eltern / du / aus / gut / **Kommst** / ?
c gehen / aus / oft / am Wochenende / **Wir** / .
d später / **Ich** / an / dich / rufe / .
e kommt / Lehrer / **Wann** / zurück / der / ?

Verben

When you use a separable verb in the present tense, the separable prefix moves to the end of the sentence or clause:

ausgehen → Wir **gehen** am Samstag **aus**.
We're going out on Saturday.

Subordinate clauses are an exception to this rule, e.g.:
... weil wir **ausgehen**. – ... because we're going out.

Using *seit*

9 Translate these sentences into English.

a Wir lernen seit zwei Jahren Spanisch.
b Ich wohne seit zehn Monaten in England.
c Er spielt seit drei Stunden Gitarre.
d Seit wann bist du Mitglied des Clubs?

Using *seit* (translation)

10 Translate these sentences into German.

a I have been learning German for three years.
b We have been in school since half past eight.
c They have been living in London for six weeks.

Verben

Seit means 'since' and is usually used with the present tense:

Ich bin **seit** 9 Uhr hier.
I've been here since 9 o'clock.

Coordinating conjunctions

11 Use *und*, *aber*, *oder* or *denn* to link each pair of short sentences.

a Ich heiße Ben. Ich bin siebzehn Jahre alt.
b Ich treibe gern Sport. Ich schwimme nicht gern.
c Am Abend gehe ich nicht aus. Ich habe viele Hausaufgaben.
d Er mag Biologie. Die Lehrerin ist sehr gut.
e Wir spielen Tennis. Wir gehen spazieren.
f Mein Freund studiert Medizin. Er will Arzt werden.

Grammatik

Coordinating conjunctions such as *und*, *aber*, *oder* and *denn* do not affect word order.

Subordinating conjunctions such as *weil* send the verb to the end.

Ich bin müde, **weil** ich nicht gut geschlafen **habe**.
I am tired because I have not slept well.

fünfundvierzig

Theme 1 — Grammar practice

Perfect tense with *haben*

12 Copy and complete the sentences in the perfect tense, using *haben* and the verb in brackets.

a Wir ___ gestern Golf ___. (*spielen*)
b Mein Bruder ___ keine Hausaufgaben ___. (*machen*)
c Ich ___ heute nicht viel ___. (*essen*)
d ___ du das Buch ___? (*lesen*)
e Meine Schwester ___ ein Eis ___. (*kaufen*)
f Ich ___ den Tag ermüdend ___. (*finden*)
g Die Kinder ___ Klettern ___. (*lernen*)
h Wie lange ___ ihr ___? (*arbeiten*)
i Meine Mutter ___ mit dem Lehrer ___. (*sprechen*)
j ___ Sie das Spiel ___? (*sehen*)

Perfect tense with *sein*

13 Copy and complete the sentences in the perfect tense, using *sein* and the verb in brackets.

a Ich ___ spät in die Schule ___. (*kommen*)
b Er ___ nach Berlin ___. (*fahren*)
c Wir ___ ins Fitness-Studio ___. (*gehen*)
d Mein Opa ___ krank ___. (*sein*)
e ___ du zu Hause ___? (*bleiben*)
f Mein Freund ___ Zahnarzt ___. (*werden*)
g Die Kinder ___ ins Wasser ___. (*fallen*)
h Am Montag ___ ich nicht schwimmen ___. (*gehen*)
i Meine Freundin und ich ___ im Park ___. (*laufen*)
j Warum ___ ihr nicht pünktlich ___ ? (*kommen*)

Verben

The perfect tense is formed using an auxiliary verb plus a past participle.

Usually the auxiliary verb is the present tense of *haben*, but in some instances – usually verbs denoting movement from one place to another, or a change of state – it is the present tense of *sein*.

The nominative and accusative cases (definite article)

14 Copy and complete each sentence, using the correct form of the definite article.

a D___ Fisch ist lecker.
b Ich habe d___ Apfel gegessen.
c D___ Kind ist zehn Jahre alt.
d Kennst du d___ Lehrerin?
e D___ beste Fach ist bestimmt Mathe.
f Wie alt sind d___ Jungen?
g Ich habe d___ Buch vergessen.
h Ich will d___ Job im Café haben.
i D___ Frau kauft d___ Bücher.
j D___ Klassenzimmer sind schmutzig.

Grammatik

Definite articles are the words for 'the'. Indefinite articles are the words for 'a'. In the **nominative** case – used for the subject of the sentence – these are as follows:

	masculine	feminine	neuter	plural
definite article	der	die	das	die
indefinite article	ein	eine	ein	-

In the **accusative** case – used for the direct object of the sentence – the **masculine singular** forms change:

	masculine	feminine	neuter	plural
definite article	den	die	das	die
indefinite article	einen	eine	ein	-

*Sie isst **den** Apfel und **einen** Kuchen.* – She eats the apple and a cake.

The nominative and accusative cases (indefinite and negative article)

15 Copy and complete each sentence, using the correct form of the indefinite or negative article.

a Martin hat e___ Schwester, aber k___ Bruder.
b Er hat e___ besten Freund, der Max heißt.
c Hast du k___ Plan für nächstes Jahr?
d Mein Onkel hat e___ nette Partnerin.
e Willst du e___ Kaffee oder e___ Cola?
f Du sollst k___ Zigaretten rauchen.
g Sie hat e___ Eis gegessen.

46 sechsundvierzig

People and lifestyle **Theme 1**

The imperfect tense of sein

16 Copy and complete each sentence with the correct imperfect form of *sein*.

a Meine Mutter ___ sauer auf mich.
b Die beiden Mathestunden ___ sehr interessant.
c Das Kind ___ traurig.
d Ich ___ nicht sportlich.
e Ihr ___ bei mir.
f Wo ___ du heute?

The imperfect tense of weak and strong verbs

17 Copy and complete each sentence with the correct imperfect tense form of the verb in brackets. The first five are regular / weak verbs, while the remaining five are irregular / strong verbs.

a Im Kindergarten ___ ich den ganzen Tag. (*spielen*)
b Die Lehrerin ___ manchmal Kekse für uns. (*kaufen*)
c Ich ___ Rechnen, Lesen und Schreiben. (*lernen*)
d Wir ___ oft Bilder. (*malen*)
e Die Kinder ___ viel Lärm. (*machen*)
f Um zwölf Uhr ___ wir zu Mittag. (*essen*)
g Einige Kinder ___ am Nachmittag. (*schlafen*)
h Du ___ viele Freunde. (*haben*)
i Es ___ keine Uniform und keine Hausaufgaben. (*geben*)
j Er ___ zum Park. (*gehen*)

Verben

To form the imperfect tense of weak verbs (e.g. *machen*), take the stem (*mach-*) and add the following endings: *ich mach**te**, du mach**test**, er / sie / es mach**te**, wir mach**ten**, ihr mach**tet**, sie / Sie mach**ten**.

For some irregular imperfect forms, see page 172.

Relative pronouns

18 Add the correct relative pronoun to complete each sentence.

a Mein Vater, ___ Lehrer ist, hat lange Arbeitszeiten.
b Die Frau, ___ Deutsch unterrichtet, ist ziemlich jung.
c Sie hat ein Kind, ___ sechs Jahre alt ist.
d Die Freunde, ___ ich heute gesehen habe, sind sehr lustig.
e Das Essen, ___ mir am besten schmeckt, ist Hähnchen mit Pommes.
f Ich hoffe, eine Arbeit zu finden, ___ mich interessiert.
g Mein Opa, ___ in der Schweiz wohnt, ist achtzig Jahre alt.
h Der beste Lehrer, ___ ich kenne, ist Herr Heckelsmüller.
i Ich mag alle Fächer, ___ ich dieses Jahr lerne.
j Ich liebe Bananen, ___ sehr gesund sind.

Grammatik

Relative pronouns (who, whom, which, that) vary according to the gender and case of the word they refer to.

In this sentence, the relative pronoun refers to a feminine noun (*Schwester*) and is the subject of the relative clause, so it is in the nominative case:

*Meine Schwester, **die** Wissenschaftlerin ist …*
My sister, who is a scientist …

In this sentence, the relative pronoun is masculine and is the object of the relative clause, so it is in the accusative case:

*Mein Bruder, **den** ich gestern gesehen habe …*
My brother, who I saw yesterday …

Using um … zu

19 Translate the sentences into German.

a We eat fruit in order to be healthy.
b I work hard in order to get good marks.
c She went to London to see the family.
d What do you do to keep fit?
e He's going out to see a film.

Grammatik

To express 'in order to', use *um … zu …*:
*Ich werde einen Job finden, **um** Geld **zu** verdienen.*
I will find a job in order to earn money.

siebenundvierzig **47**

Theme 1 — Higher Vocabulary

Words that are highlighted in grey in this list are words that may be useful, but you won't need to know them for the exam.

Introductory

aber but
Aktivität (f) activity
alt old
älter als older than
Arbeit (f) work
ärgerlich annoying
Arzt (m), Ärztin (f) doctor
Augen (pl) eye
auskommen mit to get on with
aussehen to look like
Autor (m), Autorin (f) author
Bauer (m), Bäuerin (f) farmer
beide both
bekannt known, famous
bezahlen to pay
Beziehung (f) relationship
bleiben to stay
böse bad, mad, naughty, angry
braun brown
Brille (f) glasses
Bruder (m) brother
Chef (m) boss
denken to think
der Vorteil (m) advantage
Deutsch German
dort there
Erdkunde (f) geography
ermüdend tiring
essen to eat
Familie (f) family
Frau (f) woman, wife
furchtbar terrible
Fußball spielen to play football
geduldig patient, patiently
gefährlich dangerous
gehen to go
Geige (f) violin
gemeinsam in common
Gemüse (nt) vegetables
geschieden divorced
gesund healthy
Gesundheit (f) health
glücklich happy

groß tall, big
Grüß dich! Greetings! Hello!
gut good, well
Haare (pl) hair
Haus (nt) house
Hausaufgaben (pl) homework
helfen to help
hilfsbereit helpful
im Freien in the open air
sich interessieren für to be interested in
joggen to jog
jung young
Junge (m) boy
jünger als younger than
Keks (m) biscuit
Kellner (m), Kellnerin (f) waiter, waitress
Klasse (f) class
Klavier piano
klein small
Klima (nt) climate
Kontakt (m) contact
Kuchen (m) cake
Kunst (f) art
kurz short
lang long
Lehrer (m), Lehrerin (f) teacher
lesen to read
lieb kind
lieben to love
links left, on the left
lustig funny, enjoyable
machen to make, to do
malen to paint
Mann (m) man, husband
Mathe (f) maths
Mensch (m) person, human being
mitkommen to come with
Musik (f) music
Nachmittag (m) afternoon
Natur (f) nature
nett nice
Noten (pl) marks / grades
Obst (nt) fruit
Oma (f) grandma
Onkel (m) uncle
Opa (m) grandpa

Park (m) park
Polizist (m), Polizistin (f) police officer
Problem (nt) problem
rechts right, on the right
Roman (m) novel
ruhig calm, quiet
Schauspieler (m), Schauspielerin (f) actor
schlank slim, thin
schmecken to taste
schreiben to write
Schule (f) school
Schwester (f) sister
schwierig difficult
schwimmen to swim
sein to be
Sohn (m) son
spannend exciting
spielen to play
Sport (m) sport, PE
sportlich sporty
stief- step-
streng strict
Studium (nt) study, studies
Stunde (f) hour, lesson
Tag (m) day
Tante (f) aunt
tanzen to dance
Tochter (f) daughter
tragen to wear
Tschüß! Bye!
und and
Uni (f) uni, university
unterrichten to teach
verdienen to earn
vergessen to forget
verheiratet married
Wasser (nt) water
Welt (f) world
wichtig important
witzig funny
Woche (f) week
wohnen to live
Zeit (f) time
ziemlich quite
zu Hause at home
Zukunft (f) future
Zwillinge (pl) twins

1.1F Ich und die Meinen

.. Jahre alt ... years old
bei uns with us, at our house
Cousin (m), Cousine (f) cousin
Einzelkind (nt) only child
Eltern (pl) parents
es gibt there is, there are
fahren to go, to drive
Film (m) film
Freund (m) friend, boyfriend
Freundin (f) friend, girlfriend
fünfzehn fifteen
Geschwister (pl) siblings, brothers and sisters
heißen to be called
Katze (f) cat
kein no, not any
Kind (nt) child
Kino (nt) cinema
manchmal sometimes
mein my
mit dem Auto by car
mit dem Bus by bus
Mutter (f) mother
Name (m) name
nicht weit von not far from
niedlich cute
oft often
Partner (m), Partnerin (f) partner
sechzehn sixteen
sehen to see
sehr very
siebzehn seventeen
sprechen to speak
treiben to do (e.g. sport), to drive, to pursue
Vater (m) father
vierzig forty
weit far
zusammen together

1.1H Meine Leute und ich

arbeiten to work
auf dem Land in the countryside
beginnen to begin
blau blue
die Schweiz Switzerland

48 achtundvierzig

Theme 1

draußen outside
dunkel dark
Farbe (f) colour
Ferien (pl) holidays, school break
freundlich friendly
genießen to enjoy
grau grey
hoffen to hope
im Moment at the moment
immer always
Kleidung (f) clothes, clothing
Klettern (nt) climbing
Konzert (nt) concert
Land (nt) country, countryside
lernen to learn
Lesen (nt) reading
Mädchen (nt) girl
mir to me, me (indirect obj)
musikalisch musical
rot red
schlafen to sleep
schön beautiful
schwarz black
Schwimmen (nt) swimming
verbringen to spend (time)
versuchen to try
Wochenende (nt) weekend
zwölf twelve

1.2F Lebensweisen und Lebensbeziehungen

sich amüsieren to enjoy oneself
ausgehen to go out
denn because
dich you, yourself (familiar singular, direct object pronoun)
sich duschen to shower
euch you, yourself (familiar plural, direct object pronoun)
faul lazy
*Freund*in (m/f), Freund*innen (pl)* friend, friends (gender neutral)
sich freuen auf to look forward to
gemein mean
getrennt separated
heiraten to marry
Hochzeit (f) wedding
Jahr (nt) year

jedes Wochenende every weekend
jetzt now
kennen to know (people)
langweilig boring
Lebenspartnerschaft (f), zivile Partnerschaft (f) civil partnership
ledig single
meistens mostly
mich me, myself (direct object pronoun)
mit wem with whom
Mutti (f) Mum, Mummy
nächstes Jahr next year
neunzehn nineteen
nie never
Partnerschaft (f) partnership
sich himself/herself/yourself (formal)/themselves (direct object pronoun)
streiten to quarrel, to argue
ungeduldig impatient
uns us, ourselves (direct object pronoun)
Vati (m) Dad, Daddy
verlobt engaged
Verlobte (m or f) fiancé(e)
verstehen to understand
sich verstehen mit to get on with
warum why
sich waschen to wash (oneself)
wer who
wie how

1.2H Wichtige Beziehungen

ab und zu now and again
aktiv active
allein alone
alles everything
ankommen to arrive
anrufen to phone, to ring
sich beschäftigen (mit) to be busy (with), to be dealing (with)
beschreiben to describe
Ehe (f) marriage
ehrlich honest
einander each other
einige a few, some
einkaufen to shop

sich entspannen to relax
erlauben to allow
etwas something
etwas Positives something positive
Freiheit (f) freedom
Gruppe (f) group
heute today
Interesse (f) interest
jemand someone
kaum hardly
Kleinigkeit (f) minor thing, trivial matter
sich kümmern um to take care of, to concern ourselves about
leben to live
Leben (nt) life
miteinander with each other
Monat (m) month
morgen tomorrow
natürlich natural, naturally, of course
neu new
normalerweise normally, usually
nötig necessary
Person (f) person
positiv positive
Restaurant (nt) restaurant
schlecht bad
seit since, for
seit … Jahren for … years
selten rare, rarely
spät late
toll great
traurig sad
trinken to drink
Kaffee (m) coffee
über about, above, over
verantwortlich responsible
wenn if, when, whenever
wunderbar wonderful
zum Beispiel for example
zurück back

2.1F Wir essen gern!

abends in the evening
Apfel (m) apple
benutzen to use
Brot (nt) bread
Cola (f) cola
dreimal three times, thrice

Ei (nt) egg
Ernährung (f) food, diet
Essen (nt) food, meal
Fastfood (nt) fast food
finden to find
Fisch (m) fish
Fleisch (nt) meat
frisch fresh
Frühstück (nt) breakfast
genug enough
gestern yesterday
Glas (m) glas
Hähnchen (nt) chicken
heute Morgen this morning
Information (f) information
Joghurt (m or n) yoghurt
Kartoffeln (pl) potatoes
Käse (m) cheese
Käsebrot (nt) bread and cheese
kochen to cook
Lebensmittel (pl) food, foodstuffs, groceries
lieblings- favourite
Liter (m or nt) litre
Milch (f) milk
mindestens at least
Morgen (m) morning
nützlich useful
österreichisch Austrian
Österreich Austria
Pizza (f) pizza
Pommes (pl) chips, fries
Portion (f) portion
Pyramide (f) pyramid
Reis (m) rice
Salat (m) salad
Tasse (f) cup
Tee (m) tea
Wurst (f) sausage
zweimal two times, twice

2.1H Ein gesundes Leben

an der frischen Luft in the open air
andere other
sich aufstehen to get up
ausprobieren to try out
Banane (f) banana
besser better

neunundvierzig 49

Theme 1 — Higher Vocabulary

Club (m) club
Computer (m) computer
das erste Mal the first time
eines Tages one day
Energie (f) energy
erklären to explain
sich ernähren to feed yourself
Fanatiker (m) fanatic, endie Aktithusiast
faszinierend fascinating
Frage (f) question
Freiwasserschwimmen (nt) wild swimming
Gefühl (nt) feeling
hoffentlich hopefully
in der Nähe near, in the vicinity
interessant interesting
Internet (nt) internet
jeden Tag every day
Jugendliche (f) young person, adolescent
Juni June
kalt cold
krank ill
Lebensstil (m) lifestyle
Mahlzeit (f) meal
Meer (nt) sea, ocean
mehr more
Mitglied (nt) member
müde tired
nächst- next
Rauchen (nt) smoking
sagen to say
Schock (nt) shock
Schokolade (f) chocolate
sofort immediately, straight away
später later
Spiel (nt) game, match
suchen to seek, to look for
surfen to surf
Toastbrot (nt) toast
Vegetarier (m), Vegetarierin (f) vegetarian
verbessern to improve
vor einem Jahr a year ago
Weg (m) path, way

2.2F Glück und Gesundheit

Aktivität (f) activity
Aspekt (m) aspect
auch also
auch nicht … not … either
bekommen to receive, to get
Bewegung (f) movement
Buch (nt) book
dann then
deshalb therefore
einfach simple, simply
einladen to invite
erleben to experience
ernst nehmen to take seriously
erstens, zweitens, drittens first(ly), second(ly), third(ly)
Erwachsene (m or f) adult
fast almost
fliegen to fly
Freitag Friday
Freizeit (f) free time
ganz whole, all the, quite
gar nicht not at all
geben to give
genau exact, exactly
hören to hear, to listen to
kaufen to buy
lachen to laugh
laufen to run
leider unfortunately
letzte Woche last week
lösen to solve, to loosen
meiner Meinung nach in my opinion
möglich possible
müssen must, to have to
nicht der Fall not the case
Regel (f) rule
regelmäßig regular, regularly
richtig right, correct
Schlaf (m) sleep
schließlich finally, eventually
Schularbeit (f) schoolwork
sitzen to sit
Stress (m) stress
stundenlang for hours
teilen to share
um … Uhr at … o'clock
unmöglich impossible
viele a lot, many
werden to become
Zimmer (nt) room
zuletzt in the end

2.2H Pass gut auf dich!

Alltag (m) daily routine, everyday life
Änderung (f) change
Anfänger (m) beginner
aufpassen (auf) to pay attention (to), to take care (of)
bestimmt certain, definite, certainly, definitely
dass that
doch however, but
eifersüchtig jealous, envious
ein bisschen a bit
empfehlen to recommend
erreichen to reach, to achieve
fernsehen to watch TV
sich fühlen to feel
funktionieren to function, to work
für for
halten to stop, to hold
hier here
in letzter Zeit recently
informieren to inform
Intensität (f) intensity
klingen to sound
können can, to be able to
Kraft (f) strength, power
langfristig long-term
Lebensweise (f) way of life
lecker delicious
leicht light, easy
mental mental
Methode (f) method
Minute (f) minute
mittel (mittlere) medium
pro per
Rad fahren to cycle, to go by bike
schon already
schrecklich terrible
Schritt (m) step
sondern (but) rather
sonnig sunny
spazieren gehen to go for a walk
steigen to rise, to increase, to climb
Treppe (f) flight of stairs
Vorteil (m) advantage
wandern to go for a walk, to hike
warm warm
wenig little
weniger als less than
Wetter (nt) weather
Wirkung (f) effect
Ziel (nt) goal
zu Fuß gehen to go on foot, to walk
zuerst first of all

3.1F Eine gute Ausbildung

am Ende at the end
besuchen to visit, to go to
Biologie (f) biology
danach afterwards, after
Deutsch (nt) German
dienstags on Tuesdays
Doppelstunde (f) double lesson
Englisch (nt) English
etwa about, approximately
Fach (nt) subject
Französisch (nt) French
freitags on Fridays
Gesamtschule (f) comprehensive school
Geschichte (f) history
Grundschule (f) primary school
gut good
Gymnasium (nt) grammar school
Hauptschule (f) secondary school
Kantine (f) canteen
Lieblingsfach (nt) favourite subject
Mittagspause (f) lunch break
nach Hause gehen to go home
nachmittags in the afternoons
Pause (f) break
Physik (f) physics
Religion (f) relignion, religious studies
Schüler (m), Schülerin (f) student, pupil
Schultag (m) school day

Theme 1

Stadt (f) town
Stundenplan (m) timetable
Unterricht (m) lessons, classes, teaching
Wirtschaft (f) economics, economy
zu Ende finished, at the end
zwischen between

3.1H Nun heißt's lernen!

Adresse (f) address
aufnehmen to take (photos), to record (videos), to pick up
ausreichend satisfactory
befriedigend fair
direkt direct, directly
enttäuschend disappointing
erlaubt allowed
Fahrrad (nt) bicycle
Foto (nt) photo, photograph
Gebäude (nt) building, buildings
gesamt whole, entire
Handy (nt) mobile phone
Idee (f) idea
in Ordnung in order, all right
Kaugummi (m or nt) chewing gum
mangelhaft poor
Naturwissenschaften (pl) natural sciences
Prüfung (f) exam
pünktlich punctual, in/on time
regnen to rain
schicken to send
schlimm terrible
schnell fast, quick, quickly
Schulgelände (nt) school grounds
ungenügend inadequate, unsatisfactory
Verkehr (m) traffic
verlassen to leave
Video (nt) video
während during

3.2F Jetzt geht's an die Arbeit!

Beruf (m) job, career
berühmt famous
Büro (nt) office
Busfahrer (m), Busfahrerin (f) bus driver
Café (nt) café
erfolgreich successful
Firma (f) firm
Flughafen (m) airport
frei free
Geld (nt) money
Geschäft (nt) business, shop
glauben to believe
gut bezahlt well paid
Hotel (nt) hotel
Informatiker (m), Informatikerin (f) computer scientist
Job (m) job
Journalismus (m) journalism
Journalist (m), Journalistin (f) journalist
Jura (m) law
Kellner (m), Kellnerin (f) waiter, waitress
Kollege (m), Kollegin (f) colleague
Krankenhaus (nt) hospital
kreativ creative
Medien (pl) (the) media
Nebenjob (m) extra job, side job
Oberschule (f) grammar school
Paket (nt) package
Post (f) post, mail, post office
reich rich
studieren to study
Tagung (f) conference, session
Technologie (f) technology
Theater (nt) theatre
Vielfalt (f) variety
vollzeit full time
weil because
willkommen welcome
Zusteller (m), Zustellerin (f) delivery agent

3.2H Ein schönes Stück Arbeit

Abendschule (f) evening/night school
Arbeitsplatz (m) workplace, place of work
Ausbildung (f) training, education, development
Auto (nt) car
Bibliothek (f) library
Charakter (m) character
dauern to last
eigen own
Eigenschaft (f) quality
Erfahrung (f) experience
Fähigkeit (f) ability
fleißig hardworking, diligent
Fremdsprachen (pl) foreign languages
Industrie (f) industry
inzwischen in the meantime
Kenntnis (f) knowledge
Kunde (m), Kundin (f) customer
Kurs (m) course
Kutur (f) culture
Land (nt) country, land, state
Lust (f) desire
Polizei (fl police
Reise (f) journey, trip
Reisebüro (nt) travel agency
Rezeption (f) reception
schaffen to create
Sommer (m) summer
Stelle (f) place, job
Tourismus (m) tourism
Traum (m) dream
um … zu … in order to …
vielleicht perhaps
Vorstellungsgespräch (nt) job interview
Zufriedenheit (f) contentment

Kultur

Abitur (nt) school leaving exams, A level equivalent
Alpen (pl) the Alps
Art (f) type, kind
Ausrüstung (f) equipment
Ball (m) ball
bauen to build
damals then, at that time
einzig only, single
sich entwickeln to develop
Fan (m) fan, supporter
fördern to promote
früher earlier
geboren born
genannt called
heutig current
Kapitän (m) captain
Linie (f) line, route (e.g. bus)
Mannschaft (f) team
Ort (m) place, town, location
Pfleger (m), Pflegerin (f) carer, keeper
privat private
Privatleben (nt) private life
Profi- professional
sanft gentle
Schwarzwald (m) Black Forest
Spaß machen to be fun
Spieler (m), Spielerin (f) player
Strand (m) beach
Tier (nt) animal
Tor (nt) goal, gate, gateway
traditionell traditional, traditionally
umweltfreundlich environmentally friendly
Verband (m) association
Wasserfall (m) waterfall
Wettbewerb (m) competition

German is a language with grammatical genders, so some of the words in this list have a masculine and feminine form, which are used for referring to different people. You will not be marked down in the exam for your preferred ways of referring to yourself and others through the use of pronouns, gendered language and grammatical agreement.

Theme 1 — Test and revise: Higher Listening

1 🎧 **You hear a Swiss student talking about his school life. Complete each sentence in English.**

   a He thinks the school day ___. **1 mark**
   b He hates ___. **1 mark**
   c He thinks that maths and ___ are useful for the future. **1 mark**

> **Tipp**
> This task is about listening for specific details within the passage you hear. Before you start, read the incomplete sentences carefully and try to predict what language you might hear. For example, for the second sentence, you will need to listen out for a negative opinion.

2 🎧 **You hear a German podcast about what makes people happy with their lives. Of the eight aspects of life listed here, which three are mentioned in the podcast?**

1	pets
2	a new car
3	good relationships
4	a nice place to live
5	holidays abroad
6	having lots of money
7	good health
8	having fun

3 marks

3 🎧 **Two young people are talking about work. For each person, note something they did in the past (P), something they do now (N) and something they are planning for the future (F).**

   a P _____
       N _____
       F _____ **3 marks**
   b P _____
       N _____
       F _____ **3 marks**

> **Tipp**
> For this type of task, you need to listen out for time references. You could break this down by first listening to the verbs used in the audio and deciding whether they are in the past, present or future tense. Secondly, listen out for time phrases, such as *vorher* or *heute*.

4 🎧 **Your Austrian friend, Finn, is talking about his relationships with family and friends. Which statements are true (T) and which are false (F)?**

   a Finn's parents are divorced. **1 mark**
   b Finn has an older sister. **1 mark**
   c Finn's father has remarried. **1 mark**
   d Finn sees his father every weekend. **1 mark**
   e Finn doesn't get on with his mum. **1 mark**
   f Finn has a good relationship with his sister. **1 mark**

People and lifestyle — Theme 1

5 🎧 **Listen to what this researcher says about a study of young people's lifestyles in Germany.**

Answer the questions in English.

5.1

a What do many young people see as an important part of life? **1 mark**

b According to the study, how often do most young people do this? **1 mark**

5.2

c What were the study's findings about smoking in the 12–17 age group? **1 mark**

d What does the figure of 21% represent? **1 mark**

e What has gone up dramatically? **1 mark**

der / die Befragte	person questioned / participant
der Konsum	consumption

Tipp

It is a good idea to listen to the whole of the relevant section of the recording before you fill in your answer. Try not to react to the first thing you recognise, as it may be a red herring.

6 🎧 **You hear a podcast about handball, a very popular sport in Germany. Complete the sentences in English.**

a Handball is a relatively ___ sport. **1 mark**

b It is played in Europe, ___ and ___. (**two** details) **2 marks**

c It has been an Olympic sport since ___. **1 mark**

d A handball team has ___ players. **1 mark**

e The aim is to ___ the handball into the goal. **1 mark**

f The goal measures 7.2 by ___ metres. **1 mark**

7 🎧 **Dictation A**

You will now hear **five** short sentences in German (a–e).

Listen carefully and, using your knowledge of German sounds, write down in German exactly what you hear for each sentence.

You will hear each sentence **three** times: the first time as a full sentence, the second time in short sections and the third time again as a full sentence.

Use your knowledge of German sounds and grammar to make sure that what you have written makes sense. Check carefully that your spelling is accurate.

a Sentence 1
b Sentence 2
c Sentence 3
d Sentence 4
e Sentence 5 **10 marks**

8 🎧 **Dictation B**

You will now hear **five** more sentences in German (a–e).

Write down in German exactly what you hear for each sentence.

a Sentence 1
b Sentence 2
c Sentence 3
d Sentence 4
e Sentence 5 **10 marks**

Tipp

You will have two minutes to check your work at the end of the exam. Take advantage of this time to make sure everything is clear and says what you want it to say.

Theme 1 — Test and revise: Higher Speaking

1 Role play

You are talking to a German friend.

Your teacher will play the part of your friend and will speak first.

You should address your friend as *du*.

When you see this – **?** – you will have to ask a question.

In order to score full marks, you must include a verb in your response to each task.

1 Say whether healthy eating is important to you, and why / not.
2 Say what you've done recently to keep fit. (Give **two** details.)
3 Say what you do to deal with stress.
4 **?** Ask your friend about their diet.
5 Say how you want to relax this evening. (Give **two** details.)

10 marks

Tipp

Remember that you are allowed to take notes for all tasks in the speaking exam. You can refer to these at any point during the test. Use this to help you!

Tipp

For the role play, the most important thing is to convey the message clearly. Double-check how many pieces of information you are required to give for each point. Keep your sentences short and accurate.

2 Reading aloud

When your teacher asks you to do so, read aloud the following German text.

> Ich versuche, gesund zu sein, weil mir meine Gesundheit wichtig ist.
>
> Ich esse täglich Obst und Gemüse, ich trinke genug Wasser und ich rauche nicht.
>
> Mein Traum ist, in der Zukunft Fußballspieler zu werden.
>
> Ein großes Problem für Jugendliche heute ist, dass es viel Schulstress gibt.
>
> Das finde ich schlecht.

You will then be asked four questions **in German** that relate to the topic of a **healthy lifestyle**.

Make sure you **answer all four questions as fully as you can.**

15 marks

Tipp

You need to communicate your responses clearly and in as much detail as possible. Try to answer all the questions and extend your sentences by giving opinions, using other tenses and linking your ideas to make longer sentences with conjunctions.

People and lifestyle — Theme 1

3 Photo card

- During your preparation time, look at the two photos. You may make as many notes as you wish on an Additional Answer Sheet and use these notes during the test.
- Your teacher will ask you to talk about the content of these photos. The recommended time is approximately **one and a half minutes. You must say at least one thing about each photo.**
- After you have spoken about the content of the photos, your teacher will then ask you questions related to **any** of the topics within the theme of **People and lifestyle.**

Tipp

You must say at least one thing about each photo. Try to give as much information, in accurate language, as you can.

The follow-up conversation is an opportunity to show off a variety of tenses, adjectives, adverbs, pronouns and intensifiers (e.g. words like 'very' and 'really') in your answers.

25 marks

Photo 1

Photo 2

fünfundfünfzig 55

Theme 1 — Test and revise: Higher Reading

1 Read the rules for a healthy lifestyle. Answer the questions in English.

Die acht Regeln für ein gesundes Leben

- **Regel 1:** Unterschiedliche Lebensmittel essen
- **Regel 2:** Täglich Obst und Gemüse essen
- **Regel 3:** Pflanzenfette wählen
- **Regel 4:** Zu viel Zucker vermeiden
- **Regel 5:** Wenig Salz essen
- **Regel 6:** Genug Wasser trinken
- **Regel 7:** Sich Zeit nehmen beim Essen
- **Regel 8:** In Bewegung bleiben

unterschiedlich	varied
Pflanzenfette (pl)	vegetable fats

Which rule (1–8) …

a mentions fruit? **1 mark**
b mentions sugar? **1 mark**
c mentions exercise? **1 mark**
d mentions vegetable fats? **1 mark**
e suggests eating a range of different foods? **1 mark**

f How often should you eat fruit and vegetables? **1 mark**
g How much salt should you have? **1 mark**
h What does Rule 7 advise? **1 mark**
i What advice is given about drinking water? **1 mark**
j What is the advice about sugar? **1 mark**

2 Some young people are messaging about school and future plans. Read what they say and then match the statements (a–j) below to **Emily (E), Noah (N), Jonas (J)** or **Meryem (M)**.

Emily
Mein bestes Fach dieses Jahr ist Biologie, und ich bekomme gute Noten, weil ich alles logisch finde. Chemie mag ich auch, aber das finde ich ein bisschen schwieriger. Nach dem Abitur will ich Naturwissenschaften studieren.

Noah
Ich finde die Schule meistens eine Zeitverschwendung. Fast nichts, was ich jetzt lerne, ist nützlich für mich. Ich interessiere mich meistens für Autos und Flugzeuge und will die Schule verlassen und bei der Armee als Mechaniker arbeiten.

Jonas
Mein Plan für die Zukunft ist, ein bekannter Schauspieler zu werden. Deshalb sind meine Lieblingsfächer Englisch und Theater, weil wir viel lesen und interessante Ideen diskutieren. Letztes Jahr habe ich in einem Theaterstück gespielt, und das war wunderbar.

Meryem
Ich besuche seit drei Jahren mein Gymnasium und bin mit meinem Schulleben total zufrieden. Ich mag alle Fächer, aber am liebsten lerne ich Fremdsprachen. Nach der Uni will ich in diese Stadt zurückkommen und in dieser Schule Französisch unterrichten.

a I want to be famous. **1 mark**
b Most school subjects don't interest me. **1 mark**
c I have been in a play. **1 mark**
d I like all the subjects I'm studying. **1 mark**
e I see my future in the field of science. **1 mark**
f I want to join the armed forces. **1 mark**
g I love discussing literature. **1 mark**
h I am very happy with my life at school. **1 mark**
i I plan to live and work in my home town. **1 mark**
j I like studying something that is logical. **1 mark**

Tipp

Read the texts carefully and work out the gist (overall meaning) before looking at the statements in English. Once you have understood the main ideas, you should find it easier to decide who says what. If you are still unsure of one of them, put in a name rather than leaving the answer blank.

People and lifestyle — Theme 1

3 Read this extract from an online article about friendship. Answer the questions in English.

Warum wahre Freunde wichtig sind

Wahre Freunde sind schwer zu finden. Das ist kein Geheimnis. Eine tiefe Freundschaft braucht nicht nur viel Zeit – auch die Chemie zwischen beiden Personen muss richtig sein. Man muss miteinander „auf einer Wellenlänge" sein.

Wenn wir älter werden, ist es nicht so einfach, Verbindungen zu neuen Personen aufzubauen. Deshalb lernen wir unsere Freunde meistens schon in den jungen Jahren kennen.

Jeder Mensch ist natürlich ganz individuell, aber enge Freunde haben meistens die gleichen Interessen oder Hobbys. Daher gibt es auch immer etwas zum Reden.

Mit unseren wahren Freunden können wir über alles sprechen. Das heißt, dass wir in harten Zeiten nie allein sind – Hilfe ist immer zur Hand. Unsere Freunde kümmern sich um uns und machen unser Leben glücklicher.

Für viele Menschen steht die Familie über allem – auch über den besten Freunden. Aber Freundschaften sind unabhängig von der familiären Situation. Das heißt, dass wir die Probleme, die wir nicht mit unserer Familie besprechen wollen, mit Freunden teilen.

das Geheimnis	secret
die Wellenlänge	wavelength

a What does the article say is 'no secret'? **1 mark**
b What two key elements are needed for a true friendship? (**two** details) **2 marks**
c When do we form most of our friendships? Why is this the case? (**two** details) **2 marks**
d Why do friends never run out of things to talk about? **1 mark**
e According to the article, what do friends do when things are difficult? (**two** details) **2 marks**
f How do many people feel about their family? **1 mark**
g In what situation are friends sometimes more necessary than family? **1 mark**

Tipp

In this task, it's important to give the correct number of details for each question: check the numbers in bold and the marks in brackets.

4 Translate these sentences into English.

a Ich besuche seit vier Jahren diese Gesamtschule.
b Wir wollen später einkaufen gehen, wenn wir Zeit haben.
c Die Schüler tragen nicht gern eine Uniform, weil sie altmodisch aussieht.
d In letzter Zeit habe ich begonnen, bessere Noten in den Klassenarbeiten zu bekommen.
e Mein Bruder versteht sich gut mit seiner Freundin, aber manchmal streiten sie sich.

10 marks

5 Translate these phrases into **English**.

a Ich habe eine gute Beziehung zu meiner Schwester.
b Es ist wichtig für mich, Sport zu treiben und gesund zu essen.
c Ich habe die Stunde langweilig gefunden, weil Physik schwierig ist.
d Wir haben ein schönes Wochenende gehabt und haben mit Freunden einen Spaziergang gemacht.
e In der Zukunft will ich auf die Uni gehen, um Mathe zu studieren.

10 marks

Tipp

When translating into English, you will need to get across the meaning of the whole sentence, although without necessarily translating it word for word. If you are missing a word, try not to leave a gap; it is better to choose a similar word (e.g. noun, adjective, adverb) that fits the context.

siebenundfünfzig

Theme 1 — Test and revise: Higher Writing

1 Translate the sentences into German.

   a She always comes back late.
   b Every morning at 7 o'clock he goes to work by bus.
   c It is important to see friends and to relax.
   d I do not want to stay at school next year to do A-levels.
   e My mother was angry because I did not do my homework.   **10 marks**

> **Tipp**
>
> The priority in the translation task is to convey the correct meaning. Therefore, it's important to use the correct tense and to choose the correct subject pronouns ('I', 'you', etc.).

EITHER Question 2.1 OR Question 2.2:

2.1 You are writing to a Swiss friend about your lifestyle.

Write approximately **90** words in **German**.

You must write something about each bullet point.

Describe:
- what you usually eat and drink
- a sports activity you have done recently
- how you will spend the evening.   **15 marks**

Or:

2.2 You write a post about your relationships with the people in your life.

Write approximately **90** words in **German**.

You must write something about each bullet point.

Describe:
- a good relationship you have with someone
- a recent problem with a friend or family member
- how you will make new friends in the future.   **15 marks**

> **Tipp**
>
> For this task, you will have to write something about all the bullet points, but there is no need to cover them equally. Your message must be conveyed clearly and you should also take this chance to show you can use varied vocabulary and grammar. Include all three time frames in your answer.

People and lifestyle — **Theme 1**

EITHER Question 3.1 OR Question 3.2:

3.1 You are writing a post on a German forum for young people.

Your post is about making career choices.

Write approximately **150** words in **German**.

You must write something about both bullet points.

Describe:
- your opinion of the subjects you are studying this year
- your ideal future job and why you think it's a good choice. **25 marks**

Or:

3.2 You are writing an article about your healthy lifestyle.

Write approximately **150** words in **German**.

You must write something about both bullet points.

Describe:
- why good health is important to you
- what you have done to improve your lifestyle and fitness. **25 marks**

Tipp

For this task, your answer will need to include something about both bullet points, but you don't need to cover them equally. Your ideas should be communicated clearly and using a variety of language is important too. Start by looking for the bullet point on each card that isn't asking about the present and decide which topic gives you the best chance of handling different tenses well in your answer.

neundundfünfzig 59

Theme 2
Popular culture

Free-time activities

1 📖 Read what Tanya says about her local dance venue. Write down what type of music you can hear on each day of the week.

Tanya

In unserer Stadt gibt es nur einen Club, aber das macht nichts, denn es gibt jeden Tag neue Musik: montags gibt es elektronische Musik und Techno, dienstags gibt es Popmusik, mittwochs gibt es R&B, Hip Hop und Reggae, donnerstags gibt es Rockmusik und freitags gibt es deutsche Musik (Schlager). Am Wochenende gibt es dann Konzerte. Diesen Monat kommen ein klassisches Orchester, ein Gospelchor und eine englische Rockband.

montags	every Monday / on Mondays
dienstags	every Tuesday / on Tuesdays
mittwochs	every Wednesday / on Wednesdays
donnerstags	every Thursday / on Thursdays
freitags	every Friday / on Fridays
Schlager (pl)	pop songs
Konzerte (pl)	concerts

2 📖 Read what Sam says about music. Fill the gaps with the words in the yellow box.

Musik ist mein Leben!

Ich **a** ___ morgens, mittags und abends Musik, weil es mich glücklich macht und entspannend ist. Ich liebe Rockmusik, aber ich höre auch Soulmusik und klassische Musik. Ich spiele Gitarre und **b** ___ mit meinen Freunden eine Band. Tom **c** ___ Keyboard und Ayush **d** ___ . Zusammen heißen wir 3Jam und wir **e** ___ immer freitags. Ich **f** ___ die Liedtexte und manchmal **g** ___ mein Bruder Videos von uns für YouTube.

Meine Schwester **h** ___ an der Universität Musik Management, und ich will das auch studieren.

schreibe			studiert
singt	spielt		höre
macht	üben		habe

die Band	band
üben	to practise
der Liedtext	lyrics
das Video	video

3 🎧 Look at the photo and listen to the statements (a–j). Which five of the statements about the photo are correct?

60 sechzig

Popular culture — Theme 2

4 🎧 **Listen to five people talk about what they have been watching. For each person (a–e), write down which programmes and films (1–10) they mention.**

die Sportsendung	sports show
toll	great
der Dokumentarfilm	documentary
der Horrorfilm	horror movie
Science Fiction-Filme (pl)	sci-fi films
der Liebesfilm	romance
der Fantasiefilm	fantasy movie
der Krimi	crime show / film
der Zeichentrickfilm	cartoon, animation
die Komödie	comedy
der Abenteuerfilm	adventure film

5 📖 **Copy and complete each sentence with a suitable adjective from the box.**

a Dokumentarfilme interessieren mich nicht, ich finde sie ___ .

b Meine kleine Schwester sieht jeden Tag *Peppa Pig*, aber ich finde das total ___ .

c Ich sehe nicht gern Horrorfilme, weil sie ___ sind.

d Meine Mutter sieht gern Komödien, weil sie ___ sind.

e Am liebsten sehe ich Abenteuerfilme, denn sie sind ___ .

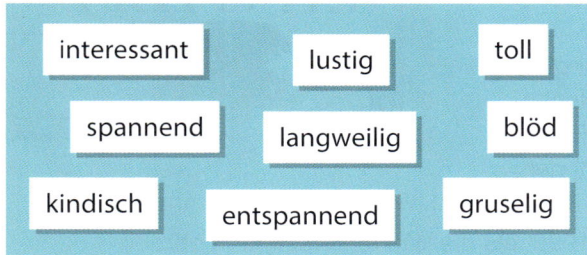

6 📖 **Pair up the words with similar meanings.**

Theme 2 — Popular culture

Customs, festivals and celebrations

7 📖 Match the sentences (a–f) to the dates (1–6).

a Ich freue mich immer auf Weihnachten, weil ich Zeit mit meiner ganzen Familie verbringe.
b Die Karnevalssaison beginnt! Karneval ist das Lieblingsfest meines Bruders, weil er die Kostüme und Umzüge mag.
c Ich mag den Valentinstag nicht, weil ich wieder Single bin.
d Der Maifeiertag ist das Lieblingsfest meiner Freundin, weil es im Frühling stattfindet und das Ende des Winters bedeutet.
e Meine Freund*innen und ich feiern Silvester in Berlin. Es ist auch mein Geburtstag!
f Meine Mutter fährt zum Oktoberfest nach München.

Umzüge (pl)	processions
feiern	to celebrate
der Frühling	Spring

8 🎧 Listen to Naya talking about is discussing her birthday. Answer the questions in English.

a What day of the week is Naya's birthday?
b How old will she be?
c Who will she celebrate with?
d What will they do first?
e What will they eat?
f What will they do after eating?
g When will Naya open her presents?
h What **two** things does she hope to get?

zuerst	first (of all)
gemeinsam	together
danach	afterwards

9 📖 Read the article about a German national holiday and complete the sentences in English.

a German Unity Day is on the ___ .
b It commemorates the unification of ___ and ___ Germany.
c Since 1990 it has been a ___ ___ .
d Unification was officially ___ in 1990.

Der 3. Oktober ist der Tag der Deutschen Einheit. Es erinnert an die deutsche Wiedervereinigung, als sich die Deutsche Demokratische Republik (Ostdeutschland) der Bundesrepublik Deutschland (Westdeutschland) anschloss.

Der Tag ist seit 1990, als die Wiedervereinigung offiziell vollzogen wurde, ein deutscher Nationalfeiertag.

die Einheit	unity	die Bundesrepublik Deutschland (BRD)	Federal Republic of Germany (FRG)
die Wiedervereinigung	reunification	sich anschließen	to join
die Deutsche Demokratische Republik (DDR)	German Democratic Republic (GDR)	vollziehen	to complete
		der Nationalfeiertag	national holiday

Popular culture — Theme 2

Celebrity culture

10 📖 Read how Luca, Anja and Moritz describe their favourite actors, then complete the table.

Luca: Mein Lieblingsschauspieler ist aus Amerika. Er spielt oft in Liebesfilmen. Er ist sehr groß, blond und freundlich.

Anja: Meine Lieblingsschauspielerin ist aus Deutschland. Sie spielt oft in Komödien, und ich finde sie sehr lustig. Sie ist ziemlich klein, so wie ich.

Moritz: Mein Lieblingsschauspieler ist aus China. Er spielt oft in Actionfilmen und ist sehr stark und cool.

stark — strong

	Country of origin	Typical genre	Physical and character description
Luca			
Anja			
Moritz			

11 📖 Two influencers are describing their careers. Read the statements (a–f) below and decide which person, Freya or Karl, each one applies to.

Freya
Ich war erst siebzehn, als ich berühmt wurde. Es macht Spaß, Content mit meinen Followern zu teilen. Ich mache Videos über Musik und Politik, denn beide sind mir sehr wichtig. Es ist mir aber auch wichtig, ein Offline-Leben zu führen.

Karl
Ich bin als Gamer bekannt und habe fast 400 000 YouTube-Abonnenten. Vor kurzem habe ich angefangen, mit vielen Gaming-Marken zusammenzuarbeiten. Es ist toll, aus einem Hobby eine Karriere zu machen! Ich chatte auch sehr gern mit meinen Fans.

es macht Spaß	it's fun
teilen	to share
führen	to lead
Abonnenten (pl)	subscribers
Marken (pl)	brands
zusammenarbeiten	to work together, to collaborate

Which person …
a works with brands?
b thinks politics is very important?
c became famous at seventeen?
d loves having a hobby that is a career?
e likes talking to fans?
f finds sharing content fun?

12 🎧 Listen to Markus, an actor, giving advice about managing fame. Which four things does he recommend?

a try to lead a normal life
b don't talk to the press
c be nice to your fans
d don't use social media
e use social media
f travel
g have some savings
h stay healthy

4.1F Sportstars der Zukunft

OBJECTIVES
- Talking about free time activities
- Using *gern* and *lieber*
- The future tense with *werden*
- Pronunciation: *w*

1 Read about Aisha and Stefan's sporting plans. Decide whether the phrases (a–e) in English below refer to Aisha (A) or Stefan (S).

Aisha

Ich werde im September mein Fußballtraining bei der Allianz FC Bayern Akademie beginnen und freue mich sehr. Das ist eine einmalige Chance. Ich werde in einem Apartment auf dem FC Bayern Campus wohnen und jeden Tag drei Stunden trainieren. Ich werde viele talentierte Jungen und Mädchen kennenlernen. Am ersten Tag werden wir unsere Trainer treffen und nach drei Wochen werden wir unser erstes Spiel gegen die U16 Mannschaft von Freiburg spielen. Hoffentlich werde ich ein Tor schießen!

Stefan

Ich werde nächste Woche mein Training mit dem Team Berlin Junior beginnen. Ich kann sehr gut Basketball spielen, aber ich bin ein bisschen nervös, denn es wird nicht leicht sein. Wir werden nächstes Jahr an der Junioren Weltmeisterschaft teilnehmen. Ich werde an meiner Technik arbeiten und mein Bestes leisten.

a will start their new training next week
b will train three hours per day
c will take part in an international competition
d feels nervous
e will move into new accommodation

2 Read the texts from activity 1 again and find the following phrases.

a a unique opportunity
b our first match
c to score a goal
d it won't be easy
e I will work on my technique.

Verben

The future tense with *werden*

The future tense is formed using the present tense of *werden* plus the infinitive.

ich werde	Sport machen
du wirst	Basketball spielen
er / sie / es wird	ein Buch lesen
wir werden	schwimmen gehen
ihr werdet	
sie / Sie werden	

Remember that the infinitive goes to the end of the sentence or clause:
*Ich **werde** in einem Apartment **wohnen**.* – I will live in a flat.

Free-time activities 4.1F

3 Translate the following into German. Use activity 1 to help you.

a I will start
b I will live
c I will get to know
d we will meet
e we will play
f it will be
g we will take part

4 Listen to Heiko, Tina and Mustafa talk about the sport they play. Copy and complete the table in English.

	Sport	Next event	When	Opinion
Heiko			next week	
Tina	tennis			
Mustafa				it will be fantastic

5 Translate the sentences into German. Use the *Grammatik* box to help you.

a I like swimming.
b I don't like going shopping.
c I like playing tennis, but I prefer playing football.
d Do you like watching television?
e Do you prefer playing basketball or tennis?

Grammatik

Using *gern* and *lieber*

When you want to say you like doing something, use the adverb *gern*. It comes after the verb:
Ich spiele gern Handball. – I like playing handball.

Use *lieber* to say what you prefer doing:
Ich lese nicht gern. Ich höre lieber Musik.
I don't like reading. I prefer listening to music.

6 What will your classmates do in the future? Working in pairs, take turns to ask and answer the following questions using the future tense. Give justifications if you can, using *weil* or *denn*:

Wer wird Rockstar werden?

Lena wird Rockstar werden, weil sie sehr gern singt.

a Wer wird Tennisprofi werden?
b Wer wird Fußballer werden?
c Wer wird heute Formel 1 schauen?
d Wer wird nach der Schule trainieren?
e Wer wird in der Zukunft eine Medaille gewinnen?
f Wer wird eine Rockband haben?
g Wer wird im Theater arbeiten?

Aussprache

w

The *w* sound in German is like the 'v' sound in English. Take care with *wer*, *wird* and *werden* in activity 6!

7 Write a paragraph about an activity you are planning in the future (50 words). Use the table to help you and mention:
- what you will do
- when you will do it
- why you want to do it
- what you think it will be like.

Ich werde		Tennis spielen, Musik hören,	weil ich	(sehr) gern	lese/singe ...
Morgen Danach Nächste Woche	werde ich	ein Buch lesen, in die Stadt gehen,		mich für ... interessiere.	
Das wird		toll/lustig/fantastisch	sein!		

funfundsechzig 65

4.1H Extremsportarten für alle

OBJECTIVES
- Talking about sports and extreme sports
- Using *beim / am* + infinitives as nouns
- The present tense of *wissen*

1 📖 **Decide whether the following statements describe advantages (A) or disadvantages (D) of extreme sports.**

a Beim Skateboarden kann man sich selbst und andere verletzen.

b Beim Tieftauchen kann man seine Angst überwinden.

c Eisschwimmen ist sehr erfrischend.

d Beim Snowboarden fühlt man sich frei.

e Das Schlimmste am Tieftauchen ist, dass es nicht gut für die Natur ist.

f Sportarten wie Wildwasser Rafting sind sehr gefährlich.

g Klettern hilft der Konzentration.

h Bungeespringen ist sehr teuer für zwei Minuten Spaß.

i Jugendliche, die in der Stadtmitte Parkour machen, sind egoistisch.

j Das Beste am Sport ist, dass man aktiv ist und Probleme vergessen kann.

2 📖 **Match the photos (1–6) to the sports mentioned in activity 1 (a–j).**

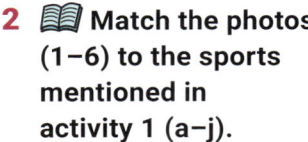

3 📖 **Read Nils's blog and answer these questions in English.**

a What two sports did Nils do when he was young?

b What does he pay attention to when he does parkour?

c What happens sometimes when they do their tricks?

d What is the best thing about mountain biking?

e What is part of the fun for him?

f What did he think of his bungee jump? (two details)

g What does he love? (two details)

h What has his mum accepted about him?

unvergesslich	unforgettable
überwinden	to overcome

Kultur

The Swiss alps and the German Black Forest count as two of the best places to go mountain biking. Berlin is known as one of the best cities for skateboarding worldwide.

> Ich bin totaler Adrenalinjunkie. Ich habe schon als Kind Gymnastik gemacht und Fußball gespielt, aber jetzt ist Extremsport mein Leben. Ich treffe mich mit meinen Freunden, und wir machen Parkour oder fahren Skateboard. Ich weiß, wo man das gut machen kann, ohne andere Leute zu nerven. Manchmal haben wir aber Zuschauer, die unsere Tricks spannend finden. Am Wochenende gehe ich hier im Schwarzwald Mountainbiken. Das Beste am Mountainbiken ist die Geschwindigkeit. Das kann manchmal gefährlich sein, und ich hatte auch schon einige Unfälle, aber zum Glück nichts Schlimmes. Mir macht Sport am meisten Spaß, wenn es gefährlich ist. Letztes Jahr war ich zum ersten Mal beim Bungeespringen, und es war unvergesslich, mein Herz ist fast explodiert. Ich liebe die Herausforderung und ich mag meine Angst überwinden. Meine Mutter macht sich manchmal Sorgen, aber sie weiß, dass ein Fitness-Studio nichts für mich ist.

— Nils

Free-time activities 4.1H

4 Copy and complete the sentences with the correct present tense form of *wissen*.

  a Meine Mutter ___, wann ich nach Hause komme.
  b Wir ___, wo man gut schwimmen kann.
  c ___ du, wie viel ein Bungeesprung kostet?
  d ___ ihr, dass Mountainbiken ohne Helm sehr gefährlich ist?
  e Ich ___, dass ich noch viel üben muss.
  f Malte und Imke ___ noch nicht, wo sie im Sommer klettern werden.

5 Translate the sentences from activity 4 (a–f) into English.

6 Put the jumbled parts of these sentences into the correct order, then translate them into English.

  a Wir wissen nicht, werden kommen wie viele Zuschauer .
  b Ich weiß, an meinem Geburtstag was machen werde ich .
  c Melanie weiß, Extremsport dass für sie ist nichts .
  d Weißt du, später Training du dass hast ?

7 Translate the first five sentences (a–e) from activity 1 into English. Use the *Grammatik* box to help you.

8 Listen to Herr and Frau Meyer talking about their daughter's hobby, then copy and complete the sentences (a–g) with the missing words.

  a Herr Meyer findet, dass Heikes Sport viel zu ___ ist.
  b Heike hat sich schon oft ___.
  c Er denkt, dass es nur eine Frage der Zeit ist, bis sie sich ___ ___ ___ ___ ___ bricht.
  d Heike hat beim letzten Wettbewerb ___.
  e Heike hat viel Spaß am ___.
  f Herr Meyer findet das Hobby etwas ___.
  g Frau Meyer findet es gut, dass ___ ___ ___.

9 Read the following statement aloud, then use it as a model to give your own opinion on extreme sports.

> Meiner Meinung nach sind Extremsportarten viel zu gefährlich, und Leute, die diesen Sport machen, sind sehr egoistisch. Man kann sich verletzen und deshalb ist traditioneller Sport besser für junge Leute.

10 Write around 150 words in German on the following points. Use activities 1 and 3 to help you.
  • Your past experience of sport.
  • Pros and cons of extreme sport.

Verben

The present tense of *wissen*

ich weiß	I know
du weißt	you know
er/sie/es weiß	he/she/it knows
wir wissen	we know
ihr wisst	you (plural) know
sie/Sie wissen	they/you (formal) know

Wissen is used for knowing facts (for knowing people and places, use *kennen*). Note the word order in clauses following *wissen*:

Ich **weiß**, **was** du gesagt **hast**.
Wir **wissen**, **wo** man gut Skateboard fahren **kann**.

Grammatik

Using *beim* / *am* + infinitives as nouns

You can say 'while doing something' by turning the verb into a noun and using *beim* before it:

Beim Fernsehen entspanne ich mich.
I relax **while watching TV**.

When you say what is the best or worst thing about (*das Beste / Schlechteste am …*) an action, e.g. climbing, the verb becomes a noun:

Das Beste **am Klettern** ist die Herausforderung.
The best thing **about climbing** is the challenge.

Achtung!

When giving opinions, use phrases such as:
Ich denke, dass … (verb to the end)
Ich glaube, dass … (verb to the end)
Ich weiß, dass … (verb to the end)
Meiner Meinung nach … (verb next)

4.2F Auf geht's zum Konzert!

OBJECTIVES
- Making plans
- Question words
- *mögen* and *wollen*
- Pronunciation: *o* and *ö*

1 Match the German words to their English translations.

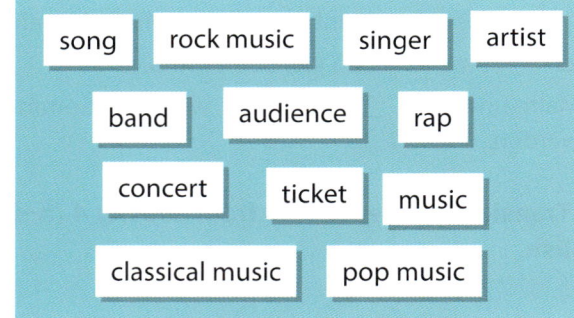

2 Read these texts, then answer the questions in English.

Hi! Ich heiße Fatimah und ich mag Popmusik. Meine Lieblingssängerin ist Taylor Swift, und ich möchte sie im Konzert sehen, weil ich ein totaler Fan bin. Ich will mit meinen Freunden Karten für das Konzert im August kaufen, aber es ist ein bisschen teuer.

Ich bin Max und mag Rap. Ich höre auch manchmal Rock, aber am liebsten höre ich Tupac. Im Sommer will ich zum Splash! Festival gehen, das ist das bekannteste HipHop Festival in Deutschland. Ich will mit meinem Bruder dorthin fahren und viele meiner Lieblingskünstler sehen.

Hallo, ich bin Jamal und ich mag Rockmusik. Meine Freunde und ich möchten zu Rock am Ring fahren, wenn wir achtzehn Jahre alt sind. Ich will im Publikum springen und alle Lieder mitsingen.

a Who thinks that the tickets are a bit expensive?
b Who will wait until they are 18 before going to a concert?
c Who wants to go with their brother?
d Who likes rock music?
e Who wants to see many of their favourite artists?
f Who wants to sing along?

Kultur

Rock am Ring is one of the most famous music festivals in Germany. It started in 1985 and, as the name suggests, features rock music. It takes place at the Nürburgring which is usually used for Formula 1. Its audiences have numbered up to 90 000 and it has hosted bands such as Coldplay, Metallica and Foo Fighters.

3 Read the texts from activity 2 again and find the following phrases. What do you notice about the sentence structures?

a I want to buy tickets.
b I want to go to the festival.
c I want to see many of my favourite artists.
d I want to jump around in the crowd.
e I want to sing along to all the songs.

achtundsechzig

Free-time activities 4.2F

4 ✂ **Translate the sentences into German. Use the *Verben* box to help you.**

a I like pop music.
b My sister likes rock music.
c We like rap.
d I want to go to the concert.
e I want to see Harry Styles.
f We want to sing the songs.

5 🎧 **Listen to Anke talk about her plans and select the correct option to complete each sentence.**

a Anke will go to   **1** a pop concert.   **2** a reggae festival.
b Anke wants to go with   **1** her friends.   **2** her sister.
c They want to buy the tickets   **1** in August.   **2** next week.
d Anke wants   **1** to dance and sing.   **2** to take photos.
e They want to wear   **1** green, yellow and red.   **2** purple.

6 ⭐ **Place the words in the correct order to form questions and then translate them into English.**

a Wer / dein / Lieblingssänger / ist / ?
b dein Lieblingslied / ist / Was / ?
c du / Wann / gehst / auf das Konzert / ?
d ist / Was / Musikfestival / das bekannteste / ?
e kostet / Wie viel / eine Karte / ?
f gesungen / Wer / hat / Bohemian Rhapsody / ?

7 💬 **Working in pairs, ask and answer the questions.**

- Was für Musik magst du?
- Was für Musik mögen deine Freunde?
- Welchen Sänger oder welche Sängerin willst du live sehen?
- Auf welches Konzert oder Festival willst du gehen?
- Wann willst du auf das Konzert / Festival gehen?
- Was willst du auf dem Konzert / Festival machen?

8 ✏ **Write down your answers to the six questions in activity 7 (aiming for 50 words).**

Ich mag Meine Freunden mögen		Rockmusik / klassische Musik / Rap / Popmusik...	
Ich will Meine Freunden wollen		Billie Eilish Khalid Drake	live sehen.
Nächstes Jahr Im Sommer	will ich wollen wir	zum ... Festival gehen.	
Dort	will ich wollen wir	tanzen. alle Lieder mitsingen.	

Verben

mögen and *wollen*

Mögen (to like) and *wollen* (to want) are both modal verbs. The present tense of *mögen* is usually followed by a noun:

Ich mag Rockmusik. – I like rock music.

Wollen works with an infinitive to say what you want to do:

Ich will auf das Konzert gehen.
I want to go to the concert.

Here are the present tense forms in full:

	mögen	wollen
ich	mag	will
du	magst	willst
er / sie / es	mag	will
wir	mögen	wollen
ihr	mögt	wollt
sie / Sie	mögen	wollen

Remember that *ich will* means 'I want', not 'I will'!

Grammatik

Question words

was	what	wann	when
wer	who	warum	why
wie	how	wo	where

When we ask a question with a question word, the verb is the second idea as normal.

Aussprache

o and *ö*

In German, *o* sounds either like the 'o' in 'hot' or like the exclamation 'oh':

Wir wollen auf ein Konzert oder ein Festival gehen.
We want to go to the concert or a festival.

When an umlaut is added to make *ö*, it sounds like the English hesitation 'er':

Wir mögen das Konzert.
We like the concert.

neunundsechzig

4.2H Filme, die man sehen muss

OBJECTIVES
- Talking about films
- Using the demonstrative adjective *dies-*
- Using *ich möchte* to say what you would like

1 📖 Three young people say which films they would like to see. Match each description (a–c) to the correct photo (1–3).

a Ich möchte diesen Film sehen, weil ich Horrorfilme liebe. Ich habe gehört, dass die Spezialeffekte sehr gut sind, und der Film ist super gruselig. Ich liebe die Spannung, wenn ich einen Film sehe. Ich kann Komödien nicht leiden, weil ich sie albern und kindisch finde.

b Ich möchte diesen Film sehen, weil ich ein Fußballfan bin. Der Film erzählt die Geschichte von Deutschlands Sieg bei der Fußball-Weltmeisterschaft 1954 in Bern. Die Schauspieler sind alle sehr talentiert und beeindruckend. Der Film hat gute Kritiken und hat sogar die Goldene Leinwand 2003 gewonnen.

c Ich möchte diesen Film sehen, weil ich Zeichentrickfilme liebe und weil ich einen Film sehen will, der mich zum Lachen bringt. Ich werde den Film mit meiner Familie sehen, weil wir ihn alle genießen können. Meine kleine Schwester kann keine Horrorfilme sehen, sonst bekommt sie Alpträume.

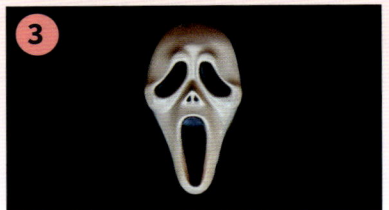

(super) gruselig	(very) scary	beeindruckend	impressive
albern	silly	Zeichentrickfilme (pl)	cartoons
kindisch	childish	Alpträume (pl)	nightmares

2 📖 Find the following phrases in the texts from activity 1.

a the movie is very scary
b I love the suspense
c I can't stand comedies
d silly and childish
e the actors are all very talented
f which makes me laugh
g because we can all enjoy it
h otherwise she gets nightmares

Kultur

The Berlinale is the international film festival which takes place every year in Berlin. It was founded in 1951 and now has similar status to the film festivals of Venice and Cannes, with tens of thousands of visitors each year. Instead of Oscars, actors and producers are awarded the golden or silver bear, as the *Bär* is a symbol of Berlin or *Bärlein* (little bear) which is a pun on the city's name.

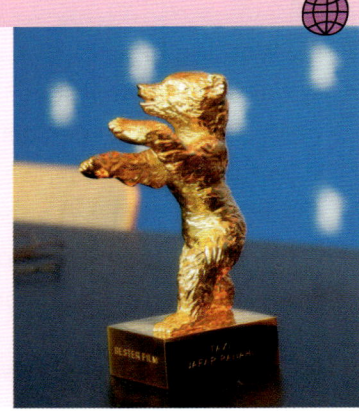

3 🎯 Copy and complete each sentence with the correct form of *möchten*.

a Ich ___ ins Kino gehen.
b Er ___ eine Komödie sehen.
c Meine Schwester ___ Tom Holland treffen.
d Wir ___ den Soundtrack kaufen.
e Meine Eltern ___ einen Dokumentarfilm sehen.
f ___ du ins Kino gehen?

Verben

Using *ich möchte* to say what you would like

Ich möchte is the easiest way to say politely what you want to do:
Ich möchte ins Kino gehen. – I would like to go to the cinema.
Möchtest du mitkommen? – Would you like to come too?

Möchten is the conditional form of the verb *mögen* and is formed as follows:

| ich möchte | er/sie/es möchte | ihr möchtet |
| du möchtest | wir möchten | sie/Sie möchten |

Like *wollen*, it sends the infinitive to the end of the sentence.

siebzig

Free-time activities 4.2H

4 🎧 **Jannik is talking about Star Wars. Listen and then answer the questions in English.**

  a Why does Jannik say everyone must watch these films?
  b When was the first Star Wars film released?
  c For which **three** categories did the films get awards?
  d Which film is Jannik's personal favourite?
  e What does Jannik say about John Boyega?

5 🎧 **Listen to three sentences and transcribe each one.**

6 ⭐ **Copy and complete the sentences with the correct demonstrative adjective, using the *Grammatik* box to help you. The gender of the noun is given in brackets, but the case is also important!**

  a Ich möchte ___ Film (m) nicht sehen.
  b ___ Schauspielerin (f) hat viele Preise gewonnen.
  c ___ Kino (n) zeigt den Film nur um 22 Uhr.
  d Ich habe ___ Film (m) schon gesehen.
  e Ich liebe Romanzen. ___ Filme (m, pl) machen mir gute Laune.
  f Ich finde alle *Fast and Furious* Filme toll. Du musst ___ Filme (m, pl) sehen.

Grammatik

Using the demonstrative adjective *dies-*

In German, *dies-* works like the English words 'this'/'these'. You use it when describing a specific thing or person. The endings change according to the gender, number and case of the noun being described:

Dies**er** (nom, masc) Film ist super. – This film is super.

Ich liebe dies**e** (acc, fem) Schauspielerin / dies**en** (acc, masc) Schauspieler.
I love this actress / actor.

Es gibt viele Spezialeffekte in dies**em** (dat, masc) Film.
There are many special effects in this movie.

	masculine	feminine	neuter	plural
nominative	dieser	diese	dieses	diese
accusative	diesen	diese	dieses	diese
dative	diesem	dieser	diesem	diesen

7 💬 **Working in pairs, take turns to interview each other on your film preferences. Use the table to help you extend your answers.**

- Wer ist dein Lieblingsschauspieler oder deine Lieblingsschauspielerin? Warum?
- Welchen Film möchtest du am Wochenende sehen? Warum?
- Möchtest du den Film zu Hause sehen oder im Kino? Warum?

Ich finde Komödien / Liebesfilme / Zeichentrickfilme / Horrorfilme	toll / interessant / langweilig / doof / spannend / beeindruckend / albern / kindisch	weil	sie mich zum Lachen bringen. weil sie mir gute Laune machen. weil sie … sind.
Ich möchte … sehen,	weil dieser Film	für die ganze Familie ist. gute Spezialeffekte / gute Schauspieler / einen guten Soundtrack hat. viele Preise gewonnen hat.	
Ich möchte den Film zu Hause sehen,	weil es bequem / billiger / entspannend ist.		
Ich möchte den Film im Kino sehen,	weil die Filmqualität / der Ton / die Atmosphäre besser ist. weil es Spaß macht.		

8 ✏️ **Write a film recommendation (150 words). Mention:**

- what type of film it is
- who the main actors are
- when it was released
- prizes it has won
- what is special about it.

einundsiebzig

5.1F Alles Gute zum Geburtstag!

OBJECTIVES
- Describing celebrations
- Word order: time, manner, place
- The modal verbs *dürfen*, *können*, *mögen* and *wollen*
- Pronunciation: long and short vowels

1 Three young people describe their birthdays. Read the texts, then answer the questions in English.

 **Thomas**

An meinem Geburtstag darf ich immer machen, was ich will. Ich darf stundenlang X-Box spielen und ich darf viele Süßigkeiten essen. Mein Geburtstag ist auch toll, weil ich von meinen Eltern und Großeltern Geschenke bekomme, und wir abends zusammen in ein Restaurant gehen. Mein Opa hat mir zum letzten Geburtstag Geld geschenkt, und ich will mit dem Geld ein neues Fahrrad kaufen.

 **Ayushi**

Nächste Woche ist mein Geburtstag, und ich möchte eine kleine Party mit meinen Freunden feiern. Wir können am Samstagabend bei mir zu Hause Bollywood Filme ansehen und Karaoke singen. Meine Oma wird für uns Samosas vorbereiten, und meine Freunde dürfen bei mir übernachten. Das wird super!

 **Kojo**

Mein Vater wird dieses Jahr fünfzig Jahre alt und er möchte ein großes Fest in unserem Garten feiern. Meine Tanten, Onkel und Cousinen aus Ghana werden kommen und ihn überraschen. Mein Vater will seine Kultur feiern, und wir werden traditionelle Kleidung tragen, High Life Musik hören und viel tanzen. Ich darf auch ein paar Schulfreunde zu der Party einladen, aber wir dürfen nach Mitternacht nicht laut sein, weil sich sonst unsere Nachbarn ärgern.

a What is Thomas allowed to do on his birthday? (two details)
b Who usually gives him birthday presents? (two details)
c What does he want to do with the money he received last year?
d What is Ayushi going to do for her birthday party? (two details)
e What is her grandmother going to do?
f What will be the surprise for Kojo's dad?
g How will they celebrate Ghanaian culture? (three details)
h What do they need to be mindful of?

Verben

The modal verbs *dürfen*, *können*, *mögen* and *wollen*

Remember the modal verbs you have learnt so far:

dürfen may, to be allowed to
können can, to be capable of
mögen to like
wollen to want

When these verbs are paired with an infinitive (as they often are), this second verb goes to the end of the sentence or clause:

Ich will Musik hören. – I want to listen to music.
Ich darf keine Süßigkeiten essen.
I'm not allowed to eat any sweets.

2 Read the texts in activity 1 again and note down all the modal verbs you can find, including the subject (noun or pronoun). Then translate these into English.

Customs, festivals and celebrations **5.1F**

3 Put the words in these sentences into the correct order, then translate them into English. The first word is in bold.

a **Ich** / am Wochenende / mit meinen Freunden / gehe / auf eine Party / .

b **Wir** / im Sommer / zusammen / feiern / ein Familienfest / in Köln / .

c darf / am Samstag / bei meinem Freund / **Ich** / übernachten / .

d werden / **Wir** / um Mitternacht / mit dem Bus / fahren / nach Hause / .

e mit meiner Familie / an meinem Geburtstag / **Ich** / möchte / gehen / ins Restaurant / .

4 Listen to Anastasia talking about a special party, then answer the questions in English.

a Who got married?
b Where did the person get married?
c Describe the decoration of the venue.
d How many guests were there?
e What did they do in the evening? (two details)
f What happened at midnight?
g What are Anastasia's wedding plans?

5 Working in pairs, take turns to ask and answer the following questions. Advice on how to answer is supplied in brackets.

- Was machst du normalerweise an deinem Geburtstag? (*Say what you usually do on your birthday.*)
- Feierst du lieber mit deinen Freunden oder mit deiner Familie? Warum? (*Say how you prefer to celebrate and why.*)
- Was hast du an deinem letzten Geburtstag geschenkt bekommen? (*Say what you received for your last birthday.*)
- Was möchtest du an deinem nächsten Geburtstag machen? (*Say what you'd like to do for your next birthday.*)

6 Write down your answers to the questions in activity 5 (50 words). Make sure that you include reasons, opinions and a variety of connectives.

Grammatik

Word order: time, manner, place

When you talk about **when** (time), **how** (manner) and **where** (place) you do something, you always give the time first, then the manner, then the place.

	Time	Manner	Place
Ich feiere meinen Geburtstag	am Samstag	mit meinen Freunden	in der Disko.
Wir fahren	morgen	mit dem Zug	nach Bern.

Aussprache

Long and short vowels

In German, vowels can be pronounced as either long or short.

Vowel	Long sound	Short sound
a	'ar' as in 'car' – *Spaß*	'a' as in 'cat' – *Stadt*
e	'ay' as in 'hey' – *Regen*	'e' as in 'red' – *Tennis*
i	'ee' as in 'street' – *ihnen*	'i' as in 'hit' – *Wind*
o	'oh' as in 'go' – *geflogen*	'o' as in 'hot' – *toll*
u	'oo' as in 'who' – *gut*	'u' as in 'foot' – *Wohnung*

Achtung!

When doing a writing task, have a checklist of grammatical features you want to include:

- *weil* / *da*
- *ich denke, dass*
- modal verb + infinitive
- present tense
- past tense
- future tense

dreiundsiebzig **73**

5.1H Weihnachtszeit in Deutschland

OBJECTIVES
- Talking about Christmas traditions
- Revising modal verbs
- Revising subordinate clauses

1 🎧 📖 Read and listen to the lyrics of the Christmas carols and find the German phrases for a–f below.

Alle Jahre wieder
Kommt das Christuskind
Auf die Erde nieder,
Wo wir Menschen sind.

Stille Nacht, heilige Nacht
Alles schläft; einsam wacht
Nur das traute hochheilige Paar.
Holder Knabe im lockigen Haar,
Schlaf in himmlischer Ruh!
Schlaf in himmlischer Ruh!

Advent, Advent,
ein Lichtlein brennt.
Erst eins, dann zwei,
dann drei, dann vier,
dann steht das Christkind vor der Tür.

Schneeflöckchen, Weißröckchen
Wann kommst du geschneit?
Du wohnst in den Wolken
Dein Weg ist so weit.

a the Christ child
b down to Earth
c a small light is burning
d holy night
e the most holy couple
f little snowflake

Kultur

Christmas carols are an important part of German Christmas traditions. While many have religious texts, these songs are widely enjoyed by Christians and non-Christians. Traditionally, German children believe that either the *Weihnachtsmann* or the *Christkind* (or *Christuskind*) bring the presents.

2 📖 Read about *Stille Nacht* (Silent Night), then copy and complete the fact file in English.

Im Jahr 1816 schreibt ein Pfarrer namens Joseph Mohr im Fürstentum Salzburg ein Gedicht mit dem Titel „Stille Nacht, Heilige Nacht". **Er will aber, dass dieses Gedicht ein Lied wird**, also bittet er zwei Jahre später, am 24. Dezember, Franz Gruber, der Organist und Lehrer ist, eine Melodie zu dem Text zu komponieren. Noch am selben Heiligabend ist Gruber fertig mit der Komposition und singt zusammen mit Mohr und Gitarrenbegleitung das Lied in der Kirche in Oberndorf. Heute kann man **das Lied, das eines der bekanntesten Weihnachtslieder ist**, in 140 Sprachen hören.

Title of the song: _____
Original form: _____
Author's name: _____
Author's profession: _____
Year of first performance: _____
Place of first performance: _____
Number of translations: _____

der/die Pfarrer/in	vicar
komponieren	to compose
die Gitarrenbegleitung	guitar accompaniment
die Kirche	church

3 🔀 Translate the phrases in bold from activity 2 into English, saying what you notice about the position of the verbs.

74 vierundsiebzig

Customs, festivals and celebrations 5.1H

4 Join the two sentences to make one sentence, using the subordinating conjunction given in brackets.

a Ich bleibe zu Hause. Es schneit. (*weil*)
b Wir fangen mit dem Essen an. Alle Gäste sind da. (*wenn*)
c Viele Menschen feiern Weihnachten. Sie sind nicht religiös. (*obwohl*)
d Das Haus sieht schön aus. Es ist weihnachtlich geschmückt. (*wenn*)
e In meiner Stadt gibt es einen Weihnachtsmarkt. Er ist sehr berühmt. (relative clause with *der*)
f Meine Mutter backt Plätzchen. Sie sind lecker. (relative clause with *die*)

schmücken	to decorate
Plätzchen (pl)	biscuits

5 Listen to Rebekka and Katja talk about Christmas food and activities. Write down the German words for a–f.

a goose
b red cabbage
c potatoes
d honey
e nuts
f biscuits

6 Listen again to the conversation from activity 5 and decide whether the following activities take place in the past, present or future.

a food shopping
b going to the Christmas market
c decorating the tree
d baking biscuits
e buying presents
f wrapping presents

Verben

Revising modal verbs

Remember that modal verbs such as *müssen*, *können*, *mögen* and *wollen* work with an infinitive which goes to the end of the sentence or clause:

Wir **müssen** Zutaten für das Weihnachtsessen **kaufen**.
We have to buy ingredients for the Christmas dinner.

However, if it is a subordinate clause, the main verb (the modal) goes to the very end, with the infinitive before it:

Ich weiß, dass wir Zutaten für das Weihnachtsessen **kaufen müssen**.
I know that we have to buy ingredients for the Christmas dinner.

Grammatik

Revising subordinate clauses

You have come across subordinate clauses – parts of sentences where the verb goes to the end – which follow the following conjunctions: *weil, da, obwohl, wenn, ob, dass*:

Ich denke, **dass** Weihnachten eine wichtige Tradition **ist**.
I think Christmas is an important tradition.

When the verb has two parts in the clause, they both go to the end. The auxiliary verb which works with the subject (not an infinitive or a past participle) goes last:

Ich weiß nicht, **ob** es **geschneit hat**.
I don't know if it has snowed.

Another form of a subordinate clause is a relative clause. In these clauses you give extra information about something or someone:

Wir haben **einen Nachbarn, der** Weihnachten blöd **findet**.
We have a neighbour who thinks Christmas is stupid.

7 Put the words in the sentences into the correct order. The first word is in bold.

a möchte / kochen / **Anna** / Gans und Kartoffeln / .
b unserem Vater / **Wir** / müssen / helfen / .
c gehen willst / wollte fragen, / ob du / auf den Weihnachtsmarkt / **Ich** / .
d **Ich** / weil / ich / einpacken / muss / kann nicht mitkommen, / die Geschenke / .

8 Working in pairs, take turns to say who can do the different tasks in preparation for a festive party as given below.

Ich kann / muss / darf / will …, und du kannst / musst / darfst / willst …

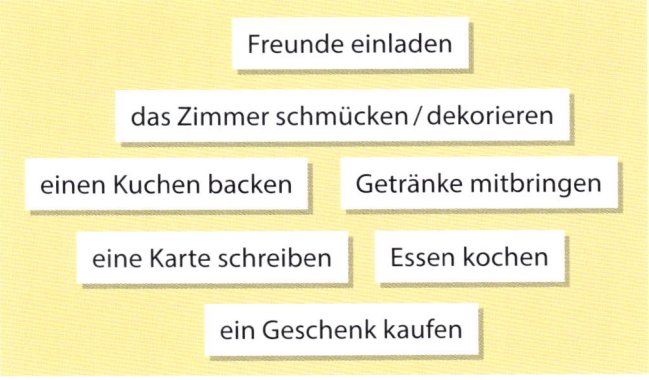

Freunde einladen
das Zimmer schmücken / dekorieren
einen Kuchen backen
Getränke mitbringen
eine Karte schreiben
Essen kochen
ein Geschenk kaufen

9 Write a piece about preparing for a celebration (90 words). Use some of the examples from activity 8 to help you.

5.2F Schöne und seltsame Traditionen

OBJECTIVES
- Talking about typical festivals
- The negatives *nicht* and *nie*
- The modal verbs *sollen* and *müssen*
- Pronunciation: two-vowel combinations (dipthongs)

1 📖 Read the text about a festival and select the correct option each time for a–e.

a When is St Nikolaus Day?
- 6th December
- 16th December
- 5th December

b What are typical attributes of St Nikolaus?
- red hat and black boots
- red hat and white beard
- red hat and white shirt

c What do children need to do the night before?
- put their boots outside the door
- eat nuts
- make presents

d What do they often learn in school?
- the history of St Nikolaus
- a special poem
- a special song

e What is Krampus supposed to do?
- carry presents
- make music
- scare naughty children

2 🔀 Translate the phrases in bold from the text for activity 1 into English.

St Nikolaus und Krampus

In Deutschland, Österreich und der Schweiz feiert man am sechsten Dezember St Nikolaus, aber in Südtirol gibt es an dem Tag **eine besondere Tradition**, die **nicht nur schön, sondern auch schrecklich** ist.

Der Nikolaus in seinem roten Kostüm, mit roter Mütze und weißem Bart bringt den Kindern kleine Geschenke, **wenn sie nett waren**. Dazu müssen die Kinder am Abend des fünften Dezember ihre Stiefel vor die Tür stellen und am nächsten Morgen finden sie Schokolade, Nüsse und Mandarinen in den Stiefeln. Manche Familien laden auch einen Nikolaus nach Hause ein. **Er hat eine Liste und weiß alles** über die Kinder. Oft lernen Kinder in der Schule ein Nikolausgedicht für diesen Tag.

Der Krampus jedoch bringt keine Geschenke, sondern er soll den bösen Kindern Angst machen. Er ist wie **ein Dämon und trägt eine schreckliche Maske**. In Südtirol gibt es am fünften Dezember Krampusläufe, wo man Monster mit lauter Musik durch die Straßen ziehen sieht.

Verben

The modal verbs *sollen* and *müssen*

While *müssen* (must) expresses what you must or have to do, *sollen* is used for what you should do.

	müssen	sollen
ich	muss	soll
du	musst	sollst
er/sie/es	muss	soll
wir	müssen	sollen
ihr	müsst	sollt
sie/Sie	müssen	sollen

3 🎯 Read this conversation about *Sankt Martin* and fill the gaps for a–e with the correct form of *sollen* or *müssen*.

Was **a** ___ man über Sankt Martin wissen?

Er war ein guter Mann, der alles mit armen Menschen geteilt hat. Wir feiern das Fest am elften November mit einem Laternenumzug, aber es ist kein deutscher Feiertag, also **b** ___ wir an dem Tag zur Arbeit und zur Schule gehen.

Wie **c** ___ ich mich auf den Tag vorbereiten?

Du **d** ___ eine Laterne bauen und Martinslieder lernen. Du **e** ___ dich auch warm anziehen.

der Laternenumzug — lantern procession

Customs, festivals and celebrations 5.2F

4 🎧 **Listen to Mario talking about his festival experiences (a–e). For each, choose the name of the festival from the box and whether the experience was positive (P), negative (N) or positive and negative (P+N).**

Aschermittwoch	Karneval
Martinstag	Neujahr
Oktoberfest	Ostermontag
Tag der Arbeit	Weihnachten

5 ⭐ **Turn the sentences into negatives using *nicht* or *nie*.**

a Ich trage gern Kostüme.
b Ich werde auf den Weihnachtsmarkt gehen.
c Es war kalt auf dem Laternenumzug.
d Ich habe den Krampus gesehen.
e Der Krampus ist sehr nett.

Grammatik

The negatives *nicht* and *nie*

To turn a statement into a negative, you can use **nicht** (not) or **nie** (never). Usually these negatives follow the verb:
*Ich gehe **nicht** zum Karneval.* – I don't go to the carnival.
*Ich gehe **nie** zum Karneval.* – I never go to the carnival.

However, when there is an object in the sentence, *nicht* or *nie* follow the object:
*Mir gefällt der Krampuslauf **nicht**.*
I don't like the Krampuslauf.

Aussprache

Two-vowel combinations (diphthongs)

Listen and repeat the following phrase to help you pronounce the combinations *au* and *eu*:
Aua sagt die Eule, Ich glaub' ich hab 'ne Beule. Au Au Au. Die kleine Eule hat eine Beule.
Ouch, said the owl, I think I have a bump. Ow ow ow. The little owl has a bump.

6 💬 **Prepare a short talk on a celebration of your choice, mentioning the points given below. Use the text to help you, by replacing the sections in bold. Mention:**
- when it is celebrated
- what you usually do and what your opinion of it is
- what other people think of it
- what people should do to prepare for it
- what you did last time.

Wir feiern **Halloween** am **31. Oktober**.
Normalerweise feiere ich **Halloween** mit **meinen Freunden**. **Ich verkleide mich, und wir gehen abends von Haus zu Haus**. Ich denke, dass **es Spaß macht**.
Mein Vater mag **Halloween** nicht, weil **er** es **kindisch** findet.
Wenn man **Halloween** feiert, soll man **ein Kostüm kaufen und sich verkleiden**.
Letztes Jahr habe ich **mich als Hexe verkleidet**. Meiner Meinung nach war **mein Kostüm sehr gruselig**. Ich bin **mit meinen Freunden durch die Stadt gegangen,** und wir haben **viele Süßigkeiten bekommen**.

7 **Write a short piece (90 words) based on your presentation for activity 6.**

siebenundsiebzig

5.2H Wenn ich reich wäre …

OBJECTIVES
- Talking about festivals from other parts of the world
- The genitive case for possession
- Conditional clauses

1 📖 Read Lennard's article and answer the questions (a–f) in German.

Meine Traumreise nach China

Wenn ich mehr Geld hätte, würde ich gern das chinesische Neujahrsfest, das auch Frühlingsfest heißt, in Hongkong feiern, weil ich mich für die Kultur des Landes interessiere. Das chinesische Neujahr findet nicht wie bei uns am ersten Januar statt, sondern beginnt nach dem chinesischen Mondkalender. Das Fest dauert 15 Tage von Ende Januar bis Mitte Februar. Es ist ein großes Fest mit Tanz, Musik und leckerem Essen. Familien putzen und dekorieren ihre Häuser und reisen oft weit, um mit der Familie zu feiern. Sie geben sich am letzten Tag rote Umschläge mit Geldgeschenken. Es gibt auch Umzüge mit Tänzern und tanzenden Drachen, da der Drache Glück bringen soll. Die Träger der Drachen müssen sehr stark und akrobatisch sein, und das Spektakel ist wirklich beeindruckend! Wenn ich bei so einem Umzug wäre, würde ich tausend Fotos von dieser einmaligen Erfahrung machen. Natürlich gibt es auch ein Feuerwerk, weil diese aus China stammen.

a Warum will Lennard das chinesische Neujahrsfest feiern?
b Wann findet das Fest statt? (von … bis …)
c Wie bereitet man sich auf das Fest vor? (*two details*)
d Was ist ein typisches Geschenk zum chinesischen Neujahr?
e Was symbolisiert der Drache?
f Warum sind Feuerwerke beliebt in China?

nach	according to
der Mondkalender	lunar calender
putzen	to clean
Umschläge (pl)	envelopes
der Umzug (pl: **Umzüge**)	procession
der Drache (pl: **Drachen**)	dragon
Träger (pl)	carriers
beeindruckend	impressive
einmalig	unique

2 ✂ Translate these two phrases from activity 1 into English.

a Wenn ich mehr Geld hätte, würde ich gern das chinesische Neujahrsfest in Hongkong feiern.
b Wenn ich bei so einem Umzug wäre, würde ich tausend Fotos machen.

3 ✂ Translate these sentences into English, using the *Verben* box to help you.

a Silvester in New York wäre fantastisch.
b Ich hätte beim chinesischen Neujahrsfest viel Spaß.
c Wenn ich Vegetarier wäre, wäre meine Ernährung gesünder.
d Wenn ich viel Geld hätte, würde ich einen Ferrari kaufen.
e Wohin würdest du reisen, wenn du viel Geld hättest?

Verben

Conditional clauses

You have already come across the conditional form with *möchte* (the conditional of *mögen*). To say what you would do, you usually use *ich würde, wir würden*, etc. (from the verb *werden*, which you know from the future tense):

Ich würde um die Welt fahren.
I would travel around the world.

The conditional is often used with *wenn* clauses:

Wenn ich reich wäre, würde ich um die Welt fahren.
If I were rich, I would travel around the world.
Wenn wir viel Geld hätten, würden wir ein Auto kaufen.
If we had lots of money, we would buy a car.

Note that *hätte* is used instead of *würde haben*, and *wäre* instead of *würde sein*.

Customs, festivals and celebrations 5.2H

Grammatik

The genitive case for possession

The genitive case is often used to show possession / belonging, e.g: the father's birthday = *der Geburtstag des Vaters*. You add **-s** or **-es** to masculine and neuter nouns in this case. Feminine nouns stay the same.

	masculine	feminine	neuter	plural
the	des Brud**ers**	der Schwester	des Kind**es**	der Kinder
a	eines Brud**ers**	einer Schwester	eines Kind**es**	-
not a	keines Brud**ers**	keiner Schwester	keines Kind**es**	keiner Kinder
my	meines Brud**ers**	meiner Schwester	meines Kind**es**	meiner Kinder
this	dieses Brud**ers**	dieser Schwester	dieses Kind**es**	dieser Kinder

Find these genitive phrases in the text from activity 1:

a the country's culture **b** the carriers of the dragons

4 ⭐ Copy and complete the sentences with the correct genitive form of the noun in brackets, using the correct form of the definite article.

a Die Besucher ___ ___ kommen aus der ganzen Welt. (*das Fest*)
b Die Kleider ___ ___ sind sehr bunt. (*die Frauen*)
c Die Häuser ___ ___ sind schön dekoriert. (*die Stadt*)
d Der Lärm ___ ___ ärgert die Nachbarn. (*die Kinder*)
e Das bekannteste Fest ___ ___ ist das Oktoberfest. (*das Land*)

5 🎧 **Listen to Beate talk about her dream festival, then decide which five of the statements (a–i) are true.**

a Beate has found out a lot of information about the Holi Festival.
b The festival is celebrated at the beginning of February.
c The length of the festival changes from region to region.
d The festival starts with a big fire.
e The fire symbolises the demon.
f The next day people visit the temples and pray.
g They wear white clothes to go to the temple.
h On the second day they have a big party.
i At the party people throw coloured powder at each other.

6 💬 Working in pairs, take turns to ask and answer the following questions.
- Welches Fest möchtest du gern feiern?
- Was weißt du darüber?
- Wie wäre das?

7 ✏️ Using the table to help you (as well as your own ideas), write about what you would do if you were rich (150 words).

Wenn ich reich wäre,	würde ich	um die Welt / nach … fahren. ein Haus / ein Auto … kaufen. … besuchen.
	hätte ich	keine Sorgen. viele Tiere.
	wäre ich	glücklich / traurig / berühmt	, weil …
Es wäre mein Traum,		… zu tun / machen / kaufen / besuchen, usw.

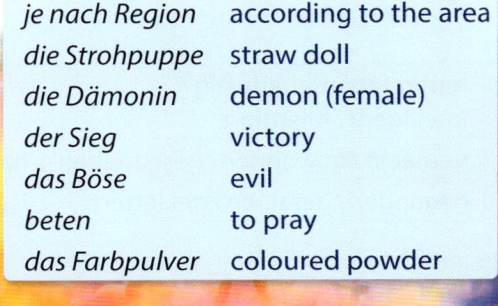

je nach Region	according to the area
die Strohpuppe	straw doll
die Dämonin	demon (female)
der Sieg	victory
das Böse	evil
beten	to pray
das Farbpulver	coloured powder

neunundsiebzig 79

6.1F Alt und cool

OBJECTIVES
- German-speaking celebrities from the past
- Adjective endings in the nominative and accusative cases
- Revising the perfect tense

1 📖 Read the articles about these celebrities. Select the correct past participle from the words provided to complete each gap.

| bekommen | gespielt | geklettert |
| geschrieben | gereist | gegangen |

Name: Reinhold Messner
Geburt: 17.09.1944 in Brixen, Südtirol, Italien
Beruf: Abenteurer
Leistungen: Er ist 1978 mit Peter Habeler als erster Mensch ohne Sauerstoffflasche auf den Mount Everest **a** ___. Er ist auch durch die Antarktis und die Wüste Gobi **b** ___.
Anderes: Er hat mehr als achtzig Bücher über seine Abenteuer und Expeditionen **c** ___.

Name: Marlene Dietrich
Geburt: 27.12.1901 in Berlin, Deutschland
Beruf: Schauspielerin
Leistungen: Sie hat in vielen Hollywood Filmen **d** ___ und hat sogar einen Stern auf dem Hollywood Boulevard. Sie war zu ihrer Zeit eine der bestbezahltesten Schauspielerinnen.
Anderes: In der Nazizeit ist Dietrich nach Amerika **e** ___. 1947 hat sie eine Medaille für ihre Hilfe im Zweiten Weltkrieg **f** ___.

die Sauerstoffflasche	oxygen bottle
klettern	to climb
die Wüste	desert

Kultur

Reinhold Messner was born in South Tyrol, Italy. A majority of people in this part of northern Italy speak German as their first language.

Across the world around 7.5 million people in 42 countries belong to a German-speaking minority. For instance, in the American states of North and South Dakota, German is the most common language spoken in the home after English.

2 🎧 Listen and check your answers for Activity 1.

3 📖 Find the German for these expressions in the texts for activity 1.

a as the first person
b more than 80 books
c even has a star
d in her time
e a medal for her help

4 💬 Working with a partner, take turns to ask and answer the following questions. Use the table to help you construct your answers.

- Wie findest du Reinhold Messner und Marlene Dietrich?
- Sind sie gute Vorbilder?
- Was ist für dich beeindruckend?

Ich finde, Reinhold / Marlene ist ein gutes Vorbild, weil er / sie	mutig / abenteuerlustig / intelligent / talentiert	war.
Ich finde beeindruckend, dass er / sie …	gemacht / gewonnen / geschrieben	hat.
	gegangen / gefahren / geklettert	ist.

achtzig

Celebrity culture 6.1F

5 Put the sentences (a–f) into the perfect tense.
  a Sie spielt in vielen Filmen.
  b Er spricht Deutsch und Italienisch.
  c Schreibst du ein Buch?
  d Ich fahre nach Österreich.
  e Wir spielen Fußball.
  f Sie bekommt ein Geschenk.

Verben

Revising the perfect tense
To form the perfect tense you need:
- the present tense of *haben* or *sein* as an auxiliary verb
- a past participle, which usually starts with *ge-*.

Ich habe Musik gehört. I listened to music.
Ich bin ins Kino gegangen. I went to the cinema.

6 Choose the correct option for each sentence. Then translate the sentences into English.
  a Ich finde den **deutsch / deutschen / deutsche** DJ, Robin Schulz, beeindruckend.
  b Ich liebe die **talentierte / talentierten / talentiert** Schauspielerin.
  c Ich habe die **interessante / interessantes / interessanten** Bücher von Reinhold Messner gelesen.
  d Das **neue / neuen / neues** Lied ist mein Lieblingslied.
  e Er hat für die **nationalen / nationale / nationales** Mannschaft gespielt.

Grammatik

Adjective endings in the nominative and accusative cases
When adjectives are used before a noun in the sentence, their endings reflect the gender and case of the noun:
Die deutsche Schauspielerin hat einen Preis gewonnen.
The German actor won a prize.
Ich habe das neue Buch von Reinhold Messner gelesen.
I have read the new book by Reinhold Messner.
Here are the endings for the nominative and accusative cases after the definite article ('the').

	masculine	feminine	neuter	plural
nominative	der gut**e**	die gut**e**	das gut**e**	die gut**en**
accusative	den gut**en**	die gut**e**	das gut**e**	die gut**en**

Remember that the nominative case is used for the subject of a sentence, and the accusative for the direct object:

Subject		Direct object	
Die deutsche Schauspielerin	hat	*das neue Buch*	*gekauft.*

7 Listen to Lars talking about his idol and answer the questions below.
  a What is his idol's name? (one detail)
  b What sport does she do and how old was she when she started? (two details)
  c What activity did she do before? (one detail)
  d Where did she go to train?
  e In which years was she an Olympic champion? (two details)
  f What two qualities does Lars say that his idol has? (two details)

8 Write a short biography of a person from the past (50 words).
Mention:
- when and where the person was born.
- what they were known as (e.g. sportsperson)
- their achievements
- what you think they were like as a person.

… ist am … in … geboren.
Er / Sie war …
Er / Sie hat … gewonnen / gespielt / geschrieben.
Ich denke, dass er / sie … war.

einundachtzig 81

6.1H Berühmt und beliebt?

OBJECTIVES
- Famous German-speaking people
- Adjectival nouns after *viel, etwas, nichts* and *alles*
- Different ways to use *werden*
- Pronunciation: *w* and *v*

1 Read the article on Angela Merkel and answer the questions in English.

Die erste Kanzlerin

Angela Merkel ist eine deutsche Politikerin. Sie ist am 17. Juli 1954 in Hamburg geboren. Als Kind ist sie mit ihrer Familie in die DDR umgezogen. Sie hat in Leipzig Physik studiert.

2005 wurde sie die erste Bundeskanzlerin Deutschlands, die erste Frau in dieser Rolle. Sie war auch die erste Person aus Ostdeutschland in diesem Amt.

2021 trat sie von ihrem Amt zurück. Mit 5860 Tagen als Kanzlerin kam sie dem Rekord von Helmut Kohl, der 5870 Tage Kanzler war, sehr nahe.

Kultur

After the Second World War, Germany was divided into two countries: the Federal Republic of Germany (West Germany, or *die Bundesrepublik Deutschland*, aligned with the Allied countries), and the German Democratic Republic (East Germany, or *die Deutsche Demokratische Republik*, aligned with the Soviet Union). The two countries became one again in 1990, a year after the Berlin Wall fell.

Although Angela Merkel was born in Hamburg, she grew up in East Germany. She went into politics in 1989. After the reunification of Germany, she had several government positions before becoming the chancellor / head of government in 2005.

a Where did Angela Merkel's family move to?
b What did she do in Leipzig?
c How was she different from all the chancellors before her? (two details)
d What record did she almost beat?

die DDR (Deutsche Demokratische Republik) — German Democratic Republic

2 Translate the sentences into German. Use the *Verben* box to help you.

a I will study German.
b They became very famous.
c Would you move to Germany?
d I would never do that.
e He became the best footballer.
f She is going to buy the book.

Verben

Different ways to use *werden*

You have encountered the verb *werden* (to become) in various contexts. You use the present tense + another verb to talk about the future:
Sie wird Physik studieren.
She will study physics.

The imperfect form of *werden* (*wurde*) is used in the text for activity 1:
2005 wurde sie die erste Bundeskanzlerin.
She became the first female chancellor.

You use *würde* (the conditional form) to talk about what you would do:
Ich würde nicht gern in die Politik gehen.
I wouldn't like to go into politics.

Take care not to confuse *wurde* and *würde*!

Celebrity culture 6.1H

3 🎧 **Listen to the podcast on the actor and politician Arnold Schwarzenegger. What do each of the following numbers represent?**

a 1947
b 19
c 21
d 5
e (more than) 40
f 2003

4 💬 **Working in pairs and using the table below, talk about what you would do if you were famous.**

Was würdest du machen, wenn du berühmt wärst?

Ich würde	mich für Umweltschutz / Tierschutz / Gleichberechtigung / Menschenrechte	einsetzen / engagieren.
	gegen Ungerechtigkeit / Rassismus / Armut	kämpfen.
	viel Geld	ausgeben / spenden.

wärst were (conditional form)

5 🎧 💬 **Read the words below with your partner, taking care with the *v* and *w* sounds. Then listen to the audio to compare and check.**

Viele Fußballer sind **w**underbare **V**orbilder.
Ich **w**ill **w**irklich **v**iel **v**erdienen, so **w**ie mein **V**ater.

6 ⭐ **Complete the sentences with the correct form of the adjectival noun.**

a Es gibt hier nichts (*interessant*).
b Sie hat etwas (*wichtig*) gesagt.
c Ich habe viel (*nützlich*) von ihm gelernt.
d Man kann hier viel (*alt*) und (*neu*) sehen.
e Sie sind für alles (*schlecht*) verantwortlich.

7 🔀 **Translate the passage into English.**

Meiner Meinung nach ist es nichts Besonderes, berühmt zu sein, aber es ist etwas Nützliches, Gutes für die Welt zu tun. Ich mag Sportler, die nicht nur sportlich, sondern auch hilfsbereit sind. So will ich auch werden.

8 ✏️ **Write two or three short paragraphs profiling a famous person of your choice, using activity 1 as a model.**

Aussprache

w and v

The spelling of the *w* and *v* sounds in German are rather tricky for English speakers. Remember that *v* sounds like 'f' and *w* sounds like 'v'!

Grammatik

Adjectival nouns after *viel, etwas, nichts* and *alles*

Adjectives can be used as nouns and these are usually neuter (*das Gute, das Böse*). When used with *viel, etwas, nichts* and *alles*, the adjective needs to end in **-es**:

*Sie hat **viel Gutes** getan.*
She has done **many good things.**

However, after *alles*, the adjectival noun ends in **-e**:

***Alles Gute** zum Geburtstag!*
Best wishes (literally: everything good) on your birthday!

dreiundachtzig 83

6.2F Superstars

OBJECTIVES
- Talking about celebrities
- Checking adjective endings
- Modal verbs in the imperfect tense (singular forms)

1 📖 Match the sentences (a–d) to the images (1–4).

a Ich wollte als kleines Kind Sänger sein.
b Ich musste Englisch lernen.
c Bis ich 12 war, durfte ich kein Haustier haben.
d Ich konnte es nicht glauben, als ich den Preis gewonnen habe!

2 🔀 Translate the sentences (a–d) from activity 1 into English. Use the *Verben* box to help you.

3 📖 Read the story of the German singer Nena, then answer the questions in English.

Verben

Modal verbs in the imperfect tense (singular forms)

Here is the imperfect tense (singular forms) for the modal verb *müssen* (must):

ich	musste
du	musstest
er/sie/es	musste

The first person endings for other modal verbs you know follow the same pattern as for *müssen*:

wollen (to want) → *ich wollte* I wanted to

dürfen (to be allowed to) → *ich durfte* I was allowed to

können (to can) → *ich konnte* I could

Kultur

99 Luftballons was written during the height of the Cold War, when Germany, and Berlin itself, was divided into two parts and people were very worried about war between the US-aligned West and the Soviet East. The song imagines what it would be like if a balloon drifted over the border between East and West and was mistaken for a weapon, leading to a nuclear war.

The English version of the song is called 99 Red Balloons.

a For how long has Nena been making music?
b What happened in 1983?
c Which other language has Nena's famous song been translated into?
d How old was Nena when she had her first band?
e What could people do in Berlin in the 80s? (two details)

Alles über Nena

Nena ist eine der berühmtesten Sängerinnen Deutschlands mit einer Karriere von über vierzig Jahren. Im Jahr 1983, als Nena 23 Jahre alt war, hatte sie einen internationalen Hit, der bis heute beliebt und berühmt ist: 99 Luftballons. Das Lied gibt es auch in Englisch.

Mit 17 Jahren hatte Nena ihre erste Band. Sie ist in Hagen geboren, aber sie wollte schon als Jugendliche nach Berlin fahren. In Berlin konnte man coole Kleidung kaufen und internationale Trends miterleben. Berlin in den 80er Jahren war sehr interessant!

Celebrity culture 6.2F

4 🎧 **Listen to Tina's school project about her idol, Annika Zeyen, then copy and complete the statements in English.**

a Annika won a ___ medal at the 2020 Paralympics.
b She had a riding accident when she was ___.
c At first, wheelchair ___ was just a hobby.
d She took part in the world championship when she was ___.
e After several ___ medals she wanted to try something new.
f She is now world champion at ___.

5 ⭐ **Rewrite the sentences with the correct adjective endings for the words in brackets.**

a Meine Mutter wollte eine (*bekannt*) Sängerin werden.
b Mein Bruder konnte das (*letzt*) Konzert seiner Lieblingsband nicht sehen.
c Gestern musste ich mit meiner Mutter einen (*langweilig*) Film ansehen.
d Als meine Oma jung war, durften Mädchen keine (*kurz*) Haare haben.

6 ✂ **Translate the sentences from activity 5 into English.**

Grammatik

Checking adjective endings

Adjective endings change only if they go before a noun:
Der Apfel ist grün. – The apple is green.
Ich habe einen grünen Apfel. – I have a green apple.
The ending you choose depends on the gender and article of the noun being described, whether it is plural or singular, and the case:

	masculine	feminine	neuter	plural
nominative	der grün**e** Apfel	die grün**e** Tasse	das grün**e** Kleid	die grün**en** Blätter
	ein grün**er** Apfel	eine grün**e** Tasse	ein grün**es** Kleid	die grün**en** Blätter
accusative	den grün**en** Apfel	die grün**e** Tasse	das grün**e** Kleid	die grün**en** Blätter
	einen grün**en** Apfel	eine grün**e** Tasse	ein grün**es** Kleid	grün**e** Blätter

Most endings are the same for the nominative and accusative cases, apart from the endings for masculine singular nouns.

7 ✏ **Write a short presentation about a celebrity of your choice, using the table to help you (90 words). Mention:**
- their character
- their achievements
- any extra details about their life.

8 💬 **Using your presentation for activity 7, make a list of 10 key words. Try to speak to your partner about your celebrity for one minute, using only your list for reference.**

Ich denke, dass er / sie	der beste Sänger / Schauspieler / Sportler die beste Sängerin / Schauspielerin / Sportlerin	ist.
Im Jahr … hat er / sie	die Weltmeisterschaft / eine Medaille / einen Oscar / einen Grammy	gewonnen.
	…	gesungen / gespielt.
Er / Sie musste	diszipliniert	sein.
	hart / viel / jeden Tag / …	arbeiten.
	…	lernen.
Schon als Kind wollte er / sie	Sänger(in) / Schauspieler(in) / Sportler(in) / bekannt / ein Superstar	sein.
	die Weltmeisterschaft / eine Medaille / einen Oscar / einen Grammy	gewinnen.

fünfundachtzig

6.2H Es ist nicht alles Gold, was glänzt

OBJECTIVES
- Talking about positive and negative aspects of fame
- Dative reflexive pronouns
- Modal verbs in the imperfect tense (all forms)

1 📖 Read the statements about fame and decide which is positive (P), negative (N) or both (P+N).

Fotografen (pl)	photographers
jeder	everyone
die Kleidermarke	(clothing) label
die Realität	reality

1  Ich hatte großes Glück: Ich habe schon mit 16 Jahren als Model viel Geld verdient und konnte in viele Länder reisen.

2 Jeden Tag Fotografen vor der Tür, das hat mich fast verrückt gemacht. In allen Zeitschriften gab es Fotos von mir, ich hatte kein Privatleben, weil alles in der Öffentlichkeit war. Ich war berühmt, aber nicht frei, weil jeder mein Foto wollte.

3  Ich wollte immer Fußballer werden, aber ich hatte keine Ahnung, dass Fans so böse sein können. Ich konnte X und Insta nicht benutzen. Das war sehr schwierig.

4 Ich habe mit meinem YouTube-Kanal angefangen und dann durfte ich in einem Video von Beyoncé tanzen. Jetzt habe ich meine eigene Tanzschule, Kleidermarke und mein Traum ist Realität geworden.

5 Meine Freunde und ich haben bei X-Factor mitgemacht und wir wurden sehr populär. Nach drei Jahren ging alles kaputt. Ich habe meine Freunde und Karriere verloren.

2 📖 Match one of the headings (a–e) with one or more of the speech bubbles (1–5) from activity 1:

a Opfer der sozialen Medien
b Paparazzi
c Vom Traum zur Realität
d Enttäuschung nach dem Erfolg
e Ein schönes Leben

die Enttäuschung	disappointment
der Erfolg	success

Celebrity culture — 6.2H

3 Rewrite the sentences using the imperfect tense, then translate them into English.

a Sie kann in viele Länder reisen.
b Er will Insta nicht benutzen.
c Wir dürfen in einem Video tanzen.
d Ich muss neue Freunde finden.
e Wir können das nicht verstehen.

4 Listen to Leonie and Elsa discussing the good and bad sides to fame, then answer the questions in English.

a According to Leonie, what do you always have to be if you are famous?
b What does Elsa suggest is great about being famous?
c What do famous people not have, according to Leonie?
d What do famous people often have problems with? (two details)
e How many followers do Lisa and Lena have?
f For whom are Lisa and Lena good role models?

Zwillinge (pl) twins

5 Copy and complete the sentences with the correct dative reflexive pronoun.

a Ich will ___ keine Fotos ansehen.
b Meine Mutter macht ___ oft Sorgen um mich.
c Viele Jugendliche stellen es ___ toll vor, berühmt zu sein.
d Jetzt kannst du ___ alles leisten.

6 Work with a partner to ask and answer questions based on the photo on the right.

- Sag etwas über das Foto.
- Was sind Nachteile des Ruhms?
- Was wolltest du als Kind werden? Warum?

der Ruhm fame

7 Imagine you had your own brush with fame! Write a paragraph (90 words) answering the following questions:

- Wie bist du berühmt geworden? Was hast du gemacht?
- Was durftest du als berühmte Person (nicht) tun?
- Beschreibe deine Fans. Wie waren sie?

Verben

Modal verbs in the imperfect tense (all forms)

Here is the imperfect tense for the modal verb *müssen*:

ich	musste
du	musstest
er/sie/es	musste
wir	mussten
ihr	musstet
sie/Sie	mussten

The endings are the same for the other modal verbs you have come across (*ich konnte, ich wollte, ich durfte*).

Grammatik

Dative reflexive pronouns

Some reflexive verbs use *mir* and *dir* (dative reflexive pronouns) instead of *mich* and *dich* (accusative reflexive pronouns):

*Ich mache **mir** um meine Schwester Sorgen.*
I am worried about my sister.

*Das kann ich **mir** nicht vorstellen.*
I can't imagine that.

All the other pronouns are the same in the dative and the accusative cases:

nominative	dative	accusative
ich	mir	mich
du	dir	dich
er/sie/es	sich	sich
wir	uns	uns
ihr	euch	euch
sie/Sie	sich	sich

The dictionary will give *dat.*, indicating the dative, after *sich*.

Theme 2

Kultur
Mehrsprachig und berühmt

1 Read the text on migration and multilingualism. Answer the questions in English.

Migration und Mehrsprachigkeit in Deutschland

Jedes Jahr ziehen viele Menschen aus anderen Ländern nach Deutschland. Außerdem gibt es zweite und dritte Generationen von Migranten. Mehr als 20% der Bevölkerung in Deutschland haben einen anderen kulturellen Hintergrund, deshalb gehört Mehrsprachigkeit zur Realität vieler Menschen in Deutschland.

Immer mehr Kinder und Jugendliche wachsen mehrsprachig auf. Die meistgesprochenen Sprachen in Deutschland sind Türkisch, Russisch, Arabisch, Polnisch, Rumänisch, Italienisch und Englisch. Im Jahr 2022 hatten mehr als 40% der Kinder unter fünf Jahren einen Migrationshintergrund.

Wer mehrere Sprachen spricht, hat Vorteile in der globalisierten Welt. Mehrsprachigkeit ist etwas Positives und man sollte es feiern.

die Mehrsprachigkeit — multilingualism

a What do 20% of the German population have?
b What is reality for many people in Germany when it comes to speaking other languages?
c What are the most common additional languages spoken in Germany?
d In 2022, what did more than 40% of children under five have?

Kultur

Children who already speak more than one language at school or in the home can have an advantage when it comes to learning another language. Different languages share common roots and patterns, and it can be fun to identify the similarities and differences.

2 Translate the final paragraph of the text from activity 1 into English.

3 Work with a partner. Take turns to ask and answer the following questions.
- Welche Sprache(n) sprichst du?
- Welche Sprachen sprechen andere Schüler an unserer Schule?

| Ich spreche … | Englisch / Deutsch / Ukrainisch / Polnisch … |
| An unserer Schule spricht man … | |

4 Match the descriptions to the famous people.

a Sie hat einen iranischen Vater und eine türkische Mutter. Sie hat in der deutschen Mannschaft gespielt.
b Er hat einen finnischen Vater und eine deutsche Mutter und spricht fünf Sprachen! Er ist Automobilrennfahrer.
c Er hat einen deutschen Vater und eine spanische Mutter. Er hat in deutschen, amerikanischen und spanischen Filmen gespielt.
d Sie hat einen südafrikanischen Vater und eine deutsche Mutter. Sie liebt Soul und R&B.

1 Sara Doorsoun-Khajeh (Fußballspielerin)
2 Nico Rosberg (Formel 1 Fahrer)
3 Joy Denalane (Sängerin)
4 Daniel Brühl (Schauspieler)

Theme 2

5 Read about the actress Helena Zengel. Answer the questions in English.

das Autogramm	autograph
fließend	fluent
der / die Regisseur/in	director

Ihre Karriere als Schauspielerin begann als sie mit fünf Jahren in einem Musikvideo mitspielte. Danach kamen ein paar deutsche Filmprojekte. Nachdem ihr Film „Systemsprenger" bei der Berlinale einen Silbernen Bären gewann, spielte sie sogar in einem Film mit dem amerikanischen Schauspieler Tom Hanks.

Mit elf Jahren war sie in einem Hollywood Film, ging auf Film Festivals, gab Autogramme und ging weiterhin zur Schule. Während der Filmarbeiten hatte sie eine Privatlehrerin. Sie hat in dieser Zeit ihr Englisch sehr verbessert, da das am Anfang noch nicht so gut war, und heute spricht sie fließend Englisch.

Trotz großen Erfolges muss sie für Klassenarbeiten lernen und Hausaufgaben machen. Sie will das Abitur machen und dann will sie in der Kunst arbeiten – als Regisseurin, Buchautorin oder Schauspielerin.

a When and what was Helena's first acting experience?
b What did her film 'Systemsprenger' win?
c Name three things she did when she was 11 years old.
d What did she improve a lot in while filming?
e What career plans does she have?

6 Listen to the podcast about the singer Zoe Wees. Complete the German sentences.

a Zoe Wees kommt aus ___.
b Sie hat im Jahr ___ bei *The Voice Kids* mitgemacht.
c Sie hat ___ und ___ benutzt, um Fans zu gewinnen.
d Heute hat sie mehr als ___ Follower.
e Im Jahr ___ hat sie ihre erste Single veröffentlicht.
f Es gibt eine Wachsfigur von Wees bei Madame Tussauds in ___.

| veröffentlicht | published, released |

Kultur

The Voice Kids is shown in different countries around the world (there is also a UK version). Zoe Wees appeared in the German version. This is the most popular version internationally, due in part to the fact that many contestants have a multicultural background, with one or both parents from another country,

7 Research one of these celebrities who have gained international fame and answer the questions below.

- Tom Wlaschiha
- Motsi Mabuse

Find out:
- where they are from and where they live now?
- what languages they speak?
- what is their profession?
- what successes they have had?

8 Write a short paragraph about your chosen celebrity from activity 7.

neunundachtzig

Theme 2 — Grammar practice

gern, lieber, am liebsten

1 Translate these sentences into German.
- a I like baking cakes.
- b I most like celebrating Halloween.
- c I prefer watching action movies.
- d I like training with my father.
- e My friend prefers to go hiking.

The perfect tense

2 Write the sentences in the perfect tense.
- a Ich höre Musik.
- b Ich sehe fern.
- c Ich gehe einkaufen.
- d Ich singe im Chor.
- e Wir fahren Skateboard.
- f Wir feiern Weihnachten.
- g Sie gewinnt das Spiel.
- h Er kocht das Abendessen.

Grammatik

Remember that when forming the perfect tense, most verbs take *haben* as the auxiliary verb. Verbs indicating movement to a place or a change of state take *sein*.

The present tense of *wissen*

3 Give the correct present tense forms of *wissen* (a–g) to complete the conversation.

Lehrerin: „Hallo Klasse, heute sprechen wir über deutsche Musik. Was **a** ___ ihr schon?"

Tim: „Ich **b** ___, wer 99 Luftballons gesungen hat."

Yusra: „Das ist einfach, das **c** ___ wir alle!"

Tim: „Meine Schwester **d** ___ es nicht!"

Lehrerin: „Na, wenn das so einfach ist, was **e** ___ du, Yusra?"

Yusra: „Meine Eltern **f** ___ viel über klassische Musik, und da habe ich gelernt, dass Beethoven neun Symphonien geschrieben hat."

Lehrerin: „Wow, dann **g** ___ ihr etwas über alte und neue Musik, super!"

The future tense with *werden*

4 Translate the sentences into German.
- a On Saturday I will go shopping.
- b On Sunday we will celebrate my birthday.
- c Tomorrow my brother will play football.
- d In the evening my parents will go to a concert.
- e Next month we will visit the Oktoberfest.

Verben

To say what you are going to do in the future, use the present tense of the verb *werden* plus the infinitive:

*Wir **werden** ins Kino **gehen**.*
We will go to the cinema.

*Was **wirst** du **machen**?*
What are you going to do? / What will you do?

Different uses of *werden*

5 Add the correct form of *werden* to complete the sentences.
- a Sie ___ eine berühmte Influencerin. (*She became a famous influencer.*)
- b Ich ___ ein schönes Haus kaufen. (*I would buy a beautiful house.*)
- c Sie ___ im Fernsehen auftreten. (*They will appear on TV.*)
- d Was ___ du tun, wenn du berühmt wärest? (*What would you do if you were famous?*)
- e Sie ___ ein Star ___. (*She will become a star.*)

Verben

Different uses of *werden*:

To become: *Er **wurde** Präsident.*
He became president.

Future tense: *Sie **wird** Mathe studieren.*
She will study maths.

Conditional mood: *Ich **würde** das nie tun.*
I would never do that.

Popular culture — Theme 2

Question words

6 Match the question beginnings and endings, then translate them into English.

a Wo
b Wer
c Wie
d Warum
e Wann
f Was

1 hast du gestern gemacht?
2 geht es dir?
3 bist du so traurig?
4 wohnt ihr?
5 fängt die Party an?
6 kommt mit?

Adjective endings

7 Copy and complete the sentences with the correct form of the adjective in brackets.

Morgen werde ich in das ___ (new) Stadion in Freiburg gehen. Ich werde ein ___ (red) T-Shirt tragen, weil das die Farbe des Vereins ist. Ich möchte den ___ (Austrian) Fußballer sehen, der ___ (new) im Team ist. Das ___ (old) Stadion war viel zu klein für so einen ___ (successful) Verein. Mein Vater sieht das Spiel lieber im Fernsehen, weil er die ___ (loud) Fans nervig findet.

Grammatik

When adjectives go before a noun, their endings change according to the article, gender and case, and whether the noun is singular or plural.

Modal verbs (present tense)

8 Select the correct modal verb to complete the sentences.

a Ich kann / muss viel trainieren, weil ich am Wochenende einen Wettbewerb habe.
b Ich darf / will nicht auf das Konzert gehen, weil meine Mutter denkt, dass ich zu jung bin.
c Ich will / soll auf einen Laternenumzug gehen, weil es dort schön ist.
d Du darfst / musst den Kuchen nicht essen, weil du allergisch gegen Nüsse bist.
e Auf dem Oktoberfest darf / kann man viele Touristen sehen, weil es so bekannt ist.

Modal verbs (imperfect tense)

9 Rewrite these sentences in the imperfect tense.

a Ich will berühmt werden.
b Ich darf abends nicht ausgehen.
c Ich muss jeden Tag mein Instrument üben.
d Mein Bruder kann sehr gut singen.
e Meine Schwester will Tennisprofi werden.
f Meine Eltern können meinen Traum nicht verstehen.

Verben

Here is the imperfect tense (all forms) for the modal verb *können*:

The endings follow the same pattern for the other modal verbs you have encountered (*ich musste, ich wollte, ich durfte*).

ich	konnte
du	konntest
er / sie / es	konnte
wir	konnten
ihr	konntet
sie / Sie	konnten

einundneunzig

Theme 2 — Grammar practice

The genitive case to denote possession

10 Translate these sentences into German.

a The city's museum is very famous.
b The singer's (f) voice is beautiful.
c The actor's (m) talent is tremendous.
d The band's new album is very successful.
e The team's coach is always friendly.
f The end of the movie is a bit disappointing.

Grammatik

The genitive case can be used to indicate possession:
das Zimmer des Kindes – the child's room
Masculine and neuter nouns add an extra *-(e)s* in the genitive:

	masculine	feminine	neuter	plural
the	des Mannes	der Frau	des Mädchens	der Kinder
a	eines Mannes	einer Frau	eines Mädchens	–
not a	keines Mannes	keiner Frau	keines Mädchens	keiner Kinder
my	meines Mannes	meiner Frau	meines Mädchens	meiner Kinder
this	dieses Mannes	dieser Frau	dieses Mädchens	dieser Kinder

Conditional clauses

11 Translate the sentences into English.

a Wenn ich reich wäre, würde ich nach Italien reisen.
b Wenn das Wetter besser wäre, würden wir Tennis spielen.
c Was würdest du tun, wenn du an meiner Stelle wärest?
d Wenn wir weniger Hausaufgaben hätten, könnten wir mehr Sport treiben.
e Wenn er Zeit hätte, würde er mehr Bücher lesen.

Verben

To say what you would do, you usually use *ich würde, wir würden,* etc.
Remember that *hätte* is used instead of *würde haben*, and *wäre* instead of *würde sein*.

Time, manner, place

12 Add the additional details to the sentences, bearing in mind the time-manner-place rule.

a Ich gehe ins Kino. (mit meinen Freunden, morgen)
b Sie fahren mit dem Zug. (zum Weihnachtsmarkt, am Donnerstag)
c Ich habe als Kellnerin gearbeitet. (in Bern, letztes Jahr)
d Markus wird in die Stadt fahren. (am Wochenende, mit seinen Freunden)
e Kaja hat gefrühstückt. (im Garten, heute Morgen, mit ihrer Familie)

Grammatik

When you mention when (time), how (manner) and where (place), you normally give the time first, then the manner, then the place.

Popular culture — Theme 2

nie and nicht

13 Translate the sentences into German.

a She never eats pizza.
b We're not going to the cinema.
c I will never see the film.
d They don't play football.
e We never celebrate Christmas.
f He doesn't drink coffee.

Adjectival nouns after *viel, etwas, nichts* and *alles*

14 Translate the sentences into English.

a Hier gibt es nichts Interessantes.
b Das ist etwas Besonderes.
c Alles Gute zum Geburtstag!
d Es gibt viel Spannendes in diesem Film.
e Sie haben nichts Neues gefunden.

Grammatik

Adjectives used as nouns are usually neuter. When they follow *viel, etwas* and *nichts* you add *-es*. When they follow *alles*, add *-e*.

beim / am + infinitives as nouns

15 Translate the sentences into German, using *beim* or *am* plus an infinitive as a noun.

a While reading you can relax.
b The worst thing about climbing is that it is often dangerous.
c The best thing about swimming is that it is so good for your health.
d While watching TV I fell asleep.
e While singing I can forget all my worries.

Grammatik

Remember that you can say 'while doing something' by turning the verb into a noun and using *beim* before it:

Beim Tanzen bin ich glücklich.
I'm happy **while dancing**.

When you say what is the best or worst thing about an action (*das Beste / Schlechteste am …*) the verb becomes a noun:

*Das Beste **am Tanzen** ist, dass es Spaß macht.*
The best thing **about dancing** is that it's fun.

möchte

16 Look at the questionnaire Ali filled out for his exchange partner. Write sentences in German using *Ali möchte / Ali möchte nicht*, saying what Ali would like and would not like to do, according to the questionnaire.

Möchtest du …	
a abends ausgehen?	✓
b Sport treiben?	✗
c deutsche Spezialitäten essen?	✓
d im Allgäu wandern?	✓
e das Stadtmuseum besuchen?	✗

dreiundneunzig 93

Theme 2 — Higher Vocabulary

Words that are highlighted in grey in this list are words that may be useful, but you won't need to know them for the exam.

Introductory

aber but
ab und zu now and again
allein alone
abends in the evening
Abonnent (m), Abonnentin (f) subscriber
Actionfilm (m) action film
andere other
sich anschließen to join
April April
arbeiten to work
auch also
August August
ausgehen to go out
aussehen to look like
Band (f) band, group (music)
beide both
bekannt known, famous
bekommen to receive, to get
berühmt famous
beschreiben to describe
blöd silly
brauchen to need
Chor (m) choid
cool cool
dann then
das macht nichts that doesn't matter
denn because
Dezember December
die Dokumentarsendung (f) documentary programme
die Sportsendung (f) sports programme
dienstags on Tuesdays
dort there
donnerstags on Thursdays
Einheit (f) unity
einfach simple, simply
einzig only, single
elektronisch electronic
entspannend relaxing
etwa about, approximately

etwas something
Fantasiefilm (m) fantasy film
Februar February
Feiertag (m) holiday, celebration day
Fest (nt) festival, celebration
Film (m) film
finden to find
freitags on Fridays
freundlich friendly
früher earlier
führen to lead
für for
ganz whole, all the, quite
gehen to go
genau exact, exactly
genug enough
gestern yesterday
glauben to believe
glücklich glücklich
groß big, tall
gruselig gruesome
gut good, well
heißen to be called
helfen to help
heute today
Hintergrund (m) background
hoch high
hoffen to hope
Hobby (nt) hobby
Horrorfilm (m) horror film
intelligent intelligent
interessant interesting
Januar January
jeden Tag every day
jedes Wochenende every weekend
jemand someone
Juli July
Juni June
kalt cold
Karneval (m) Carnival
Karriere (f) career
kaum hardly
kein no, not any
klassisch classical
klein small, short
Komödie (f) comedy
Konzert (nt) concert

Krimi (m) crime drama
langweilig boring
Liebesfilm (m) romance film
Lokal (nt) inn, restautant, bar, meeting place
lustig fun
Mai May
März March
mehr more
mein my
meiste most
meistens mostly
mit with
mittags at midday
mittwochs on Wednesdays
montags on Mondays
morgen tomorrow
Morgen (m) morning
morgens in the morning
Musik (f) music
Nachmittag (m) afternoon
nachmittags in the afternoons
nett nice
neu new
November November
oft often
Oktober October
Oktoberfest (nt) Munich beer festival
Orchester (nt) orchestra
Politik (f) politics
Pullover (m) pullover
Rock (m) skirt, rock music
ruhig calm, quiet
samstags on Saturdays
schlecht bad
schließlich finally, eventually
schlimm terrible
schön beautiful
schreiben to write
sehen to see
Sendung (f) programme
September September
schicken to send
schnell fast, quick, quickly
sehr very
sein to be
selten rare, rarely
Silvester (m or nt) New Year's Eve

singen to sing
sitzen to sit
sofort immediately, straight away
sonntags on Sundays
spannend exciting
sprechen to speak
stark strong, strongly
Tag (m) day
tanzen to dance
teilen to share
Text (m) text, lyric
toll great
tragen to wear
traurig sad
üben to practise
über about, above, over
Universität (f) university
Valentinstag (m) Valentine's Day
verbessern to improve
verbringen to spend (time)
verlassen to leave
versuchen to try
viele a lot, many
vollziehen to complete
Weihnachten (nt) Christmas
weil because
wenig little
Wiedervereinigung (f) reunification
Zeichentrickfilm (m) cartoon
zum Beispiel for example
zusammen together

4.1F Sportstars der Zukunft

Amerika America
Apartment (nt) flat, appartment
Basketball (m) basketball
Chance (f) chance, opportunity
ein bisschen a bit
einmalig unique
sich freuen auf to look forward to
Freundschaft (f) friendship
Fußball (m) football
gern(e) gladly, (with a verb) like to
hoffentlich hopefully

94 vierundneunzig

Theme 2

international international
leicht easy, easily
leisten to perform, to achieve
lieber more gladly, rather
Mannschaft (f) team
Medaille (f) medal
nervös nervous
schießen to shoot
Spanien Spain
Spiel (nt) game, match
spielen to play
talentiert talented
Team (nt) team
Technik (f) technology, technique
teilnehmen to take part
Tennis (nt) tennis
Tor (nt) goal, gate, gateway
Trainer (m) trainer
trainieren to train
Training (nt) training
Trainingslager (nt) training camp
treffen to meet
Verein (m) association, club
werden to become
Woche (f) week
wohnen to live
Zukunft (f) future
zuschauen to watch
zwischen between

4.1H Extremsportarten für alle

Angst (f) fear
Arm (m) arm
aufgeben to give up
Bein (nt) leg
Beste (nt) (the) best
brechen to break
Bungeesprigen (nt) bungee jumping
egoistisch selfish
sich entspannen to relax
Eis (nt) ice, ice cream
explodieren to explode
Fitness-Studio (nt) gym
Frage (f) question
frei free
sich fühlen to feel

Geburtstag (m) birthday
gefährlich dangerous
Geschwindigkeit (f) speed
gewinnen to win
Gymnastik (f) gymnastics
Helm (m) helmet
Herausforderung (f) challenge
Herz (nt) heart
jetzt now
Kind (nt) child
klettern to climb
Konzentration (f) concentration
kosten to cost
Meinung (f) opinion
Minute (f) minute
nerven to annoy, to irritate
nichts nothing
Problem (nt) problem
riskant risky
Schlimmste (nt) (the) worst
schwimmen to swim
Skateboarden (nt) skateboarding
Snowboarden (nt) snowboarding
Sorge (f) worry, care
später later
Sport (m) sport, PE
springen to jump
Stadtmitte (f) town centre
tauchen to dive
teuer expensive
tief deep
Tieftauchen (nt) deep diving
überwinden to overcome
unvergesslich unforgettable
vergessen to forget
verletzen to injure
wandern to go for a walk, to hike
wissen to know
Wochenende (nt) weekend
Zeit (f) time
Zuschauer (m) viewer, spectator

4.2F Auf geht's zum Konzert!

am liebsten best of all
billig cheap
dorthin to there
Eintrittskarte (f) entrance ticket

Farbe (f) colour
gelb yellow
grün green
ich möchte I would like
Karte (f) ticket, card
klassisch classical
Konzert (nt) concert
Künstler (m), Künstlerin (f) artist
Lied (nt) song
lila purple
mitsingen to sing along
mögen to like
obwohl although
Popmusik (f) pop music
Publikum (nt) audience, the public
Rap (m) rap (music)
rot red
Sänger (m), Sängerin (f) singer
total total, totally, completely
wann when
warum why
was what
wer who
wie how
wo where
wollen to want

4.2H Filme, die man sehen muss

(jdn) zum Lachen bringen to make (sb) laugh
albern silly
Alptraum (m) nightmare
anschauen to watch
Atmosphäre (f) atmosphere
beeindruckend impressive
bequem comfortable
dies-(er, e, es) this, that
doof stupid
Effekt (m) effect
empfehlen to recommend
erzählen to tell, to narrate
fantastisch fantastic
genießen to enjoy
Geschichte (f) story, history
gute/schlechte Laune haben (to) be in a good/bad mood | being in a good/bad mood
gute Laune machen to put in a good mood

insgesamt in all, altogether, in total
kindisch childish
Kino (nt) cinema
Kostüm (nt) costume
Kritik (f) criticism, review
Kultur (f) culture
leiden to suffer, to stand, to bear
lieben to love
Preis (m) price, prize
Qualität (f) quality
Romanze (f) romance
seitdem since then, since
Sieg (m) victory
sogar even
sonst otherwise, else
Soundtrack (m) soundtrack
Spannung (f) tension
Spezialeffekt (m) special effects
talentiert talented
Ton (m) sound, tone
Traum (m) dream
überzeugend convincing
um … zu … in order to …
und and
wichtig important
ziemlich quite
zuerst first of all

5.1F Alles Gute zum Geburtstag!

ärgern to irritate, to annoy
alles everything
Ausland (nt) foreign countries, abroad
dekorieren to decorate
dürfen (to) be allowed to, may
einladen to invite
feiern to celebrate
Feuerwerk (nt) firework
Gast (m) guest
Geld (nt) money
Geschenk (nt) present
griechisch Greek
Hochzeit (f) wedding
immer always
können can, to be able to
Kuchen (m) cake
laut loud
leider unfortunately

funfundneunzig 95

Theme 2 — Higher Vocabulary

Licht (nt) light
mir ist schlecht I feel sick
Mitternacht (f) midnight
Nachbar (m), Nachbarin (f) neighbour
organisieren to organise
Party (f) party
schenken to give as a present
Schiff (nt) ship, boat
stundenlang for hours
tausend a thousand
traditionell traditional, traditionally
überglücklich delighted, beyond happy
übernachten to spend the night
überraschen to surprise
ungefähr about, approximately
vorbereiten to prepare

5.1H Festessen und Traditionen

anfangen to start, to begin
Begleitung (f) accompaniment
bis bald bye for now, see you soon
bitten to request
bleiben to stay
brennen to burn
einpacken to wrap (up)
einsam lonely
Erde (f) Earth, ground, soil
es schneit it's snowing
Essen (nt) food, meal
fertig ready, finished
Fisch (m) fish
Gans (f) goose
gar nicht not at all
Gedicht (nt) poem
heilig holy
himmlisch heavenly
hold dear, sweet, fair
Honig (m) honey
Jahr (nt) year
Kartoffeln (pl) potatoes
Kirche (f) church
Knabe (m) boy
lecker delicious
Lehrer (m), Lehrerin (f) teacher
Lied (nt) song

lockig curly
Melodie (f) melody
Mensch (m) human being, person
Nacht (f) night
Nachtisch (m) pudding, dessert
nieder down,
Nuss (f) nut
Paar (nt) pair, couple
Pfarrer (m), Pfarrerin (f) vicar
Rotkohl (m) red cabbage
Ruhe (f) peace, calm
schlafen to sleep
Schnee (m) snow
schneien to snow
Sprache (f) language
stehen to stand
Titel (m) title
Tür (f) door
wachen to wake
Weg (m) way, path
weihnachtlich festive
Weihnachtsmarkt (m) Christmas market
weit far
wieder again
Wolke (f) cloud
Zutaten (pl) ingredients

5.2F Schöne und seltsame Traditionen

am ersten Mal the first time
Angst machen to frighten
Arbeit (f) work
Bart (m) beard
besondere special
Bier (nt) beer
denken to think
Deutschland Germany
die Schweiz Switzerland
durch through
gefallen to please
Hexe (f) witch
jedoch however
leben to live
Liste (f) list
müssen must, to have to
Mütze (f) hat
Neujahr (nt) New Year

nie never
normalerweise normally, usually
nur only
Österreich Austria
sagen to say
Schokolade (f) chocolate
schrecklich terrible
sollen should
sondern (but) rather
stellen to place, to put
Stiefel (m) boot
Straße (f) street
Süßigkeit (f) sweet
Tradition (f) tradition
Umzug (m) procession, parade
sich verkleiden to dress up, to wear fancy dress
ziehen to move, to pull

5.2H Wenn ich reich wäre …

Anfang (m) start
beginnen to begin
beten to pray
Böse (nt) evil
bunt colourful, multicoloured
chinesisch Chinese
dauern to last
Drache (m) dragon
Erfahrung (f) experience
Feuer (nt) fire
Frühling (m) Spring
Glück (nt) luck, good fortune, happiness
Haus (nt) house
Indien India
je nach depending on
Kalender (m) calander
kurz vor shortly before
mitmachen to join in
Mitte (f) middle
Mond (m) moon
natürlich natural, naturally, of course
Pulver (nt) powder
Puppe (f) doll
putzen to clean
Reise (f) journey, trip
Spektakel (nt) spectacle
stammen aus to come from

stattfinden to take place
Umschlag (m) envelope
Welt (f) world
wenn if, when, whenever

6.1F Alt und cool

Abenteuer (nt) adventure
abenteuerlustig adventurous
Algerien Algeria
alt old
arm poor
bewundern to admire
Charakter (m) character
Fan (m) fan, supporter
Flasche (f) bottle
großzügig generous
Hilfe (f) help
Italien Italy
Krieg (m) war
Leistung (f) achievement
Medaille (f) medal
Meisterschaft (f) championship
mutig courageous
national national
Olympiade (f) Olympics
Partei (f) (political) party
Preis (m) price, prize
Rassismus (m) racism
Sauerstoff (m) oxygen
Soldat (m) soldier
Stern (m) star
sympathisch kind
unterhalten to entertain
Vorbild (nt) role model
Wissenschaftler (m), Wissenschaftlerin (f) scientist
Wüste (f) desert
Zimmer (nt) room
zurück back
Zweck (m) purpose

6.1H Berühmt und beliebt ?

Amt (nt) post, position
Armut (f) poverty
ausgeben to spend
beliebt beloved
Bundesrepublik, BRD (f) Federal Republic (of Germany)

Theme 2

Deutsche Demokratische Republic (DDR) (f) German Democratic Republic
sich einsetzen für to fight for
sich engagieren für to be committed to
sich entscheiden to decide
erfolgreich successful
geboren born
Gleichberechtigung (f) equal rights
kämpfen to fight, to struggle
Kanzler (m), Kanzlerin (f) chancellor
nahe close to
nichts Besonderes nothing special, nothing particular
nützlich useful
Politiker (m), Politikerin (f) politician
Recht (nt) right, law
Rolle (f) role
Schutz (m) protection
spenden to donate
Tier (nt) animal
Umwelt (f) environment
umziehen to move (house, location)
Ungerechtigkeit (f) injustice
verantwortlich responsible
verdienen to earn
zurücktreten to resign, to step back

6.2F Superstars

Blatt (nt) sheet, leaf
danach afterwards, after
diszipliniert disciplined
hart hard
Haustier (nt) pet
in den 80er Jahren in the eighties
Luftballon (m) balloon
miterleben to experience, to live through
Rollstuhl (m) wheelchair
schon already
Sportler (m), Sportlerin (f) sportsperson
Stuhl (m) chair
Unfall (m) accident
weiter further

6.2H Es ist nicht alles Gold was glänzt

(in der) Öffentlichkeit (f) (in) public
Ahnung (f) idea
Alkohol (m) alcohol
benutzen to use
Droge (f) drug
Enttäuschung (f) disappointment
Erfolg (m) success
es gefällt mir I like, it pleases me
Fall (m) case
fast almost
Foto (nt) photo, photograph
Fotograf (m), Fotografin (f) photographer
glänzen to shine, to glitter
jeder everyone
kaputt broken, ruined
Leben (nt) life
sich leisten to perform, to achieve
Marke (f) brand
Nachteil (m) disadvantage
öffentlich public, publicly
perfekt perfect
populär popular
Privatleben (nt) private life
Realität (f) reality
Ruhm (m) fame
schwierig difficult
stressig stressful
verlieren to lose
verrückt mad
verstehen to understand
sich vorstellen to imagine

Kultur

arabisch Arabic
aufwachsen to grow up
außerdem in addition, furthermore
Autogramm (nt) autograph
Automobilrennfahrer (m), Automobilrennfahrerin (f) racing driver
Bevölkerung (f) population
deshalb therefore
Figur (f) figure
fließend fluent, fluently
gehören zu to belong to
Generation (f) generation
globalisiert globalised
Grund (m) reason
immer mehr more and more
kulturell cultural
mehrsprachig multilingual
Mehrsprachigkeit (f) multilingualism
meistgesprochen most spoken
Migrant (m), Migrantin (f) migrant
Migration (f) migration
polnisch Polish
Projekt (nt) project
Regisseur (m), Regisseurin (f) director
rumänisch Romanian
russisch Russian
Staffel (f) season, series
Teilnehmer (m), Teilnehmerin (f) participant
trotz despite
türkisch Turkish
unglaublich unbelievable, unbelievably
veröffentlichen to publish, to release
während during
weiterhin furthermore, on top of that
zeigen to show
ziehen nach to move to

Theme 2 — Test and revise: Higher Listening

1 🎧 **Two fathers, Joachim and Peter, are talking about recent Father's Day celebrations. Decide whether the statements are true (T) or false (F).**

a	They spent Father's Day together.	1 mark
b	Peter prefers to stay in bed on Father's Day.	1 mark
c	This year, the event was busier than usual.	1 mark
d	They had nice weather.	1 mark
e	There was food, drink and music.	1 mark
f	Peter's daughter played the drums at the event.	1 mark

der Musikverein — musical society

Tipp

The first time you listen, you could note which statements you think are true and false, and put a question mark next to the option(s) you're not sure about. When you listen the second time, make your final decision. If you're still unsure, it is better to guess than to leave a question unanswered.

2 🎧 **You hear a radio report about women in sport. Answer the questions in English.**

2.1

a	Why is this report on the radio?	1 mark
b	What world record does Florence Griffith-Joyner hold?	1 mark
c	When did she achieve this record?	1 mark

2.2

d	Which sport does one of the highest earning women in sports do?	1 mark
e	How much money did she make in one year?	1 mark
f	What event drew big crowds in 2022?	1 mark

3 🎧 **A Swiss actress is discussing her schedule. For each event (a–e), write Past for something that happened in the past, Now for something that is happening now and Future for something that will happen in the future.**

a	social media feed	1 mark
b	photo shoot	1 mark
c	movie premiere	1 mark
d	interviews	1 mark
e	dinner with fans	1 mark

4 🎧 **Four German teenagers are discussing how they like to spend their time. For each person (a–d), choose their favourite activity (1–9).**

1	cinema
2	ballet
3	basketball
4	phoning friends
5	football
6	reading
7	computer games
8	yoga
9	baking

a	Person A	1 mark
b	Person B	1 mark
c	Person C	1 mark
d	Person D	1 mark

Tipp

This task is about choosing the correct activity for each person. Remember that you are listening for the activity that the young people like doing most of all. There are five options which will not get used, but which may also be mentioned.

Popular culture — Theme 2

5 Kurt is talking about a meal out with family. For each item, if his opinion is **positive** write **P**, for **negative** write **N** and for positive and negative, write **P+N**.

a	eating out	1 mark
b	his starter	1 mark
c	his main dish	1 mark
d	his dessert	1 mark

6 Listen to this advertisement for celebrations in Vienna. Choose the correct answer to complete each sentence.

a The celebrations are for … **1 mark**
  1 Christmas.   2 Easter.   3 New Year's Eve.

b There will be … music. **1 mark**
  1 rock.   2 pop.   3 classical.

c There is a workshop where you can learn to … **1 mark**
  1 sing.   2 dance the waltz.   3 make pancakes.

d You should wear … **1 mark**
  1 elegant clothing.   2 casual clothes.   3 fancy dress.

e The 'Kursalon' costs … Euros. **1 mark**
  1 300   2 250   3 130

f The cost includes food, a party, an orchestra and … **1 mark**
  1 fireworks.   2 a boat trip.   3 singers.

> **Tipp**
>
> For this task, you are likely to hear the exact German words given in the answer options. Before you start listening, you could jot down the German words if you know them, so you have something to refer to when listening.

7 **Dictation A**

You will now hear **five** short sentences (a–e).

Listen carefully and, using your knowledge of German sounds, write down in German exactly what you hear for each sentence.

You will hear each sentence **three** times: the first time as a full sentence, the second time in short sections and the third time again as a full sentence.

Use your knowledge of German sounds and grammar to make sure that what you have written makes sense. Check carefully that your spelling is accurate.

a Sentence 1
b Sentence 2
c Sentence 3
d Sentence 4
e Sentence 5 **10 marks**

8 **Dictation B**

You will now hear **five** more sentences (a–e).

Write down in German exactly what you hear for each sentence.

a Sentence 1
b Sentence 2
c Sentence 3
d Sentence 4
e Sentence 5 **10 marks**

> **Tipp**
>
> Once you have written your sentences, check that they make sense. Are there any corrections you need to make to the grammar, punctuation or spelling?

neunundneunzig 99

Theme 2 — Test and revise: Higher Speaking

1 Role play

You are talking to an Austrian friend about celebrities.
Your teacher will play the part of your friend and will speak first.
You should address your friend as *du*.
When you see this – **?** – you will have to ask a question.

> **In order to score full marks, you must include a verb in your response to each task.**
>
> 1 Say which celebrity you like and why. (Give **two** details.)
>
> 2 Say where you get information about celebrities.
>
> 3 Give one advantage and one disadvantage of fame. (Give **two** details.)
>
> 4 Describe a recent trip to the cinema. (Give **two** details.)
>
> 5 **?** Ask your friend about their talents.

10 marks

Tipp

Try to make sure you include at least one verb in your response to each task (1–5) on the card. It's a good idea to keep your responses short and simple and focus on conveying your meaning accurately.

2 Reading aloud

When your teacher asks you, read aloud the following text **in German**.

> Jeden Sommer findet bei uns in der Stadt ein vierwöchiges Musikfestival statt.
>
> Die Stimmung ist fantastisch. Die Eintrittskarten sind günstig, also können sich viele Leute einen Besuch auf dem Fest leisten.
>
> Dieses Jahr wird eine französische HipHop Gruppe kommen, und ich freue mich schon sehr auf das Konzert.

You will then be asked four questions in **German** that relate to the topic of customs and celebrations.
Make sure you **answer all four questions as fully as you can.**

15 marks

Tipp

Remember to focus carefully on your pronunciation in the reading aloud task. Try to remember all the German sounds and sound combinations you have learnt.

Answer the follow-up questions as fully as possible and extend your sentences by giving your opinions, with reasons. Try to use a range of tenses and varied intensifiers and adverbs.

Popular culture   **Theme 2**

3 Photo card

- During your preparation time, look at the two photos. You may make as many notes as you wish on an Additional Answer Sheet and use these notes during the test.
- Your teacher will ask you to talk about the content of these photos. The recommended time is approximately **one and a half minutes. You must say at least one thing about each photo.**
- After you have spoken about the content of the photos, your teacher will then ask you questions related to **any** of the topics within the theme of **People and lifestyle**.

25 marks

> **Tipp**
>
> In the photo card task, try to extend your answers to the follow-up questions as much as you can. For example, you could give and justify opinions with *weil* and *denn*, and by using a variety of tenses, adjectives, adverbs, pronouns and intensifiers.

Photo 1

Photo 2

hunderteins **101**

Theme 2 — Test and revise: Higher Reading

1 Two young celebrities discuss their lifestyle. For each, choose one positive (P) and one negative (N) aspect they mention from the box below (1–8).

Sam: Ich habe seit zwei Jahren meinen eigenen YouTube-Kanal und habe schon zwei Millionen Follower. Das alles ging sehr schnell. Das Beste für mich ist, dass ich mein eigener Chef bin, aber manchmal fehlt mir mein altes privates Leben.

Carola: Seit ich bei der Talentshow teilgenommen habe, habe ich mit einigen berühmten Sängern zusammengearbeitet, und das macht wirklich viel Spaß. Mein Leben ist super, aber es gefällt mir nicht, Artikel über mich in den Medien zu lesen.

1	money
2	collaboration with stars
3	having many followers
4	not having a boss
5	lack of privacy
6	being in the media

a Sam: P ___, N ___   **2 marks**
b Carola: P ___, N ___   **2 marks**

Tipp
For this task, it's helpful to look for positive or negative adjectives, as well as changeover words and phrases such as *aber* and *nur*.

2 You read a review of a film you would like to watch in German. Choose the correct option to complete each sentence.

Dieser Film ist ein Drama und kam 2019 im Kino. Der Film hat 2020 den deutschen Filmpreis für die beste Schauspielerin gewonnen. Interessant ist, dass die Schauspielerin erst elf Jahre alt war. Ihr Talent ist unglaublich, und sie wird sicher noch eine lange Karriere haben.

Sie spielt in dem Film ein Mädchen, das sehr aggressiv und böse ist und deshalb von ihrer Mutter getrennt leben muss. Sie muss lernen, ihre Gefühle zu kontrollieren. Der Film ist revolutionär, weil er so ehrlich ist.

Als Zuschauer erlebt man die starken Gefühle. Es ist sehr bewegend, wie real das Thema dargestellt wird.

a The movie was released in …   **1 mark**
   1 2019.   2 2020.   3 2021.
b The film won a German film award for …   **1 mark**
   1 best actor.   2 best actress.   3 best script.
c The female protagonist … when she won the film award.   **1 mark**
   1 had already had a long career
   2 was very emotional   3 was still very young
d The main character struggles …   **1 mark**
   1 with her mother.   2 with school.   3 with her emotions.
e The movie is groundbreaking due to …   **1 mark**
   1 the topic.   2 its honesty.   3 an all female cast.
f Viewers will find the movie …   **1 mark**
   1 exciting.   2 outstanding.   3 emotional.

3 Read the holiday recommendation. Answer the questions in English.

Du willst nicht mit deinen Eltern den Sommer verbringen? Komm und habe Spaß mit neuen Freunden in unserem Feriencamp in Süddeutschland!

Du kannst bei uns eine Woche lang dein Sing- und Schauspieltalent verbessern und am Ende der Woche gibt es eine super Show! Oder du kannst einen neuen Sport probieren. Wir gehen Kanu fahren und klettern. Abends gibt es dann ein Fußballspiel und Würste.

1 The camp is for people who don't want to do what?   **1 mark**
2 Where is the camp?   **1 mark**
3 Visitors can improve their talents in which two things?   **2 marks**
4 What happens at the end of the week?   **1 mark**
5 Which new sporting activities might visitors try?   **2 marks**
6 What happens in the evenings?   **2 marks**

Popular culture | Theme 2

4 Read this message from your German friend. Answer the questions in English.

Liebe Sarah,

Ich freue mich schon sehr auf deinen Besuch. Wenn du kommst, werden wir auf das „Cannstatter Volksfest" gehen. Das ist eines der größten Feste Deutschlands und findet im September statt, genau wenn du mich besuchst. Jedes Jahr kommen ungefähr vier Millionen Menschen verschiedener Länder und Generationen wegen des Festes nach Stuttgart.

Auf dem Fest kannst du mit dem Riesenrad fahren, leckeres Essen essen und auf dem Markt einkaufen. Wir werden aber auch den Umzug am ersten Sonntag sehen, das ist ein tolles Ereignis. Da das Fest mehr als zweihundert Jahre alt ist, wird Tradition hier groß geschrieben. Auf dem Umzug gibt es Ochsen, Pferde, Tanz- und Musikgruppen in traditioneller Kleidung.

Ich hoffe, dass du das Fest genießen wirst und wir schöne Tage zusammen verbringen werden. Meiner Meinung nach ist es wichtig, die eigene Kultur zu feiern und neue Kulturen zu entdecken.

Bis bald
Xena

der Umzug	parade
Ochsen (pl)	oxen

a When and where does the *Cannstatter Volksfest* take place? (**two** details) **2 marks**
b What does Xena say about the visitors? (**two** details) **2 marks**
c Name **two** activities you can do at the festival. (**two** details) **2 marks**
d What will they do on Sunday? **1 mark**
e What can you see at the Sunday event? (**two** details) **2 marks**
f What does Xena hope will happen? **1 mark**
g What does Xena find important? (**two** details) **2 marks**

Tipp

Don't be overwhelmed by longer texts. Take your time and focus on what you understand. Use the questions to identify the parts of the text that you need in order to answer them. For example, in the first question, you are looking for the explanation that follows 'Cannstatter Volksfest'. You are not expected to know what the phrase means on its own.

5 Translate these sentences into English.
a Letztes Jahr sind wir auf ein Musikfestival in der Nähe von Berlin gegangen.
b Im Sommer wandern wir viel, obwohl es oft regnet.
c Normalerweise nehme ich am Schulkonzert teil.
d Es gibt so viele musikalische Schüler in unserer Schule.
e Helene Fischer wird ihre neuen Lieder auf dem Konzert singen.
10 marks

6 Translate these phrases into English.
a Hoffentlich werde ich Daniel Brühl bei der Filmpremiere sehen.
b Letztes Weihnachten habe ich von meiner Tante das beste Geschenk bekommen.
c Wenn wir auf das Konzert gehen wollen, müssen wir die Karten bald kaufen.
d Ich möchte Sänger werden und habe seit sechs Monaten meinen eigenen YouTube-Kanal.
e Ein Nachteil des Erfolgs ist, dass alle Menschen einen kennen.
10 marks

Tipp

It's a good idea to identify the main verb(s) and the tense that the sentence is in before you start translating. When you have finished, make sure your translation is complete and proofread your English translation for accuracy.

hundertdrei 103

Theme 2 — Test and revise: Higher Writing

1 Translate the sentences into German.

a My mother thinks that rappers have a bad influence.
b In the summer, I'll fly to Spain.
c Next month, I will go climbing with my stepfather.
d The correct clothing is important when you do sports.
e I celebrated my birthday in the garden.

10 marks

> **Tipp**
>
> You will need to pay careful attention to tenses and verbs when you translate into German. Look for the time markers in the English sentences (such as 'this year' or 'last spring') to help you.

EITHER Question 2.1 OR Question 2.2:

2.1 You are writing a magazine article about celebrations.

Write approximately **90** words in **German**.

You must write something about each bullet point.

Describe:
- typical food in your house
- a recent celebration
- a special event you will attend soon

15 marks

Or:

2.2 You write an email about your free time to your Swiss friend.

Write approximately **90** words in **German**.

You must write something about each bullet point.

Describe:
- sports in your area
- a recent visit to the cinema
- your plans for next weekend.

15 marks

> **Tipp**
>
> For this task, make sure you read the bullet points carefully and write something about each one. Be careful with time frames, as your verbs and time phrases need to match what each bullet point is asking you.

Popular culture — Theme 2

EITHER Question 3.1 OR Question 3.2:

3.1 **You are writing an article about sports.**

Write approximately **150** words in **German**.

You must write something about both bullet points.

Describe:
- the positive and negative effects of doing sports competitively
- your sporting achievements.   **25 marks**

Or:

3.2 **You are writing a blog about adolescent life.**

Write approximately **150** words in **German**.

You must write something about both bullet points.

Describe:
- how young people spend their free time
- a positive role model and what they have done.   **25 marks**

> **Tipp**
>
> Make sure you write something about both bullet points and communicate your message clearly. Try to develop your ideas as much as possible, using a range of complex language, and a variety of vocabulary and grammatical structures. Write about different people to show your knowledge of verb endings.

hundertfünf 105

Theme 3
Communication and the world around us

Travel and tourism

1 🎧 **Listen to eight people talking about how they get around. Match each speaker (a–h) to one of the pictures (1–8), then note whether their opinion is positive (P) or negative (N).**

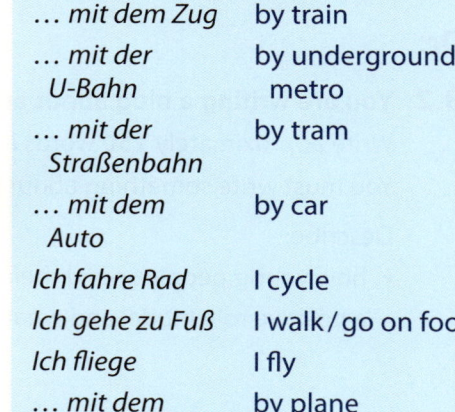

Ich fahre	I travel
… mit dem Bus	by bus
… mit dem Zug	by train
… mit der U-Bahn	by underground / metro
… mit der Straßenbahn	by tram
… mit dem Auto	by car
Ich fahre Rad	I cycle
Ich gehe zu Fuß	I walk / go on foot
Ich fliege	I fly
… mit dem Flugzeug	by plane

2 📖 **Jan is describing what he will do on one of the days during his holiday in Italy. Put the sentences (a–h) in the correct order.**

a Um achtzehn Uhr gehe ich zu meinem Hotel zurück.
b Am Nachmittag besuche ich das Schloss.
c Vor dem Frühstück schwimme ich im Pool.
d Ich esse am Abend im Restaurant.
e Nach dem Frühstück gehe ich in die Altstadt.
f Um 21.30 Uhr gehe ich am See spazieren.
g Mittags esse ich im Café.
h Um halb elf trinke ich einen Kaffee.

3 📖 **Read the sentences from activity 2 again. What will Jan do at these times of day?**

1 before breakfast   3 in the afternoon
2 at 10.30 am   4 at 6 pm

um … Uhr	at … o'clock
zurück	back
am Nachmittag	in the afternoon
vor	before
nach	after
mittags	at noon, midday

106 hundertsechs

Communication and the world around us — Theme 3

4 Unscramble these words connected with places of interest and then match each word with the correct picture (1–6).

a der sSlochs
b der zaMrkpaltt
c die eSnoygga
d die küBerc
e die sluFs
f die sheeMoc

Media and technology

5 Read the forum posts. Who likes doing which activity (a–h)? There are two activities that you do not need.

Max	Ich lese gern einen guten Roman. Meiner Meinung nach ist das sehr entspannend.
Sonja	Jede Woche schicke ich meinem Onkel WhatsApp-Nachrichten. Ich kann ihn nicht oft besuchen, weil er im Ausland wohnt.
Jürgen	Ich benutze mein Handy die ganze Zeit. Ich liebe soziale Medien, weil ich online so viele Freund*innen habe.
Brigitte	Nach der Arbeit sehe ich gern einen spannenden Krimi im Fernsehen. Das finde ich toll.
Klaus	Weil wir in einem kleinen Dorf wohnen, wo es keine Geschäfte gibt, kaufe ich fast alles online.
Lea	Ich benutze meinen Laptop, wenn ich meine Hausaufgaben mache. Das ist so nützlich.

a online shopping
b playing games
c reading a book
d watching the news
e doing homework
f sending messages abroad
g watching a movie
h using social media

lesen	to read
der Roman	novel
schicken	to send
Nachrichten (pl)	news, messages
besuchen	to visit
das Handy	(mobile) phone
der Krimi	thriller
benutzen	to use

6 Listen to five people (a–e) talking about how they use their phones. What activity (1–7) does each person mention?

1 apps
2 online games
3 talking to friends
4 e-books
5 photos
6 social media
7 the news

die Kamera	camera
Apps (pl)	apps

hundertsieben 107

Theme 3 — Communication and the world around us

The environment and where people live

7 📖 **Read these statements about the environment and answer the questions in English.**

Ich will der Umwelt helfen. Also recycle ich immer unser Glas und Papier zu Hause. Ich finde das sehr wichtig. **Julia**

Ich fliege nicht, weil ich die Luft nicht verschmutzen will. Ich fahre lieber mit dem Schiff oder mit dem Zug. **Hassan**

Meiner Meinung nach müssen wir alle Energie und Wasser sparen. Das ist wichtig für die Zukunft. **Emine**

Wir dürfen unsere Umwelt nicht zerstören. Wir brauchen unsere Berge, unsere Felder und unsere Seen. **Kevin**

Man muss die Luft in den Städten verbessern. Deswegen sollten wir immer mit öffentlichen Verkehrsmitteln fahren. **Maria**

Wir müssen die Erde schützen. Wir dürfen die Flüsse und das Meer nicht verschmutzen. **Bernd**
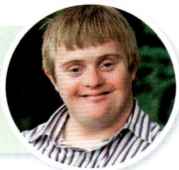

Who …
a wants to keep the rivers and sea clean?
b thinks recycling is a good idea?
c prefers to avoid flying?
d wants better air quality in towns?
e thinks we need to save natural resources?
f thinks we shouldn't destroy the countryside?

die Umwelt	environment
recyceln	to recycle
verschmutzen	to pollute
sparen	to save
zerstören	to destroy
Berg	mountains
die Luft	air
Städte (pl)	towns, cities
öffentlich	public
die Erde	earth
schützen	to protect
Flüsse (pl)	rivers
das Meer	sea

8 🎧 **Six people are describing where they live. Match the people (a–f) with the photos (1–6).**

die Wohnung	apartment, flat
das Zentrum	centre
die Nähe	vicinity
Büros (pl)	offices
gegenüber	opposite
die Post	post office
hinter	behind
weit	far
vor	in front of
neben	next to
das Krankenhaus	hospital

Communication and the world around us — Theme 3

9 Sandra and Marco are describing where they live. Read the texts and answer the questions in English.

Sandra

Wir wohnen in einer großen Stadt, die Köln heißt. Unsere Wohnung ist in einem ruhigen Viertel der Stadt und wir wohnen sehr gern hier. Die Stadt ist schön und liegt an einem Fluss. Unsere Nachbar*innen sind alle sehr freundlich, und wir haben hier keine Probleme. Im Sommer gibt es viele Touristen, aber sie wollen nur unsere Stadt sehen. Warum nicht?

Marco

Meine Eltern und ich wohnen auf dem Land in einem kleinen Dorf. Das Dorf ist schön und es gibt ein Café, aber keine Geschäfte. Wir haben eine Kirche, aber nicht so viel für Touristen. Für Jugendliche gibt es wenig zu tun. Man muss in die nächste Stadt fahren, wenn man ins Kino gehen will. Das finde ich sehr ärgerlich, da keine Busse nach 19.00 Uhr von der Stadt zu unserem Dorf fahren.

Who …
a lives in the countryside?
b has friendly neighbours?
c lives near a river?
d lives in a place with no shops?
e doesn't mind the tourists?
f doesn't have a cinema nearby?

ruhig	quiet
das Viertel	quarter
Nachbar*innen (pl)	neighbours
freundlich	friendly
Probleme (pl)	problem
nur	only
das Land	countryside
Jugendliche (pl)	young people, adolescents
wenig	little

10 Match the scrambled English names (a–f) for some places in the German-speaking world to the German names (1–6).

a oloCegn
b Bariaav
c nMuchi
d urNbergem
e enubDa
f naneVi

7.1F Was machst du gern im Urlaub?

OBJECTIVES
- Giving opinions about holidays
- Indefinite pronouns (*jemand* and *niemand*)
- Revising the perfect and imperfect tenses
- Pronunciation: *b*, *d* and *g*

1. Which of the following words refer to **eating out**, **accommodation**, or **both**? Sort them into three categories, then translate them into English.

die Speisekarte	der Blick	das Zimmer	die Rechnung	der / die Tourist / in
das Essen	der Preis	der Campingplatz	der Gast	bestellen
zahlen	das Fleisch	teuer	das Obst	das Hotel	der Urlaub

2. Read the speech bubbles and match each one (Gabi, Rohan, Mia and Tobi) to the correct photo (1–4).

   Gabi
   Ich habe immer am Strand gesessen – das war so entspannend, weil es schön warm war. Auch konnte ich den Alltag einfach vergessen. Ab und zu habe ich ein Eis gegessen. Das war lecker.

   Rohan
   Ich bin sehr gern aktiv und bleibe nicht gern den ganzen Tag im Hotel, deswegen bin ich in den Bergen gewandert. Ich habe niemanden gesehen. Es gab nur Tiere und Vögel. Der Urlaub hat mir gut gefallen.

   Mia
   Meine Familie und ich wollen nicht an einem Swimmingpool liegen. Wir sind in der Stadtmitte spazieren gegangen, weil es so viele Gebäude zu sehen gab. Wir haben alle Sehenswürdigkeiten sehr interessant gefunden.

   Tobi
   Zwei Wochen an der Küste waren mir zu lang. Ich habe es schrecklich gefunden, weil es jeden Tag geregnet hat und es nichts zu tun gab. Auch hat jemand meine Kamera gestohlen. Das nächste Mal bleibe ich zu Hause.

   1

   2

   3

   4

3. Read the texts from activity 2 again. For each person, say whether their experience was positive (P) or negative (N), and why.

4. Copy and complete these imperfect tense sentences with the correct form of the verb in brackets, then translate them into English.

   a Wir ___ keine Zeit. (*haben*)
   b Was ___ es in Berlin zu sehen? (*geben*)
   c Wo ___ Monika in den Ferien? (*sein*)
   d Das Essen ___ lecker, aber es ___ ein bisschen scharf. (*sein, sein*)

5 Copy and complete the sentences in the perfect tense, using the correct auxiliary verb and the past participle of the verb in brackets.

a   Ich ___ meine Karte ___ . (*verlieren*)
b   Unser Hotel ___ nicht zu viel ___ . (*kosten*)
c   Wir ___ jeden Tag im Meer ___ . (*schwimmen*)
d   Mein Freund ___ kein Brot ___ . (*essen*).
e   Ich ___ eine Wanderung in den Bergen ___ . (*machen*)
f   ___ Sie gestern gut ___ ? (*schlafen*)

6 Listen to Anna, Kevin and Leah talking about their holidays last year. Copy and complete the table.

Name	Destination	Transport	Accommodation	Activity
Anna				
Kevin				
Leah				

7 Copy and complete each sentence, choosing the correct word for 'someone' or 'no one'.

a   **Jemand / Jemanden** hat ihr Fahrrad genommen.
b   Es gab **niemand / niemanden** auf dem Bahnhof.
c   Gestern Abend war **jemand / jemanden** in unserem Hotelzimmer.
d   **Niemand / Niemanden** fährt heute mit dem Schiff.
e   Hast du **jemand / jemanden** gehört?
f   **Niemand / Niemanden** hat eine Kamera mitgebracht.
g   Gestern hat **jemand / jemanden** seine Tasche im Hotel vergessen.
h   Wir haben **niemand / niemanden** auf der Straße gesehen.

8 Listen to the sentence and transcribe it. You will hear it twice.

9 Working in pairs, take turns to ask and answer the following questions about a real or imaginary trip.

- Wohin bist du gefahren?
- Wie bist du gefahren?
- Wo hast du gewohnt?
- Was hast du gemacht?

10 Write four to six sentences about an imaginary holiday, mentioning the following points. Use the perfect and imperfect tenses.

- where you went
- how you got there
- where you stayed
- what you did

Verben

Revising the perfect and imperfect tenses

You can use the imperfect tense to talk about things in the past. See the full list of imperfect forms on pages 178-180.

Ich war müde. – I was tired.
Wir hatten kein Geld. – We had no money.
Es gab einen Strand. – There was a beach.

For the perfect tense, you usually use the present tense of *haben* plus the past participle which goes to the end of the sentence or clause:

*Er **hat** ein Eis **gekauft**.* – He bought an ice cream.

For verbs involving movement, use the present tense of *sein* plus the past participle which goes to the end of the sentence or clause. These verbs are irregular, so check the list on pages 178-180.

*Ich **bin** im See **geschwommen**.*
I swam in the lake.

Grammatik

Indefinite pronouns (*jemand* and *niemand*)

To say 'someone'/'somebody', use *jemand* if it is nominative. If it is accusative, use *jemanden*:

Jemand hat meine Tasche genommen.
Somebody has taken my bag.
Ich kenne jemanden in den USA.
I know someone in the USA.

To say 'no one'/'nobody', use *niemand / niemanden* in the same way as *jemand / jemanden*:

Niemand war am Strand.
Nobody was on the beach.
Heute haben wir niemanden gesehen.
We saw / have seen no-one today.

Aussprache

b, *d* and *g*

In German, if the letters *b*, *d* and *g* are at the start or in the middle of a word, they are pronounced as they are in English, but if at the end of a word, they are usually pronounced as 'p', 't' and 'k', e.g. *gib*, *Abend*, *Montag*. (However, see page 23 to see how to pronounce *ig*.)

7.1H Was hast du in den Ferien gemacht?

OBJECTIVES
- Talking about past holidays
- Plural indirect object pronouns
- Using *es gibt* and *es gab*
- Pronunciation: *er*

1 📖 **Read about Ayşe and Mehmet's holiday, then answer the questions (a–i) in English.**

a Where does Ayşe and Mehmet's uncle live? (two details)
b When did they go to see him?
c What did Ayşe and Mehmet look forward to especially?
d Why was the journey complicated?
e Who lives with their uncle?
f What is Klagenfurt famous for?
g What was an attraction for them in Klagenfurt?
h What did they see outside Klagenfurt?
i What did Ayşe and Mehmet do before saying goodbye?

Ich komme aus Berlin, der Hauptstadt Deutschlands, aber ich habe einen Onkel, der in Klagenfurt in Südösterreich wohnt. Mein Bruder und ich sehen ihn selten, deshalb hat er uns letzten Frühling eingeladen, zehn Tage bei ihm zu verbringen. Natürlich haben wir uns darauf gefreut, besonders da das unser erster Flug war.

Zuerst sind wir nach Wien geflogen, wo wir umsteigen mussten. Der Flug hat uns besonders gut gefallen, weil er so spannend war. Es gab eine Verspätung, aber schließlich sind wir am Klagenfurter Flughafen angekommen, wo mein Onkel geduldig auf uns gewartet hat. Dann hat er uns zu seiner Wohnung gebracht, und wir haben unseren Cousin Paul getroffen. Leider sind mein Onkel und meine Tante seit drei Jahren geschieden.

Klagenfurt ist für seine historische Altstadt bekannt, die wir gerne besucht haben, auch weil es viele tolle Geschäfte gab. An mehreren Tagen haben wir zusammen Ausflüge gemacht, denn diese Region ist so schön. Es gibt viele Seen und Berge. Unser Aufenthalt war bald zu Ende. Mein Onkel und Paul waren traurig, aber wir haben ihnen gedankt. Wir kommen bestimmt zurück.

umsteigen — to change (transport)

2 💬 **Working in pairs, read aloud the first paragraph of the text from activity 1. Give each other feedback on pronunciation.**

3 **Translate the first paragraph from the text for activity 1 into English.**

4 **Translate the sentences into German. Use the verb focus box to help you.**

a There is a lake nearby.
b There were lots of tourists in the Old Town.
c There is a large airport in Vienna.
d What was there to see in the town?
e There are no shops in this village.

Aussprache

er

In words where *er* is stressed, such as *Berlin* and *verbringen*, it sounds a little like 'air'. When *er* comes at the end of words, such as *Bruder*, it sounds more like 'uh'. The word *erster* includes both sounds.

Verben

Using *es gibt* and *es gab*

Use *es gibt* to say what 'there is' or 'there are'. Remember to use the accusative case afterwards:

Es gibt einen Strand (m) / *eine Stadt* (f) / *ein Dorf* (n) / *viele Geschäfte* (pl).
There is / are a beach / a city / a village / a lot of shops.

Use *kein* instead of *ein* to say what 'there isn't' or 'there aren't':
Es gibt keinen Strand / keine Stadt / kein Dorf / keine Geschäfte (pl).
There is / are no beach / no city / no village / no shops.

Use *es gab* (the imperfect tense) to say 'there was' or 'there were'. Again, use the accusative case afterwards:

Es gab einen Baum (m) / *eine Kirche* (f) / *Restaurants* (pl).
There was / were a tree / a church / restaurants.

Use *kein* instead of *ein* to say what 'there wasn't' or 'there weren't':
Es gab keinen Baum / keine Kirche / keine Restaurants.
There was / were no tree / no church / no restaurants.

Travel and tourism 7.1H

5 Copy and complete the sentences with the correct plural indirect object pronoun.

a Meine Mutter hat ___ nichts gesagt. (*to them*)
b Ich habe ___ eine Karte geschickt. (*to you, familiar, plural*)
c Hat er ___ für das Essen gedankt? (*you, formal*)
d Gestern hat er ___ Blumen geschickt. (*to them*)
e Bitte geben Sie ___ den Schlüssel. (*to us*)
f Ich sage ___ die Wahrheit. (*to you, familiar, plural*)

6 Translate the sentences into German, using the imperfect tense.

a He sent you (*familiar, plural*) a book.
b She thanked them for the money.
c They gave us a photo.
d We have sent you (*formal*) an email.
e Have you (*formal*) told them the truth?

Grammatik

Plural indirect object pronouns

Indirect object pronouns (*mir, dir, ihm, ihr*) use the dative case. Here are the plural forms:

uns – to us (the same as the accusative 'us')
euch – to you (the same as the accusative 'you')
Ihnen – to you (formal)
ihnen – to them

These are used after *danken* (to thank) and *helfen* (to help), and for the indirect object after verbs such as *schicken* (to send) and *geben* (to give):

Ich habe euch Geld gegeben.
I gave you money.

Unser Opa hat uns ein Geschenk geschickt.
Our grandad sent us a present.

Er hat ihnen gedankt.
He thanked them.

7 Listen to four German friends talking about their holidays. For each person (a–d), note down which of the following issues (1–8) is mentioned as a problem.

1 language
2 expensive
3 saw an accident
4 safety
5 unhelpful people
6 spicy food
7 wi-fi
8 poor view

8 Listen again and write down what was good about each person's holiday (a–d).

9 Write a short piece about an imaginary holiday you had (90 words), mentioning things that were good and any problems you had. Use the table to help you.

Ich bin	letzten Sommer / letztes Jahr	nach	Spanien / Deutschland / Österreich		gefahren / geflogen.
		in die	Schweiz		
Die Reise	war		interessant / langweilig / (un)bequem / zu lang.		
	hat mir		(nicht) (sehr) gut gefallen,	weil sie spannend / langweilig war.	
Ich habe	in einem Hotel		gewohnt.		
	in einer Ferienwohnung				
Es gab ein Problem	mit dem Hotel,	weil / da	es	zu kalt / schmutzig / klein war.	
	mit der Wohnung,		sie		
			es kein Wasser gab.		
Nächstes Jahr	werde ich		ein anderes Land besuchen / nach … fahren / fliegen.		
	werden wir		zurückkommen.		

10 Work with a partner to ask and answer questions based on this photo.

- Was siehst du auf dem Foto? (*Ich sehe …*)
- Was hast du letzten Sommer gemacht? (*Letzten Sommer habe / bin ich … Es war …*)
- Wie findest die Sommerferien? Warum? (*Ich finde die Sommerferien … weil ….*)
- Was möchtest du nächstes Jahr im Urlaub machen? (*Nächstes Jahr werde ich / werden wir …*)

hundertdreizehn

7.2F Was kann man hier machen?

OBJECTIVES
- Giving details about places of interest
- Singular indirect object pronouns
- Using verbal nouns
- Pronunciation: hard and soft *ch*

1 💬 Working with a partner, take turns to point at a picture (1–6) and say what you can do there, choosing an activity from the labels on the right.

> Was kann man dort machen?
>
> Dort kann man Rad fahren.

ein Schloss besuchen

im Meer schwimmen

ein Buch lesen

wandern gehen

Fotos machen

eine Bootsfahrt machen

Kultur

For people in German-speaking countries, going to the seaside isn't easy, unless you live in the north of Germany and are near the North Sea or Baltic Sea. However, people who live far from the sea but who want to swim in the open air can visit lakes such as Chiemsee or Bodensee.

Aussprache

Hard and soft *ch*

The German *ch* sound is pronounced in two ways. After the letters *a*, *o* and *u*, it is similar to the sound in the Scottish word 'Loch', as in 'Loch Ness': *danach* (afterwards), *kochen* (to cook), *Buch* (book).

After other vowels and consonants, it sounds like the 'h' sound in the English word 'huge': *sprechen* (to speak), *Milch* (milk).

2 📖 Read what each person says about their holiday preferences (a–f). Match each statement to one of the pictures (1–6) from activity 1, based on what the person says they like doing.

a Faulenzen am Strand ist bestimmt nichts für mich, weil das so langweilig ist. Ich mache lieber eine Bootsfahrt auf einem Fluss. Da kann man viel Natur sehen.

b Ich interessiere mich sehr für Geschichte und ich besuche gern Orte, wo man historische Gebäude sehen kann. Ich will nicht den ganzen Tag an einem Pool liegen.

c Berge oder Meer? Das ist eine schwierige Frage, denn sie sind beide schön, aber meiner Meinung nach ist das Wandern in den Bergen einfach wunderbar.

d An meinem letzten Geburtstag habe ich eine teure Kamera bekommen. Ich mache viele Fotos entweder in der Stadt oder am Meer, aber am liebsten mache ich Fotos auf dem Land.

e Radfahren und Joggen gefallen mir nicht – dafür braucht man zu viel Energie. Ich sitze lieber in der Sonne und lese ein Buch.

f Ich will in Form bleiben, also finde ich Sport wichtig. Mein Lieblingshobby ist Schwimmen, besonders im Meer. Das ist viel interessanter als im Pool.

114 hundertvierzehn

3 Copy and complete the sentences, using the correct verbal noun.

a Meine Schwester findet ___ langweilig. (*watching TV*)
b Mir macht ___ keinen Spaß. (*singing*)
c Unsere Freund*innen interessieren sich für ___ . (*diving*)
d ___ ist sehr gesund. (*hiking*)
e Er meint, dass ___ einfach toll ist. (*dancing*)

4 Translate the sentences from activity 3 into English.

5 Listen to the sentence and transcribe it. You will hear it twice.

6 Copy and complete the sentences by adding the correct indirect object pronoun, then translate them into English.

a Ich habe ___ die E-Mail geschickt. (*to you, singular*)
b Wir haben ___ ein Ticket gekauft. (*for her*)
c Können Sie ___ bitte den Weg zeigen? (*to me*)
d Sie hat ___ meine Kamera gegeben. (*to him*)
e Kannst du ___ die Fotos bringen? (*to her*)

7 Working with a partner or in a small group, ask what each person likes doing on holiday and why.

> Was machst du gern im Urlaub?
>> Ich finde Lesen toll, weil das entspannend ist.
> Und was machst du nicht gern?
>> Ich hasse Radfahren, da es langweilig ist.

8 Write down three things you like doing on holiday, and three things you dislike. Give a reason for each activity you mention.

9 Listen to Tanja's description of her dream holiday plans and copy and complete the summary in English.

Next **a** ___ Tanja will spend her holiday on an **b** ___. She will go **c** ___ every day and eat **d** ___ ___. She will bring lots of **e** ___ with her so that she can sit outside in the **f** ___ and **g** ___. She really enjoys **h** ___!

Verben

Using verbal nouns

A verbal noun in English often ends in '-ing':
I find **reading** relaxing. **Jogging** is fun.

To make a verb into a verbal noun is very easy in German. Take the infinitive form of the verb and give it a capital letter. Verbal nouns are always neuter:

Er findet (das) Schwimmen sehr schwer.
He finds swimming very difficult.

Ihrer Meinung nach macht (das) Kochen Spaß.
In her opinion, cooking is fun.

Note that you don't have to include the definite article ('the').

Grammatik

Singular indirect object pronouns

Indirect object pronouns take the dative case and are used after *danken* (to thank) and *helfen* (to help), and for the indirect object after verbs such as *schicken* (to send) and *geben* (to give) when the sentence includes a direct object:

Subject (Nominative)	Indirect object (Dative)	Direct object (Accusative)

Ich danke Ihnen! – I thank you!
Hilf mir! – Help me!
Ich schicke dir eine Karte. – I am sending you a card.
Du hast ihm ein gutes Buch gegeben.
You gave him a good book.

The singular forms are:

mir – to me   ihm – to him
dir – to you   ihr – to her
Ihnen – to you (formal)

You use these pronouns when you ask how people are:
Wie geht es dir? – (literally, How does it go for you?)
Es geht mir gut, danke! – (It goes well for me, thank you!)

7.2H Reiseziele, die wir lieben

OBJECTIVES
- Describing holidays
- Revising relative pronouns
- Avoiding using the passive

1 📖 Matthias and Hannah are writing about where they live. Choose the correct six statements, three for Matthias and three for Hannah.

Bern oder Bonn?

Matthias: Ich wohne sehr gern in Bern, im Tor zu den Alpen, im Herzen der Schweiz. Es ist auch die Hauptstadt der Schweiz. Nur wenige Meter vom Hauptbahnhof sieht man das Parlamentsgebäude. Sowohl für Kinder als auch Erwachsene gibt es den wunderbaren Bärenpark. Wenn man sich für Sport interessiert, dann ist Bern toll, da man hier viele Kurse für Jugendliche bietet. Auch kann ich den Bernaqua Wasserpark empfehlen, der großen Spaß macht.

Hannah: Meine Stadt heißt Bonn und ist die ehemalige Hauptstadt Deutschlands. Besonders beliebt ist die große Stadttour im Doppeldecker. Während der rund zweistündigen Tour kann man Bonn richtig kennenlernen. Auf dem Rhein mache ich gern eine Schifffahrt, die sehr entspannend ist. In Bonn gibt es auch den japanischen Garten mit seinem kleinen See und Wasserfall. Ich finde es auch einen Vorteil, dass der Freizeitpark Phantasialand nur etwa 20 Kilometer entfernt ist.

Matthias
a Bern is located in central Switzerland.
b The parliament building is on the outskirts of the city.
c It is Switzerland's second biggest city.
d People of all ages will appreciate the bear park.
e You can see other exotic animals here.
f It is a good place to come to if you like sport.

Hannah
g Bonn is the capital of Germany.
h You can go on an open-top bus tour around the city.
i The tour lasts about two hours.
j There is a lake in the Japanese Garden.
k Bonn has a large theme park.

2 💬 Read the texts again. Work with a partner to discuss which city you would like to visit and why?

Ich möchte … besuchen, weil …
In dieser Stadt kann man / gibt es …
Ich finde es …, dass man in dieser Stadt … kann.
Zuerst würde ich …, dann würde ich …

3 ✂ Translate the last three sentences of Hannah's text from activity 1 into English (*Auf dem Rhein … entfernt ist*).

Travel and tourism 7.2H

4 ⇄ **Translate these sentences into German using *man*. Use the *Verben* box to help you.**

a His passport has not been found.
b Lots of fruit is sold here.
c The money has not been paid.
d Her tickets have already been ordered.
e Our bags were stolen yesterday.

5 🎧 **Listen to this interview about supporting inclusion for school holidays, then answer the questions in English.**

a Why does Frau Schneider say summer holidays are the best time of year for children? (four details)
b How many children in Germany are unable to go on holiday?
c Where might these children spend their summer holidays? (two details)
d What low-cost possibilities for a holiday break are mentioned? (two details)
e What is the result if the children cannot have such breaks?
f What reasons are given for families staying at home? (two details)

6 ⭐ **Copy and complete the sentences by adding the correct relative pronoun.**

a Das ist der Mann, ___ in Italien wohnt.
b Hier sind die Fotos, ___ ich gestern gemacht habe.
c Das ist der Junge, ___ ich einen Apfel gegeben habe.
d Das ist der Ort, ___ uns so gefällt.
e Hast du den Strand besucht, ___ du gestern gefunden hast?
f Das Fahrrad, ___ ich letzten Monat gekauft habe, ist toll.

7 ✏ **Imagine you went on holiday to Bern, Bonn or another part of the German-speaking world. Write a status update telling people about it and try to include some relative clauses (150 words). Mention:**

- who you went with
- how you got there
- what you did there
- some opinions on your break (*Es war … / Wir fanden es …, weil …*).

8 💬 **When you have finished activity 7, take it in turns to read aloud what you have written to a partner or small group. They should listen carefully and note down any words they think you have mispronounced. See who has the fewest errors.**

Verben

Avoiding using the passive

We use the passive voice when the action in a sentence refers back to the subject, telling you what was done to it, him, her or them: Her camera was found on the train. The children were given an ice cream.

In German, these constructions can be avoided by using *man* and a 'normal' active verb:

Man hat** meine Kamera im Zug **gefunden.
(Literally, one found my camera on the train.)

Man hat** den Kindern Eis **gegeben.
(Literally, one gave the children ice cream.)

When used as a pronoun, *man* does not sound as formal in German as 'one' does in English! (Sometimes we might use an unspecified 'you'.)

Grammatik

Revising relative pronouns

Relative pronouns are the words for 'who', 'which' or 'that' when referring to someone / something already mentioned.

Remember to use the correct pronouns, the same as the words for 'the' in the nominative accusative and dative singular cases. The dative plural form is *denen*. Also don't forget to put a comma before the relative clause and move the verb to the end of it:

*Wir haben einen Freund, **der** (nom, masc.) in einem Hotel arbeitet.*
We have a friend **who** works in a hotel.

*Das ist der Garten, **den** (acc., masc.) wir gestern besucht haben.*
That is the garden **which / that** we visited yesterday.

*Sie ist die Frau, **der** (dat., fem.) ich eine E-Mail geschickt habe.*
She is the woman, to **whom** I sent an email.

*Das sind die Kinder, **denen** (dat., pl.) ich helfe.*
Those are the children I am helping.

Achtung!

In English, we don't always use a relative pronoun:
That is the book **(which)** I bought on Saturday.

In German, the relative pronoun must always be included:
*Das ist das Buch, **das** ich am Samstag gekauft habe.*

8.1F Soziale Medien – toll oder?

OBJECTIVES
- Talking about social media
- Comparatives using *als* and *so … wie*
- Revising the perfect tense of separable and reflexive verbs
- Pronunciation: *s* before a vowel

1 Identify 10 words associated with social media. Write down their meanings in English.

GESPRÄCHKONTAKTRISIKOPUBLIKUMMOBBINGGEFAHRSICHERHEITBILDSTREITWORT

2 Read about these two young people's social media usage and answer the questions in English.

Sam

Wenn ich morgens aufwache, suche ich mein Handy. Ich muss sofort sehen, wer mir eine WhatsApp-Nachricht geschickt hat. Ohne mein Handy kann ich einfach nicht leben. Vor drei Monaten habe ich es verloren und erst nach 24 Stunden habe ich es zwischen der Wand und meinem Bett gefunden. Einen ganzen Tag lang konnte ich nicht simsen, anrufen oder meine sozialen Medien benutzen. Als ich es wieder gefunden habe, war ich so glücklich.

Jennifer

Mein Handy ist mir sehr wichtig, und ich chatte gern online mit vielen Freund*innen. Gestern habe ich nach der Schule eine Stunde lang mein Handy benutzt – so habe ich mich entspannt! Jedoch weiß ich, dass soziale Medien manchmal gefährlich sein können. Deswegen muss ich vorsichtig sein, und ich versuche, sie so wenig wie möglich zu benutzen. Wenn ich in Kontakt bleiben will, schicke ich E-Mails oder simse ab und zu.

a What is the first thing that Sam does when he wakes up?
b Why does he do this?
c What happened three months ago?
d What was he unable to do as a result? (two details)
e What does Jennifer like to use her phone for?
f How did she relax after school yesterday?
g What does she think about social media?
h How does she try to be careful?
i How does she stay in touch with people?

Verben

Revising the perfect tense of separable and reflexive verbs

In the perfect tense, reflexive verbs are always used with *haben* + past participle:

Ich habe mich auf die Sommerferien gefreut.
I was looking forward to the summer holidays.

Sie hat sich für das Theater interessiert.
She was interested in the theatre.

Separable verbs use *haben* or *sein* in the perfect tense as usual, but the separable prefix now joins onto the past participle:

*Ich habe dieses Foto **hoch**geladen.*
I (have) uploaded this photo.

*Meine Freundin ist noch nicht **an**gekommen.*
My (girl)friend has not arrived yet.

3 Rewrite the sentences in the perfect tense. Use the *Verben* focus box to help you.

a Ich wasche mich um halb acht.
b Sie freut sich auf das Wochenende.
c Ich ziehe mich um sieben Uhr an.
d Er kümmert sich um seinen kleinen Bruder.
e Ich lade meine Hausaufgaben hoch.
f Der Zug fährt pünktlich ab.
g Mein Freund ruft mich heute an.
h Wir sehen uns den Film an.

4 Copy and complete these comparative sentences with the correct form of the adjective in brackets, then translate them into English.

a Das Matterhorn ist ___ als der Eiger. (*hoch*)
b Dein Laptop ist ___ als mein Laptop. (*neu*)
c Das Buch war ___ als der Film. (*langweilig*)
d England ist oft viel ___ als Griechenland. (*kalt*)
e Das Dorf ist ___ als die Stadt. (*ruhig*)

5 Write down five comparative sentences of your own, using *nicht so … wie …*

6 Transcribe the sentence which you will hear twice.

7 Listen to these four people (a–d) talking about social media. Match each person to the issue that they mention (1–6).

1 Schoolwork
2 Online dating
3 Sharing your experiences with others
4 Needing to get out more
5 Keeping in touch
6 Following celebrities

Grammatik

Comparatives using *als* and *so … wie*

To say something is 'bigger than' or 'more … than', add *-er* to the adjective followed by *als*. If the adjective contains the vowel 'a', 'o', or 'u', we usually add an umlaut:

Mein Bruder ist älter als meine Schwester.
My brother is older than my sister.

Die Zeitung ist interessanter als das Buch.
The newspaper is more interesting than the book.

However, there are exceptions: *dunkler* – darker, *ruhiger* – quieter, and the comparative for *hoch* (high) is the irregular *höher*.

To say something is 'not as … as', use *nicht so … wie*:
Mein Laptop ist nicht so teuer wie dein Laptop.
My laptop is not as expensive as your laptop.

Aussprache

s before a vowel

At the start of a word in German, the letter *s* before a vowel is pronounced like 'z' in English, e.g. *Sommer, sozial, Sonne.*

Use the same 'z' sound after a long vowel sound, e.g. *lesen, Käse, böse.*

If you see *ss*, it is always pronounced like 's' in English.

8 Working in pairs, take turns to ask and answer the following questions. Advice on how to answer is supplied in brackets.

- Was für ein Handy hast du? (*Say what kind of mobile phone you have.*)
- Wie oft benutzt du dein Handy? (*Say how often you use your phone.*)
- Wie findest du soziale Medien? Warum? (*Say what you think of social media and why.*)
- Wo benutzt du einen Computer? (*Say where you use a computer.*)
- Was machst du mit deinem Handy? (*Say what you do with your mobile phone.*)

9 Write down your answers to the above questions in German (50 words). Mention at least two details for each answer and include opinions whenever possible.

Mein Handy ist	neu / alt / groß / klein / …
	mir (sehr / nicht so) wichtig, weil …
Ich benutze mein Handy	jeden Tag / vor der Schule / sofort wenn ich aufwache … , weil … nicht so oft / fast nie …, weil …
Soziale Medien finde ich	cool / schrecklich / langweilig / wichtig / gefährlich …
Ich benutze einen Computer	in der Schule / zu Hause / in der Bibliothek …
Mit meinem Handy	chatte ich mit Freunden / simse ich / benutze ich soziale Medien …

8.1H Eine Welt ohne Medien? Unmöglich!

OBJECTIVES
- Talking about different forms of media
- Using superlative adjectives
- Revising dative reflexive pronouns

1 📖 Professor Fischer studies old and new forms of media and communications. Read the interview and answer the questions in English.

Was sind Medien Ihrer Meinung nach?
Von „Medien" sprechen wir, wenn wir das Fernsehen, das Internet, das Radio, Bücher oder Zeitungen meinen.

Und können Sie erklären, was die wichtigsten Vorteile davon sind?
Ja, natürlich existieren die traditionellen Medien – Fernsehen, Radio, Bücher und Zeitungen – schon lange, aber die digitalen Medien bieten uns spannende Gelegenheiten an. Heute haben die meisten Menschen Zugang zu elektronischen Medien und wissen auch diese zu benutzen. Was früher viele dicke Bücher im Wohnzimmer waren, das ist jetzt das Internet. Im Netz können sich fast alle über so viele verschiedene Sachen informieren. Man kann das sofort zu Hause machen.

Und die größten Nachteile?
Es ist ganz leicht, süchtig zu werden, besonders für Jugendliche. Auf der Straße sieht man so viele Leute, die die ganze Zeit auf ihr Handy gucken. Sie haben die Welt um sich herum total vergessen. Soziale Medien sind vielen Jugendlichen wichtig, aber sie müssen sich daran erinnern, dass es andere Sachen im Leben gibt.

Was sind Medien?

der Zugang — access

a Which types of media does Professor Fischer class as traditional? (four details)
b What are digital media offering?
c What can most people do nowadays? (two details)
d What has the internet replaced?
e What can you do on the internet according to Professor Fischer? (two details)
f What can easily happen when using social media, especially for young people?
g What does Professor Fischer say you see in the street?
h What should young people remember?

2 ⭐ Copy and complete the sentences with the correct dative reflexive pronoun, then translate the sentences into English.

a Er kann ___ ein neues Tablet nicht leisten.
b Ihr habt ___ einen teuren Laptop gekauft.
c Ich kann ___ ein Leben ohne mein Handy nicht vorstellen.
d Hast du ___ die Hände gewaschen?
e Wir wollen ___ die neue Sendung ansehen.
f Er hat ___ das Gesicht schon gewaschen.
g Morgen höre ich ___ dieses Lied an.
h Die Jungen kaufen ___ Karten für das Konzert.

Kultur

Remember that the word 'media' can also refer to books. You may want to try some young adult literature in German by Julia Kuhn and Felix Lobrecht.

Julia Kuhn's Ravenhall Academy series follows the adventures of the young witch Lilly Campbell. The first two books are *Verborgene Magie* and *Erwachte Magie*.

Felix Lobrecht is a comedian and presenter whose semi-autobiographical novel *Sonne und Beton* was made into a film.

Grammatik

Revising dative reflexive pronouns

Some reflexive verbs use *mir* and *dir* (dative reflexive pronouns) instead of *mich* and *dich* (accusative reflexive pronouns):
*Ich habe **mir** den Film angesehen.* I watched the film.

The dative reflexive pronouns are also used in expressions referring to parts of the body, where we use 'my', 'your', etc. in English:
*Ich habe **mir** die Hände gewaschen.*
I washed my hands. (hands are the direct object)

Note that this is different to *Ich habe **mich** gewaschen* (I washed myself), where you are the direct object.

Apart from *mir* and *dir* (for *ich* and *du*), the other dative reflexive pronouns are the same as the accusative forms.

Media and technology — 8.1H

3 🎧 Listen to these parents (a–f) discussing their children's use of the internet. For each, note whether their opinions are positive (P) or negative (N).

4 ✎ Translate these sentences into German. Use the *Grammatik* box to help you and remember to check whether the adjective is followed by a noun.

a My phone is the oldest.
b She has the most modern camera.
c Her uncle has the loudest voice.
d This laptop is the smallest.
e My favourite group plays the best music.

> ### Grammatik
> **Using superlative adjectives**
>
> Saying something is 'the most …', is called the superlative. In English we might instead add '-est' to the adjective, e.g. 'most lazy'/'laziest'.
>
> In German, when the adjective is not followed by a noun, we add *-sten* to the adjective and put *am* before it:
>
> *Sie ist **am** schnell**sten**.*
> She is the fastest.
>
> If followed by a noun, add *-st* to the adjective and the appropriate adjective ending:
>
> *Sie ist die schnell**ste** Schwimmerin.*
> She is the fastest swimmer.
>
> Note also: *gut* → *am besten / am liebsten*.

5 🎧 Listen to Kai asking Frank about his use of the internet and social media. Answer the following questions.

1 What does Frank say about using the internet? (two details)
2 What is Frank learning at the moment?
3 In what ways does he say internet access is helpful?
4 How does he feel about social media?
5 What do Frank's friends do on social media (two details)
6 What does Frank think is the worst disadvantage of social media?

6 Work in pairs to ask and answer the following questions from Kai's conversation with Frank in activity 5..

a Kannst du dir ein Leben ohne das Internet vorstellen? Warum (nicht)?
b Was machst du gern im Internet? Warum?
c Was sind die Vor- und Nachteile von sozialen Medien?

Ich kann es mir (nicht) vorstellen, weil		das Internet (nicht) so nützlich ist. man das Internet für … braucht.	
Ich	mache Hausaufgaben / sehe mir Videos an / suche Informationen	weil / da	es Spaß macht. das mir wichtig ist. es so schnell / einfach ist …
Soziale Medien sind	toll cool schrecklich	weil / da	wir Fotos hochladen können. meine Freunde Nachrichten schicken. es manchmal Mobbing gibt.

7 ✎ Working in pairs again and using third person pronouns and verb forms, write a paragraph about how your friend uses the internet and what they think of it (90 words).

- Was macht er / sie gern?
- Wie oft macht er / sie das?
- Wie findet er / sie das?

8.2F Wir streamen Sendungen

OBJECTIVES
- Talking about television
- Prepositions followed by the dative case
- Prepositions followed by the accusative case
- Pronunciation: the letter *e*

1 Unscramble each of these words (a–f) connected to television programmes, then translate them into English.

die Sendung — programme

a **doömKie**

b **feiperSone**

c **nedgrunposSt**

d **grensiTuend**

e **chinreNatch**

f **trendugunKlus**

2 Anja and her grandson Christian are talking about their TV preferences. Answer the questions in English. Write A for Anja or C for Christian.

Anja Als ich jünger war, habe ich oft Filme im Fernsehen gesehen, aber jetzt finde ich diese Sendungen zu lang. Jeden Abend sitze ich vor dem Fernseher im Wohnzimmer, weil ich gern Seifenopern sehe. Die Themen sind realistisch und spannend. Außerdem dauern die Sendungen nur eine halbe Stunde, und für mich ist das ideal.

Christian Ich will nicht zu einer bestimmten Zeit an einem bestimmten Tag im Wohnzimmer sitzen. Deswegen streame ich interessante Sendungen, wenn ich sie sehen will. Ich werde morgen eine lange Reise mit der Bahn machen, also werde ich meine Lieblingssendungen sehen. Das wird toll.

Who …
a doesn't want to spend time watching TV at home?
b often used to watch films on TV?
c likes shorter TV programmes?
d can watch programmes on the move?
e likes to watch soaps?
f watches TV at home every day?

| *der Fernseher* | TV set |
| *außerdem* | moreover / furthermore |

3 Match the sentence beginnings (a–d) and endings (1–4), then translate the sentences into English.

a Ich kann ohne mein …
b Der neue Laptop ist für …
c Wir haben nichts …
d Sie hat das Haus …

1 ohne das Tablet verlassen.
2 gegen die neue Technologie.
3 meinen Bruder.
4 Handy nicht leben.

Grammatik

Prepositions followed by the accusative case

Prepositions are short words, such as 'for', 'through', 'around'.

für for   *durch* through   *bis* until, up to
um around   *gegen* against   *ohne* without

These prepositions are always followed by the accusative case:

*für **meinen** Freund* – for my friend
*ohne **den** Laptop* – without the laptop

Media and technology 8.2F

4 Translate these phrases into German. Look at the words below to find the gender of the nouns. Use the *Grammatik* box to help you.

a opposite the theatre
b to the post office
c at my brother's (house)
d since the concert
e after the programme
f from her teacher (m)
g with the group
h out of the room

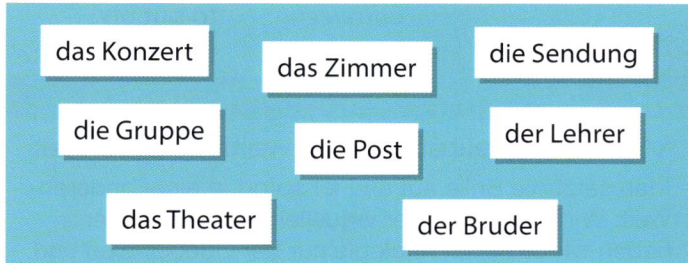

Grammatik

Prepositions followed by the dative case

These prepositions are always followed by the dative case:

mit – with, by (transport)
ab – from (time)
gegenüber – opposite
seit – since, for (a period of time)
nach – after, to
bei – at the house of, with
aus – from, out of
von – from, by, of
zu – to

Wir fahren **mit dem** Bus.
We travel by bus.

Nach dem Abendessen sehe ich fern.
I watch TV after dinner.

When plural nouns take the dative case, add an *-n* if it is not already there:

die Kinder – the children
***mit den** Kindern* – with the children

5 Listen to the six opinions about technology. For each opinion (a–f), write P for a positive opinion, N for a negative opinion and P+N for a mixed opinion.

6 Working with a partner, ask and answer questions about viewing habits using all the tenses you know. Give reasons for your responses, using the table below to help you.
- Was siehst du heute (im Fernsehen)?
- Streamst du Sendungen?
- Was hast du gestern Abend gesehen?
- Und was wirst du am Wochenende sehen?

Aussprache

The letter *e*

The letter *e* is pronounced in three different ways:
- as a long vowel sound (similar to 'b<u>ay</u>' in English) in words spelled with *ee* or *eh*, e.g. M**ee**r, s**eh**en, and also when it is followed by a single consonant, e.g. l**e**sen, g**e**ben
- as a short vowel sound (as in English 'b<u>e</u>d') when the vowel is followed by more than one consonant, e.g. B**e**tt, M**e**nsch
- similar to the ending of the English word 'bett<u>er</u>' when it comes at the end of a word, e.g. Klass**e**, Spiel**e**.

7 Write a short passage (90 words) about what you like to watch on TV. Mention:
- when and how you watch TV
- what kind of programmes you like
- something you watched recently
- what you thought of it
- something you plan on watching in the future.

Ich sehe gern		Krimis / Sportsendungen / Seifenopern / die Nachrichten.	
Ich streame Sendungen		im Fernsehen / auf meinem Handy / auf meinem Tablet / auf meinem Laptop.	
Gestern Abend	habe ich	einen Film / eine Komödie / eine Kultursendung	gesehen.
Die Sendung / Der Film war (nicht so) toll / sehr gut, Sie / Er hat mir (sehr / nicht) gefallen,		weil sie / er spannend / interessant / zu lang / komisch / traurig / langweilig	war.
Ich werde	am Wochenende	meine Lieblingssendung / eine Tiersendung	sehen.
			streamen.

8.2H Hier kommt die Zukunft

OBJECTIVES
- Talking about future technology
- Prepositions followed by dative / accusative
- Revising past, present and future tenses

1 📖 Read these articles about future technologies. Decide whether the statements (a–i) are true (T) or false (F).

übernehmen	to take over
Staus	traffic jams
Unfälle (pl)	accidents
Tote (pl)	deaths
aufsetzen	to put on
schulen	to train, educate

Technologie der Zukunft

Technologien entwickeln sich heute so schnell wie nie. Einige von ihnen haben das Potenzial, unsere Gesellschaft zu ändern.

Autos ohne Fahrer/in

Wir setzen uns ins Auto, und los geht's. So weit ist alles wie bisher, aber wir müssen es nicht selbst durch den Verkehr fahren, denn das übernimmt ein intelligentes Computersystem. Es ist nur noch eine Frage der Zeit, bis solche Autos die Straßen dominieren und sie werden miteinander kommunizieren können und so die Staus vermeiden. Deswegen wird es weniger Unfälle und Tote geben. Man experimentiert schon mit dieser Technologie, aber es gibt immer noch Gefahren.

Virtuelle Realität – eine zweite Wirklichkeit

Man setzt die Brille auf und ist sofort in einer anderen Welt: Willkommen in der virtuellen Realität! Bisher haben wir diese Technologie nur bei Videospielen und Filmprojekten gesehen. Bald wird die virtuelle Welt jedoch fester Bestandteil unseres Alltags werden. Spätere Generationen werden wohl einen größeren Teil ihrer Zeit in virtuellen Welten verbringen. Sie werden dort Aufgaben machen und neue Fähigkeiten lernen. Arbeitgeber werden wahrscheinlich öfter ihre Arbeiter in der virtuellen Realität schulen, damit diese zum Beispiel etwas über neue Maschinen lernen.

Driverless cars

a The driver will need to control the car in traffic.
b They are likely to become a reality.
c They will still get caught up in traffic jams.
d There will be fewer collisions because of them.
e Driverless cars are already safe to use.

Virtual reality

f Virtual reality is already being used in real-life situations.
g People are likely to spend longer in the virtual world in future.
h Virtual reality can be used to train people how to do things.
i Virtual reality will be used less frequently in the workplace.

2 ✂ Translate the last three sentences of the second text into English.

3 ✂ Translate these sentences into German. Remember that you can sometimes use different tenses to translate the same sentence.

a We went out at 8 o'clock.
b I shall call my friend (m) today.
c They discussed new phones.
d My cousin (f) is reading a novel.
e I ordered a shirt online.

Verben

Revising past, present and future tenses

The perfect tense uses an auxiliary verb – the present tense of *haben* or *sein* – plus a past participle.

The future tense uses the present tense of *werden* plus an infinitive:

Heute werden wir ins Kino gehen.
Today we are going to go to the cinema.

Often the future can be expressed using the present tense if the context is clear:

Morgen besuche ich ihn.
I will visit him tomorrow.

hundertvierundzwanzig

Media and technology 8.2H

4 Copy and complete the sentences with the correct form of the article. For article endings for accusative and dative cases, see pages 27 and 164.

a Sein Handy liegt auf **einen/einem** Tisch.
b Mein Freund ist in **das/dem** Theater gegangen.
c Dein Tablet war unter **deinen/deinem** Stuhl.
d Es gibt viele Fotos an **ihre/ihrer** Wand.
e Unser Hund ist aus dem Haus in **den/dem** Garten gelaufen.
f Gestern Abend hat sie ihren Mann auf **die/der** Bühne eingeladen.
g Das Bett steht zwischen **die/der** Wand und **das/dem** Fenster.
h Sie hat ihre Schuhe vor **die/der** Tür gelegt.

Grammatik

Prepositions followed by the dative / accusative

These prepositions can be followed by the dative or accusative case:

an – on (the side of), at	*über* – above, over
auf – on (top of)	*unter* – under
hinter – behind	*vor* – in front of
in – in, into	*zwischen* – between
neben – next to	

If movement from one place to another is involved ('where to'), use the accusative. If there is no movement from one place to another ('where at'), use the dative:

*Ich gehe **in das (ins)** Zimmer.*
I go **into** the room. (movement)
*Ich lese **in dem (im)** Zimmer.*
I read **in** the room. (no movement)

5 Listen to the four different opinions on technology and progress (a–d). Copy and complete the table, noting whether each opinion is positive (P), negative (N) or mixed (P+N), and giving a reason.

	Opinion	Reason
a	P	has lots of devices …
b		

Kultur

Artificial intelligence, digital personalised health, robotics and advanced manufacturing are technologies that Switzerland is developing for the future. Did you know that the longest drone delivery route in the world runs between two hospitals in Zürich and transports urgent biological samples?

6 Working in pairs, take turns to ask and answer the following questions.
- Was für Technologien benutzt du?
- Hast du einen Laptop? Warum (nicht)?
- Was hast du gestern mit Technologie gemacht?
- Was ist ein Nachteil von Technologie?
- Wie ist deine Meinung über die Technologie der Zukunft? Warum?

7 Write a paragraph (90 words), answering the following questions.
- Was sind Vor- und Nachteile der Technologie?
- Was für Technologie hast du letzte Woche benutzt?
- Wie wird die Zukunft der Technologie aussehen?

Ich benutze		einen Laptop / ein Tablet / ein Handy.		
Ich habe	einen	Laptop,	weil	ich meine Hausaufgaben darauf mache. ich immer online bin.
	keinen			sie so teuer sind. ich lieber draußen bin.
Gestern	habe ich	Videospiele gespielt. mit Freunden gesimst.		
Ein Nachteil von Technologie besteht darin, dass		alles so schnell altmodisch wird. man immer etwas Neues kaufen oder lernen muss.		
In der Zukunft wird man		alles online machen, zu Hause arbeiten,	weil	das besser für die Umwelt ist. jeder einen Computer hat.

9.1F Was sollte man machen?

OBJECTIVES
- Discussing environmental problems
- Indefinite adjectives
- Revising modal verbs
- Pronunciation: *st* and *sp*

1 📖 Match the words (a–f) to the photos (1–6).

a zu Fuß
b mit dem Bus
c Sonnenenergie
d Flugzeug
e Recycling
f Müll

2 📖 Look again at the photos (1–6) in activity 1 and match them to these statements (a–f).

a Ich fahre gern in Urlaub. Früher bin ich mit dem Flugzeug geflogen, aber jetzt will ich die Luft nicht verschmutzen. Deswegen fliege ich nicht mehr und fahre immer mit dem Zug.

b Ich wohne auf dem Land und habe kein Auto und kein Fahrrad. Also muss ich mit öffentlichem Verkehr fahren, wenn ich in die Stadt fahren will. Das ist auch sehr gut für die Umwelt.

c Ich wohne seit dreißig Jahren in dieser Stadt. Die Stadt gefällt mir sehr. In der Vergangenheit war sie so sauber, aber der Müll sieht jetzt schrecklich aus und ist schlecht für die Umwelt.

d Ich bin vierzehn Jahre alt und wohne in der Nähe von Stuttgart. Ich fahre sehr gern mit dem Auto, aber ich sollte öfter zu Fuß gehen, weil es gesünder ist.

e Meine Geschwister und ich denken an die Zukunft und wir wollen nicht in einem kalten Haus wohnen. Wir sollten Energie von der Sonne benutzen.

f Um die Umwelt zu schützen, muss man jeden Tag so viel wie möglich recyceln. Meiner Meinung nach gibt es zu viel Müll.

3 🎯 Copy and complete these sentences with the correct form of the modal verb given in brackets. Refer to page 170 for extra help.

a Ich ___ meine alten Flaschen nicht wegwerfen. (*sollen*)
b ___ du der Umwelt helfen? (*wollen*)
c Wir ___ die Tiere und die Landschaft schützen. (*müssen*)
d Man ___ die Luft und das Wasser nicht verschmutzen. (*dürfen*)
e Er ___ jeden Samstag mit dem Zug fahren. (*können*)

4 ✂ Translate the sentences from activity 3 into English. Use the *Verben* box to help you.

Verben

Revising modal verbs

Check the forms of these irregular verbs on page 170.

müssen to have to
können to be able to / can
dürfen to be allowed to
sollen should / ought to
wollen to want to
mögen to like

The verb which follows the modal verb must be in the infinitive form and goes to the end:

Man muss die Umwelt schützen.
One must protect the environment.

Wir sollten immer Plastik, Glas und Papier recyceln.
We should always recycle plastic, glass and paper.

Take care with the distinction between *müssen nicht* ('don't have to'/'not be obliged to') and *dürfen nicht* ('must not'/'not be allowed to').

Note that the conditional form *sollte* is used more often than the present tense *sollen*.

The environment and where people live 9.1F

5 Six people are talking about the environment. For each person (Emilia, Oskar, Frieda, Mohammed, Juna, Erik), decide which of the following issues (1–6) best describes their concerns.

1. air pollution
2. climate change
3. future generations
4. protecting green spaces
5. recycling
6. water pollution

6 Listen to the people talking about the environment in activity 5 again and write down as many details as you can for each person.

a What are the differences between now and earlier according to Emilia? (four details)
b What is dangerous for people and animals according to Oskar? (one detail)
c Why is the air in town less clean according to Frieda? (two details)
d Which items for recycling are mentioned by Mohammed? (three details)
e Why does Juna think we should build fewer houses? (two details)
f Why should we protect the environment according to Erik? (three details)

7 Copy and complete the sentences, choosing the correct form of the indefinite adjective.

a Die Temperatur steigt **jeder / jede / jedes** Jahr.
b **Letzten / Letztes / Letzter** Monat war der Fluss sehr schmutzig.
c **Nächstes / Nächste / Nächsten** Woche werden wir mehr Wasser sparen.
d **Letzte / Letzten / Letztes** Jahr haben wir viel Müll am Strand gesammelt.

8 Listen to this short statement and write it down in German. You will hear it twice.

9 Work with a partner and take turns to ask and answer questions based on this photo.
- Sag etwas über das Foto.
- Findest du es besser, mit dem Auto oder mit dem Zug zu fahren? Warum?
- Was hast du in letzter Zeit für die Umwelt gemacht?
- Wie wirst du in der Zukunft helfen?

10 Write a paragraph about where you live and what you do to help protect the environment (90 words).

Aussprache

st and sp

At the start of a German word, the letters *st* and *sp* are pronounced like 'sht' and 'shp' in English, e.g. *Stadt, spielen*.

This is also true when another word is joined onto the beginning of the word:

Fußballspiel – football match
Hauptstadt – capital city

In the middle or at the end of a word, they are pronounced as in English, e.g. *beste, Gast*.

Grammatik

Indefinite adjectives

Indefinite adjectives are words such as *jede* (every / each), *letzte* (last) and *nächste* (next). They are followed by a noun and will need the correct ending depending on the gender of the noun. The endings are almost the same as those for the definite article of that noun:

*Ich recycle **jeden** Tag (m).*
I recycle every day.

*Sie will **nächstes** Jahr (n) ihr Auto verkaufen.*
She wants to sell her car next year.

***Jeder** Mensch (m) muss an die Umwelt denken.*
Every person must think of the environment.

hundertsiebenundzwanzig 127

9.1H Unsere Umwelt

OBJECTIVES
- Talking about saving the planet
- Using 'it'/'them' and 'what' with prepositions
- Using *ohne/statt … zu*
- Pronunciation: *tio*

1 Read the article on protecting the environment and decide whether the statements (a–f) below are true (T) or false (F).

Einige Tipps für Umweltschutz

Versuche Gemüse statt Fleisch zu essen

Eine Studie hat gezeigt, dass Fleisch essen einen schlechten Einfluss auf die Umwelt hat. Um einen typischen Burger zu produzieren, braucht man 2 500 Liter Wasser für Tiernahrung! Im Vergleich dazu braucht man nur drei Liter zum Händewaschen, wenn das 20-30 Sekunden dauert. Für einen Burger kann man sich also ungefähr sieben Stunden lang die Hände waschen.

Versuche weniger Lebensmittel wegzuwerfen

Man sollte darauf achten, dass man so wenig Lebensmittel wie möglich verschwendet. Wenn möglich, sollte man lieber öfter zum Supermarket gehen und nur einkaufen, was man für das nächste Essen braucht. Damit spart man auch noch Geld.

Nutze öffentliche Verkehrsmittel

In Städten gibt es meistens keine guten Parkmöglichkeiten. Außerdem ist es teuer, ein eigenes Auto zu besitzen, obwohl ein Bus- und Bahnticket nicht unbedingt billig ist. In der Stadt kann man gut für kurze Wege zu Fuß gehen. Jedes Mal, wenn man sich gegen das Auto entscheidet, tut man der Erde etwas Gutes.

die Tiernahrung	animal feed
Verkehrsmittel (pl)	transport

a Producing meat uses less water than washing your hands.
b Washing your hands needs two litres of water.
c It is better to shop for what you need several times a week.
d Shopping regularly and locally is expensive.
e Doing without a car can be a sensible decision if you live in a town.
f Travel by public transport is always cheaper.

2 Copy and complete the sentences using *ohne … zu* or *statt … zu*.

a Man sollte Zeitungen und Flaschen recyceln, ___ . (*wegwerfen*)
b Man muss lernen zu leben, ___ . (*das Wasser und die Luft verschmutzen*)
c Ich gehe zu Fuß, ___ . (*mit dem Auto fahren*)
d Wir müssen weniger Häuser bauen, ___ . (*die Landschaft zerstören*)

Verben

Using *ohne/statt … zu*

Ohne … zu (without doing something) and *statt … zu* (instead of doing something) are used in a similar way to *um … zu* (in order to do something):

Wir recyceln Glas und Papier,
We recycle glass and paper …

um der Umwelt zu helfen.
in order to help the environment.

statt Glasflaschen wegzuwerfen.
instead of throwing away glass bottles.

ohne die Luft zu verschmutzen.
without polluting the air.

Zu goes after the prefix when used with a separable verb.

The environment and where people live 9.1H

3 🎧 Jan, Ella, Christoph and Rosa are discussing their school environmental project. Note down a) which problems each person mentions; and b) the solutions they propose.

4 ⭐ Replace the phrases in the bubbles with the appropriate form of *da(r)-*. Then translate your sentences into English.

a Es gibt keine Fische im Fluss .
b Wir haben von dieser Organisation gehört.
c Kannst du mir bei meinen Hausaufgaben helfen?
d Er hat nichts zu diesem Thema zu sagen.

5 ⭐ Copy and complete the questions with the correct '*wo-*' word.

a Er hat von dieser Ausstellung gehört. ___ hat er gehört?
b Sie denken an die Zukunft. ___ denken sie?
c Der Unterschied liegt in der Temperatur. ___ liegt der Unterschied?

Grammatik

Using 'it', 'them' and 'what' with prepositions

If you want to use 'it' or 'them' (referring to things) with a preposition (e.g. 'with it', 'about them'), add the preposition to the word *da-*. If the preposition starts with a vowel (e.g. *in*), add an 'r' in between (e.g. *darin*):

davon from it / them, of it / them
darin in it / them

Es gibt ein Foto an der Wand → *Es gibt ein Foto daran*. There is a photo on the wall. There is a photo on it.

If you want to use 'what' with a preposition, add the preposition to the word *wo-*. If the preposition starts with a vowel, add an 'r' (e.g. *worin*):

wovon from what, of what
worin in what
Wovon handelt das Buch? – What is the book about?

6 💬 Working in pairs, take turns to ask and answer the following questions.

* Was machst du für die Umwelt?
  Ich trenne den Müll / benutze keine Plastiktüten …
* Was sind die größten Umweltprobleme deiner Meinung nach?
  Meiner Meinung nach sind die größten Probleme …
* Was kann man machen, um diese Probleme zu lösen?
  Man / Jeder muss sofort …
* Worauf freust du dich in der Zukunft?
  Ich freue mich auf … / Ich freue mich darauf, dass …
* Wovor hast du Angst?
  Ich habe Angst vor … / Ich habe Angst davor, dass …

Aussprache

tio

The 't' in the combination *tio* is pronounced 'ts': Organisa**tio**n, funk**tio**nieren, Informa**tio**nen

7 ✏️ Write a paragraph (90 words) about environmental problems and what we should do to solve them. Use the table to help you.

Klimawandel ist ein ernstes Problem für die ganze Welt / uns alle.	
Es gibt zu viel Verschmutzung im Meer / in den Flüssen / in der Luft.	
Man denkt nicht genug an die Umwelt / die Zukunft der Erde / unsere Kinder.	
Man sollte	viel mehr für die Umwelt machen.
	Fliegen / Autos / schmutzige Fabriken verbieten.
	Lösungen für diese Probleme schneller finden.

hundertneunundzwanzig

9.2F Wie ist deine Gegend?

OBJECTIVES
- Talking about areas where people live
- Revising adjective endings
- Using the correct tense
- Pronunciation: *au* and *äu*

1 📖 Identify 11 words associated with home in the word snake. Write down their meanings in English.

GARTENKELLERWOHNZIMMERFENSTERTISCHBODENKÜCHETOILETTEBETTBADWAND

2 📖 Read what Alexander, Emma and Simon say about where they live, then answer the questions in English. Write A (Alexander), E (Emma) or S (Simon).

Alexander
Früher habe ich auf dem Land gewohnt. Unser Haus war toll, aber ich habe jeden Tag zwei Stunden gebraucht, um ins Büro zu kommen. Wir wohnen jetzt in einer modernen Wohnung im Stadtzentrum. Leider haben wir keinen Garten, aber es gibt einen wunderbaren Blick auf die ganze Stadt.

Emma
Meine Frau und ich haben ein Haus an der Küste gekauft. Wenn es sonnig ist, gehen wir gern am Strand spazieren, weil es so ruhig ist. In der Nähe ist auch ein neues Restaurant, wo wir letzten Monat gut gegessen haben. Nächsten Monat habe ich Geburtstag, also hoffe ich, dass wir dort essen werden.

Simon
Ich möchte mein Dorf beschreiben: Es ist sehr klein, und es gefällt mir, hier zu wohnen. Wir haben leider keinen Supermarkt. Natürlich kann man online einkaufen, aber das finde ich langweilig. Morgen werde ich mit dem Bus in die nächste Stadt fahren, aber das wird nicht billig sein.

Who …
a lives by the sea?
b used to live somewhere else?
c likes to live somewhere quiet?
d doesn't like shopping on the internet?
e would like to eat out soon?
f used to find it hard to get to work?
g thinks public transport is quite expensive?
h enjoys the view where they live?

Verben

Using the correct tense
When translating, remember that German has one form of the verb whereas English can have several:

Ich spiele – I play / I am playing

Ich habe gespielt
I have played / I played

Ich werde spielen
I will play / I will be playing

Don't forget the imperfect tense for *sein* (*war*) and *haben* (*hatte*):
Ich hatte – I had
Ich war – I was

When formulating questions in English, we often use 'do' or 'does', but this is just expressed with the normal present tense of the verb in German:

Spielt sie Fußball?
Does she play football? / Is she playing football?

3 ✏️ For each of the three people in activity 2, write down the tenses they use.

The environment and where people live 9.2F

4 Translate the sentences into German, paying particular attention to the tenses.
  a We are going to the cinema today because we haven't seen the film yet.
  b I have never played tennis, but on Wednesday I'll have a tennis lesson.
  c They bought a car last Friday.
  d Is he going to the beach today or will he go next week?

5 Ida and Otto are talking about where they live. Which two issues does each person mention?

  a too much noise
  b no cinema
  c lacks a stadium
  d no railway station
  e no supermarket
  f too many buildings
  g no mosque
  h lack of takeaways

Aussprache

au and *äu*

The combination *au* is pronounced like 'ow' in English, e.g. 'how', but when an umlaut is added, *äu* is pronounced like 'oy' in English:

Baum → *Bäume*.

6 Copy and complete the sentences with the correct adjective endings.

  a Wir haben ein schön___ Haus (n) in einem ruhig___ Dorf (n).
  b Die neu___ Moschee (f) ist gegenüber dem alt___ Bahnhof (m).
  c Es gibt eine groß___ Küche (f) in der modern___ Wohnung (f).
  d In dem alt___ Stadtzentrum (n) baut man ein hoh___ Gebäude (n).
  e Hier gibt es samstags einen berühmt___ Markt (m).

Grammatik

Revising adjective endings

You have learned to use adjective endings after definite and indefinite articles in the nominative and accusative cases. When using the dative case, always add *-en* to the adjective.

After the definite article ('the'):

	masculine	feminine	neuter	plural
nominative	-e	-e	-e	-en
accusative	-en	-e	-e	-en
dative	-en	-en	-en	-en

After the indefinite article ('a'/'an'), *kein* or a plural without an article:

	masculine	feminine	neuter	plural
nominative	-er	-e	-es	-e
accusative	-en	-e	-es	-e
dative	-en	-en	-en	-en

7 Transcribe the two sentences. You will hear them played twice.

8 Working with a partner, take turns to ask and answer the following questions.

- Wo wohnst du?
  Ich wohne in einem Haus / in einer Wohnung in …
  Ich finde meine Stadt / mein Dorf …
- Wo hast du früher gewohnt? (Hast du immer hier gewohnt?)
  Früher / Vor … Jahren habe ich in … gewohnt.
  Ich habe immer in … gewohnt.
- Wo wirst du in zehn Jahren wohnen, glaubst du?
  In zehn Jahren möchte ich / werde ich …, weil …

9 Using *ich möchte* or the future tense with *werden*, write two or three sentences about where you will or would like to live in the future (50 words). Give reasons.

9.2H Wie kann man die Gegend verbessern?

OBJECTIVES
- Talking about places to live
- Using the genitive after certain prepositions
- The imperative

1 📖 Read Fariha's story about moving from Syria to Germany, then answer the questions in English.

Meine Familie und ich wohnen seit letztem Oktober in Regensburg in Süddeutschland. Es gefällt uns, denn vor drei Jahren sind wir aus Syrien nach Deutschland gezogen. Wegen des Kriegs war das Leben dort unmöglich: Es gab wenig zu essen, und das Wasser war nicht immer sauber. Auch hatten wir kein Schulgebäude mehr, denn man hat viele Straßen, Brücken, Schulen und Krankenhäuser zerstört. Dazu gab es hohe Arbeitslosigkeit und mein Vater konnte einfach keine Arbeit finden. Wir waren sehr arm und wollten dieses Leben verändern. Deshalb haben wir wie mehr als fünf Millionen andere Flüchtlinge unsere ehemalige Heimat verlassen. Nach einer langen Reise sind wir endlich in München angekommen. Hier haben wir uns zum ersten Mal seit langer Zeit sicher gefühlt. Und jetzt? Mein Vater hat einen Job bekommen und meine Geschwister und ich freuen uns, dass wir wieder in die Schule gehen können.

a How long has Fariha's family lived in Germany?
b Why were living conditions difficult in Syria? (two details)
c Which buildings had been destroyed? (two details)
d Why could her father not find a job?
e How many refugees have fled Syria?
f How did Fariha's family feel when they got to Germany?
g How does Fariha feel about going to school?

2 ✏️ Copy and complete the sentences with the correct form of the infinitive given in brackets.

a Henry, ___ nicht ins Wasser! (*fallen*)
b Herr Schultz, ___ ___ bitte! (*warten*)
c Aylin und Kim, ___ morgen mit dem Bus! (*fahren*)
d Clara, ___ deine Freundinnen später! (*treffen*)
e Maja, ___ dein Zimmer sauber, bitte! (*machen*)
f Frau Weber, ___ ___ um 10 Uhr zu uns! (*kommen*)

Verben

The imperative

The imperative is used when telling someone to do something, and needs an exclamation mark at the end of the sentence.

For someone you know well or someone your age, use the *du* form of the verb, but remove the *du* and the *-st*:
Du ziehst. → *Zieh!*

If the *du* form includes the letter 'ä', omit the umlaut:
Du fährst. → *Fahr!*

For more than one person you know well or someone your age, use the *ihr* form and remove *ihr*:
Ihr freut euch. → *Freut euch!*

For adults or someone you don't know well, take the *Sie* form and swap around the verb and *Sie*:
Sie kommen … an → *Kommen Sie … an!*

The environment and where people live 9.2H

3 **Translate these sentences into English. Use the *Grammatik* box to help you.**

a Während des Kriegs sind viele Flüchtlinge nach Deutschland gekommen.

b Trotz der Verschmutzung wohne ich lieber in der Stadtmitte.

c Morgen wird er während der Pause Obst essen.

d Wegen des Regens konnten wir nicht ausgehen.

4 **Listen to these people (a–f) and their opinions about where they live. For each, note whether the opinion is positive (P), negative (N) or a mixture of both (P+N).**

Grammatik

Using the genitive after certain prepositions

You use the genitive case after these prepositions: *statt* (instead of), *trotz* (in spite of / despite), *während* (during), *wegen* (because of):

statt des Autos – instead of the car

trotz des Wetters – in spite of the weather

Articles for the genitive case are as follows:

	masculine	feminine	neuter	plural
definite article	des	der	des	der
indefinite article	eines	einer	eines	

Note that masculine and neuter nouns get an added *-s* in the genitive:

wegen des Regens – because of the rain

5 **Translate this paragraph into English.**

Ich wohne mit meiner Mutter in einem kleinen Dorf. Es gefällt mir, hier zu wohnen, weil es so schön ist, aber es kann auch ein bisschen langweilig sein. Mein bester Freund wohnt 10 km entfernt. Wegen der schlechten öffentlichen Verkehrsmittel können wir uns nur am Wochenende sehen.

6 **Working with a partner, ask and answer the following questions about where you both live.**

- Was gibt es in deiner Gegend?
- Was sind die Vor- und Nachteile?
- Wie kann man in der Zukunft die Gegend verbessern? Was würdest du machen?

7 **Write a description of your ideal place to live (150 words). What sorts of things would you find there? Why would it be such a good place? Give justifications.**

Ich möchte in … wohnen, weil …

Dort gibt es …

In der Zukunft werde ich …

In meiner Gegend gibt es …	einen Fluss / viele Berge / ein großes Stadtzentrum …
Ein Vorteil ist, dass …	ich viele Freunde hier habe. es immer etwas zu tun gibt. man Arbeit finden kann.
Ein Nachteil ist, dass …	diese Gegend zu ruhig ist. es kein Kino gibt. es zu viel Verschmutzung gibt.
Um meine Gegend zu verbessern …	könnnte man	Bäume pflanzen. neue Häuser bauen. den öffentlichen Verkehr verbessern. gegen Verschmutzung kämpfen.
	würde ich	

hundertdreiunddreißig

Theme 3

Kultur
Erfinder, Erforscher und Entdecker

1 Match each statement (a–d) with the correct photo (1–4) below.

a Otto Lilienthal war der erste erfolgreiche Gleitflieger der Geschichte.
b 1908 hat Melissa Bentz den Kaffeefilter erfunden.
c Im Jahr 1922 hat Hans Riegel das berühmte Gummibärchen erfunden.
d Die Kontaktlinse wurde 1888 von Adolf Eugen Fick in Zürich erfunden.

Kultur

Otto Lilienthal's glider plane was developed in the 1890s and played a significant role in the history of aviation. The Wright brothers studied the wing design when developing the powered plane. Lilienthal died in 1896 in Berlin after crashing his glider. His tombstone reads 'Opfer müssen gebracht werden'.

2 Read about the German polar researcher Stefanie Arndt. Answer the questions in English.

a What did Stefanie study at university?
b Where is Bremerhaven?
c Where had the 'Polar Star' been?
d What was the purpose of the trip?
e How long was Stefanie on the expedition?
f What is she researching?
g What happened while Stefanie was away from home?

Forschung in der Arktis

Stefanie Arndt ist 1988 in Berlin geboren. Sie studierte Meteorologie an der Universität in Berlin und dann später in Hamburg und Spitzbergen, Norwegen. Jetzt arbeitet sie am Alfred-Wegener-Institut für Polar- und Meeresforschung in Bremerhaven an der Nordseeküste.

Im Oktober 2020 kam das Forschungsschiff „Polarstern" nach einer Arktis-Expedition nach Bremerhaven zurück. Das Schiff war mehr als ein Jahr lang im Nordpolarmeer unterwegs gewesen. Auf der Mosaic-Expedition hatten ungefähr 300 Wissenschaftler*innen viele Daten gesammelt, und als Teilnehmerin hatte die Meereisphysikerin Stefanie sechs Monate an Bord verbracht. Ihr Forschungsprojekt handelt vom Schnee auf antarktischem Meereis.

Als sie nach Hause kam, war sie plötzlich mitten in der Covid-Pandemie. In der Arktis hatte man davon nichts gewusst!

die Forschung	research
handeln von	to be about

Theme 3

3 **Listen to the podcast about a landmark invention from the German-speaking world and complete the quiz.**

a Gutenberg invented the printing press in
  1 1456
  2 1465
  3 1486.

b The information revolution involved the printing of
  1 books
  2 newspapers and magazines
  3 books, newspapers and magazines.

c Scientists, politicians and philosophers were able to
  1 write more books
  2 spread their ideas more quickly
  3 run their own presses.

d The first printing of the Bible in Latin took
  1 three weeks
  2 three months
  3 three years.

e This produced
  1 200 books
  2 20 books
  3 2,000 books.

f Gutenberg died in
  1 1488
  2 1468
  3 1487.

g By the time he died he was
  1 very rich
  2 not rich
  3 world famous.

die Druckpresse — printing press
zugänglich machen — to make available
die Leistung — achievement

4 **Working with a partner, research the answers to these questions about technology.**

a Name six German car manufacturers.
b Who invented the following?
   Bunsen burner   diesel engine   aspirin
c What did these people invent?
   Katharina Paulus   Walter Linderer
   Christian Hülsmeyer
   Marga Faulstich   Karl von Drais
   Heinrich Focke   Hedy Lamarr

Kultur

Much of the most important research today involves collaboration across different nations. This is one of the reasons why learning a language can be really useful. German has historically been seen as the language of science and technology and it remains important in particular scientific communities and disciplines. Scientists and researchers who have more than one language can have an extra edge over those who don't!

Theme 3 — Grammar practice

Using the perfect tense

1 Rewrite the sentences in the perfect tense.

a Ich sehe heute Abend meine Lieblingssendung.
b Meine Schwester kommt sehr spät nach Hause.
c Jeden Morgen schwimmen wir im Meer.
d Kaufst du schon ein neues Handy?
e Diesen Sommer bleiben wir zu Hause.
f Am Sonntag besuchen sie das Schloss.
g Mein Vater fliegt im September in die USA.
h Mein Freund und ich fahren jeden Tag Rad.

Verben

Things to check when forming the perfect tense:
- should the auxiliary verb be *haben* or *sein*?
- how do you form the past participle?
- has the past participle been put at the end of the clause (unless the auxiliary has been sent to the end of a subordinate clause)?

Relative pronouns

2 Copy and complete the sentences with the correct nominative or accusative relative pronoun.

a Helena, hier ist der Laptop, ___ ich gestern gekauft habe.
b Unser Hotel, ___ im Stadtzentrum war, war sehr bequem.
c Das ist die Fabrik, ___ den Fluss verschmutzt.
d Die Busse, ___ ziemlich schmutzig sind, sind auch unpünktlich.
e Hast du deinen Schlüssel gefunden, ___ du gestern verloren hast?
f Das ist die Moschee, ___ meine Familie und ich besuchen.
g Die Seifenoper, ___ viermal pro Woche im Fernsehen kommt, ist meine Lieblingssendung.
h Können Sie den Computer beschreiben, ___ jemand heute Morgen gestohlen hat?

Grammatik

Relative pronouns (who, whom, which, that) vary according to the gender and case of the word they refer to. For the nominative and accusative cases, they are the same as the definite articles.
*Meine Tante hat **drei Kinder**, **die** alle nett sind.*
My aunt has three children, who are all nice.
*Hast du das **Handy** gekauft, **das** so viel gekostet hat?*
Did you buy the mobile phone that cost so much?

Using the imperative

3 Complete the sentences with the correct imperative form of the infinitive given in brackets.

a Leah, ___ pünktlich anzukommen! (*versuchen*)
b Hans und Johanna, ___ bitte den richtigen Laptop für euch beide! (*wählen*)
c Frau Lehmann, ___ Sie uns so bald wie möglich ___! (*anrufen*)
d Jürgen, ___ mit deinem Lehrer! (*sprechen*)
e Kinder, es gibt viel Verkehr, ___ vorsichtig! (*sein*)
f Mariam, ___ deine Hausaufgaben, bevor du ausgehst! (*machen*)
g ___ dir diesen Vogel ___ , Maria! (*ansehen*) Er ist so schön.
h Bitte, ___ mir das Handy, Claudia! (*geben*)

Communication and the world around us — Theme 3

Using the superlative

4 Translate the sentences into German.

a She has the most expensive camera.
b This river is the dirtiest.
c My aunt has bought the cheapest phone.
d Our village is the quietest.
e This building is the oldest.
f We have the biggest tent.
g My ice cream tastes the best.
h This train goes the fastest.

Using prepositions followed by the accusative or dative case

5 Copy and complete the sentences by adding the correct endings to the definite or indefinite articles.

a Jemand hat ein altes Fahrrad in d___ Fluss geworfen.
b Wenn wir in ein___ Hotel wohnen, muss es bequem sein.
c Morgen möchte ich einen Ausflug an d___ Meer machen.
d Mein Bruder hat sein Handy unter d___ Bett gefunden.
e An ein___ schönen Tag im Juli haben wir einen Spaziergang gemacht.
f Meine Stiefschwester hat Fotos von ihrem Lieblingssänger an d___ Wand.
g Ihre Eltern haben eine Wohnung in d___ Stadtmitte.
h Zwischen d___ Kirche und d___ Bahnhof ist ein Imbiss.

Grammatik

The following prepositions can take the dative or accusative case:

an, auf, hinter, in, neben, über, unter, vor, zwischen

If movement from one place to another is involved, use the accusative:

*Ich gehe **ins** Kino.*
I go to the cinema. (movement from one place to another)

If there is no movement from one place to another, use the dative:

*Ich bin **im** Kino.*
I'm in the cinema. (no movement from one place to another)

Using the perfect tense of separable and reflexive verbs

6 Rewrite the sentences in the perfect tense.

a Ich wasche mich um halb acht.
b Mein Bruder freut sich über die Osterferien.
c Die Straßenbahn kommt schon an.
d Wir rufen unsere Tante in den USA an.
e Heute lade ich mein Lieblingslied herunter.
f Das Konzert findet vor dem Rathaus statt.
g Um wie viel Uhr fängt der Film an?
h Nach der langen Reise entspannen wir uns neben dem Pool.

Verben

In the perfect tense, reflexive verbs are always used with *haben* + past participle:

Ich habe mich darauf gefreut.
I looked forward to it.

Separable verbs use *haben* or *sein* in the perfect tense as usual, but the separable prefix now joins onto the past participle:

Ich bin ausgegangen.
I went out.

Theme 3 — Grammar practice

Using dative reflexive pronouns

7 Complete the sentences with the correct dative reflexive pronoun.

a Wir haben ___ diesen Film angesehen.
b Jeden Morgen wäscht er ___ das Gesicht.
c Könnt ihr ___ ein Leben ohne Fernsehen vorstellen?
d Heute habe ich ___ eine neue Sendung im Fernsehen angesehen.
e Kannst du ___ einen neuen Laptop nicht leisten?
f Vor dem Essen wasche ich ___ immer die Hände.
g Morgen Abend werden ___ meine Freundinnen einen Imbiss online bestellen.
h Ich möchte ___ diesen neuen Film ansehen.

> **Grammatik**
> Some reflexive verbs use *mir* and *dir* (dative reflexive pronouns) instead of *mich* and *dich* (accusative reflexive pronouns). Dative reflexive pronouns are the same as for the accusative in all other cases.

Using 'it / them' with prepositions

8 Replace the noun in bold in the sentences with 'it', using *da-* or *dar-* plus the relevant preposition.

a Es war kein Geld in **der Tasche**.
b Wir setzten uns auf **die Bank**.
c Die Katze spielt mit **dem Ball**.
d Wir alle sind für **die Krise** verantwortlich.
e Ich denke oft über **das Problem** nach.

> **Grammatik**
> If you want to use 'it' or 'them' (referring to things) following a preposition, add the preposition to the word *da-*. If the preposition starts with a vowel, add it to d*ar-*, e.g.:
>
> *Sie freuen sich **auf die Party**.* →
> They are looking forward to the party.
> *Sie freuen sich **darauf**.*
> They are looking forward to it.

Indefinite adjectives

9 Copy and complete the sentences, choosing the correct form of the indefinite adjective.

a Wir fahren **jeden / jeder / jedes** Tag mit dem Bus.
b **Nächstes / Nächsten / Nächste** Monat fahren sie nach Deutschland.
c **Jedes / Jeder / Jede** Mensch ist für die Umwelt verantwortlich.
d **Nächsten / Nächstes / Nächster** Samstag werde ich meine Großeltern besuchen.
e **Jeder / Jeden / Jede** Firma sollte eine Webseite haben.

Using *ohne / statt ... zu*

10 Put the sentences into the correct order. The first word is in bold.

a **Er** / ein Wort / zu sagen / ging, / ohne / .
b mit dem Auto / gehen / zu fahren, / sollten / **Statt** / wir / zu Fuß / .
c gehen, / zur Schule / ohne / kann nicht / zu / frühstücken / **Ich** / .
d mein neues Buch / ich / **Statt** / werde / fernzusehen, / lesen / .
e auszugeben / viel / hatten / **Wir** / Spaß, / Geld / ohne / .

11 Translate the sentences from activity 10 into English.

Communication and the world around us — Theme 3

Using the genitive after some prepositions

12 Translate the sentences into English.
 a Trotz des Wetters hat das Wochenende Spaß gemacht.
 b Statt des blauen Fahrrads habe ich das rote gewählt.
 c Während des Films haben sie Popcorn gegessen.
 d Wegen der Kosten werden wir nicht ins Ausland fahren.
 e Trotz des Regens haben wir einen Spaziergang gemacht.
 f Ich werde die Pizza statt der Nudeln essen.

Grammatik

You use the genitive case after these prepositions: *statt* (instead of), *trotz* (in spite of), *während* (during), *wegen* (because of).

Masculine and neuter nouns get an added *-s* or *-es* in the genitive.

The imperfect tense

13 Rewrite the sentences in the imperfect tense.
 a Hier darf ich mein Handy nicht benutzen.
 b Heute wollen wir eine Stadttour machen, weil das Wetter so schön ist.
 c Jeden Tag kann ich mich im Wohnzimmer entspannen.
 d Mein Freund will eines Tages auf dem Land wohnen.
 e Ich mag meine Stadt nicht, da sie zu laut ist.
 f Am Dienstag muss ich einen neuen Laptop kaufen, weil mein alter Laptop kaputt ist.
 g Sie kann in diesem Hotel nicht schlafen, weil es einfach zu viel Lärm gibt.

Recognising tenses

14 For each of the following sentences, note down which tenses are being used.
 a Ich habe einen Freund, der Til heißt. Im Sommer werden wir zusammen zum Strand gehen.
 b Letzten Oktober habe ich meine Cousine in Österreich besucht. Sie wohnt in Wien.
 c Am Wochenende gab es ein Problem mit meinem Handy, aber jetzt funktioniert es richtig.
 d Meine Familie und ich fliegen nicht mehr, weil das schlecht für die Umwelt ist.
 e Vor zwei Jahren hat Michael in Süddeutschland gewohnt, aber seine Mutter hat letzten Monat ein Haus in Norddeutschland gekauft.
 f Hast du ein neues Tablet bekommen oder benutzt du immer noch dein altes Tablet?
 g Wir konnten nicht ins Kino gehen, weil wir kein Geld hatten.
 h Wenn du in Spanien bist, wo wirst du wohnen?

Theme 3 — Higher Vocabulary

Words that are highlighted in grey in this list are words that may be useful, but you won't need to know them for the exam.

Introductory

aber but
allein alone
alles everything
alt old
am ersten Mal the first time
am liebsten best of all
andere other
anfangen to start, to begin
App (f or nt) app
arbeiten to work
auch also
ausgehen to go out
sich aussehen to look like
beginnen to begin
beide both
bekommen to receive, to get
Berg (m) mountain
beschreiben to describe
bestellen to order
Brücke (f) bridge
Büro (nt) office
danach afterwards, after
dann then
denken to think
denn because
Dorf (nt) village
dürfen (to) be allowed to, may
ein bisschen a bit
einfach simple, simply
Erde (f) earth
etwa about, approximately
etwas something
fahren to go, to drive
fast almost
Feld (nt) field
finden to find
Fluss (m) river
Frage (f) question
früher earlier
ganz whole, all the, quite
gar nicht not at all
gegenüber opposite

gehen to go
genau exact, exactly
genießen to enjoy
Geschäft (nt) business, shop
gestern yesterday
glauben to believe
glücklich glücklich
groß big, tall
gut good, well
Handy (nt) mobile phone
Haus (nt) house
heißen to be called
helfen to help
heute today
hinter behind
hoffen to hope
hoffentlich hopefully
hübsch pretty
ich möchte I would like
immer always
insgesamt in all, altogether, in total
interessant interesting
Jahr (nt) year
je nach depending on
jeden Tag every day
jeder everyone
jedes Wochenende every weekend
jetzt now
Kamera (f) camera
kein no, not any
Kino (nt) cinema
Kirche (f) church
klein small, short
können can, to be able to
Krankenhaus (nt) hospital
Krimi (m) crime drama, thriller
Laptop (m) laptop
leben to live
lesen to read
leicht light, easy, easily
leider unfortunately
lieben to love
lustig fun, funny, enjoyable
Luft (f) air
Markplatz (m) market square
Medien (pl) media
Meer (nt) sea, ocean

mehr more
mein my
meistens mostly
mit dem Auto by car
mit dem Bus by bus
mit dem Flugzeug by plane
mit dem Zug by train
mit der Straßenbahn by tram
mit der U-Bahn by underground
mittags at midday
mögen to like
möglich possible
morgen tomorrow
Morgen (m) morning
morgens in the morning
Moschee (f) mosque
Museum (nt) museum
müssen must, to have to
Nachbar (m), Nachbarin (f) neighbour
Nachmittag (m) afternoon
nachmittags in the afternoons
Nähe (f) vicinity
natürlich natural, naturally, of course
neben next to
neu new
nichts nothing
nie never
normalerweise normally, usually
nur only
nützlich useful
obwohl although
oft often
Papier (nt) paper
recyceln to recycle
Roman (m) novel
ruhig calm, quiet
sagen to say
schicken to send
schlecht bad
Schloss (nt) castle
schon already
schön beautiful
schrecklich terrible
schützen to protect
schwierig difficult
sehen to see
sehr very

sein to be
sitzen to sit
sogar even
sollen should
sondern (but) rather
sonst otherwise, else
sozial social
spannend exciting
sparen to save
später later
spielen play
sprechen to speak
Stadt (f) town
stehen to stand
Supermarkt (m) supermarket
Synagoge (f) synagogue
Tag (m) day
teilnehmen to take part
teuer expensive
toll great
traurig sad
treffen to meet
über about, above, over
um … zu … in order to …
und and
verbessern to improve
verbringen to spend (time)
Verkehr (m) traffic
verschmutzen to pollute
Viertel (nt) quarter
vor in front of
während during
wann when
warum why
was what
weil because
weit far
weiter further
wenig little
wenn if, when, whenever
wer who
werden to become
wichtig important
wie how
wissen to know
wo where
Woche (f) week
Wochenende (nt) weekend

Theme 3

wohnen to live
Wohnung (f) flat, apartment
wollen to want
Zentrum (nt) centre
zerstören to destroy
ziemlich quite
zuerst first of all
zum Beispiel for example
zurück back
zusammen together
zwischen between

7.1F Was machst du gern in Urlaub ?

ab und zu now and again
Alltag (m) daily routine, everyday life
Ausflug (m) excursion, trip
Bahnhof (m) train station
Blick (m) view
Campingplatz (m) campsite
Ferien (pl) holidays, school break
Gast (m) guest
Gebäude (nt) building, buildings
Hotel (nt) hotel
jemand someone
kosten to cost
Küste (f) coast
liegen to lie
neben next to
niemand no one
Pension (f) guest house
Preis (m) price, prize
Rechnung (f) bill
regnen to rain
scharf spicy, sharp, hot
Schiffahrt (f) boat trip
See (m or f) sea if feminine, lake if masculine
Sehenswürdigkeit (f) sights, things worth seeing
Speisekarte (f) menu
Stadtmitte (f) town centre
stehlen to steal
Strand (m) beach
Straße (f) street
Tasche (f) pocket, bag
übernachten to spend the night
Urlaub (m) holiday
verlieren to lose

verstehen to understand
versuchen to try
Vogel (m) bird
Wald (m) forest, wood

7.1H Was hast du in den Ferien gemacht ?

Altstadt (f) old town
Aufenthalt (m) stay
bald soon
Baum (m) tree
bequem comfortable
bestimmt certain, definite, certainly, definitely
Blume (f) flower
danken to thank
deshalb therefore
einladen to invite
Flug (m) flight
sich freuen auf to look forward to
sich fühlen to feel
geduldig patient, patiently
gefährlich dangerous
Geld (nt) money
günstig cheap, favourable
Hauptstadt (f) capital city
Herbst autumn
historisch historic
Landschaft (f) landscape
langsam slow, slowly
Region (f) region
schade a shame
schließlich finally, eventually
schlimm terrible
Schlüssel (m) key
schmutzig dirty
schnell fast, quick, quickly
Schuld (f) blame, fault
selten rare, rarely
umsteigen to change (transport)
Unfall (m) accident
Verspätung (f) delay
Wahrheit (f) truth
warten auf to wait for
Wetter (nt) weather
WLAN (nt) wifi
Wort (nt) word

7.2F Was kann man hier machen ?

besuchen to visit, to go to
bleiben to stay
Bootsfahrt (f) boat trip
E-Mail (f) email
entweder … oder … either … or …
faulenzen to laze about
in Form bleiben to keep fit
Insel (f) island
joggen to jog

7.2H Reiseziele, die wir lieben

Ausland (nt) foreign countries, abroad
ausschlafen to sleep in, to have a lie-in
Balkon (m) balcony
Bärenpark (m) bear park
bieten to offer
billig cheap
ehemalig former
ein paar a few
empfehlen to recommend
entfernt distant, away
Fahrrad (nt) bike, bicycle
Garten (m) garden
genug enough
Herz (nt) heart
japanisch Japanese
kennenlernen to get to know
Kilometer (m) kilometre
Kurs (m) course
Meter (m) metre
Möglichkeit (f) possibility
noch still, yet
Ort (m) place, town, location
Reise (f) journey, trip
sicher safe, secure, certain, sure
solange as long as
sowohl both … and
stimmen to be correct
Tor (nt) gate, gateway, goal
Wasserpark (m) water park
zweistündig two-hour

8.1F Soziale Medien – toll oder?

Bett (nt) bed
Bibliothek (f) library
Bild (nt) picture
chatten to chat
Computer (m) computer
Gefahr (f) danger, risk
Gespräch (nt) conversation
hoch high
hochladen to upload
jedoch however
Kontakt (m) contact
Mobbing (nt) bullying
Nachricht (f) news, message
Note (f) mark, grade
reden to talk
Sicherheit (f) safety, security
simsen to text
sofort immediately, straight away
Streit (m) argument, fight
vorsichtig careful
Wand (f) wall
Zeitung (f) newspaper

8.1H Eine Welt ohne Medien ? Unmöglich!

Brief (m) letter (mail)
Daten (pl) data
davon of it, of them
dick fat
digital digital
sich erinnern to remember
Gelegenheit (f) opportunity
Gesicht (nt) face
gucken to look, to watch
hacken to hack
Hand (f) hand
Internet (nt) internet
meinen to mean
meiste most
Netz (nt) net, network
neulich recently
persönlich personal, personally
Radio (nt) radio
Sache (f) thing, matter
schreiben to write

hunderteinundvierzig

Theme 3   Higher Vocabulary

süchtig addicted
süß sweet
Tablet (nt) tablet (computer)
Tierheim (nt) animal refuge
total total, totally, completely
um sich herum around themselves
unmöglich impossible
vergessen to forget
sich vorstellen to imagine
sich waschen to wash (oneself)
Wohnzimmer (nt) living room

8.2F Wir streamen Sendungen

ab from (time)
aus from, out of
außerdem in addition, furthermore
bei at the house of, with
bis until, up to
brauchen to need
darstellen to portray
durch through
für for
gegen against
halb half
ideal ideal
komisch funny
mit with
ohne without
Programm (nt) program (IT), channel (TV)
realistisch realistic, realistically
Seifenoper (f) soap opera
Sendung (f) programme
streamen to stream
Technologie (f) technology
Theater (nt) theatre
Thema (nt) theme
verlassen to leave

8.2H Hier kommt die Zukunft

ändern to change
anders different
Arbeitgeber (m) employer
Artikel (m) article
Aufgabe (f) task
aufsetzen to put on
Auto (nt) car
Bestandteil (m) component part, element
bisher until now, up to now, yet
Brille (f) glasses
Bühne (f) stage
dominieren to dominate
sich entwickeln to develop
Entwicklung (f) development
experimentieren to experiment
Fähigkeit (f) skill, capability
Fenster (nt) window
fest fixed
Fortschritt (m) progress
Generation (f) generation
Gesellschaft (f) society
immer noch still
Kanal (m) channel (TV), canal
kaum hardly
kommunizieren to communicate
Maschine (f) machine
Potenzial (nt) potential
schulen to school, to train, to educate
Stau (m) traffic jam
System (nt) system
übernehmen to take over
vermeiden to avoid
virtuell virtual
wahrscheinlich probable, probably
zufrieden happy, content
Zukunft (f) future

9.1F Was sollte man machen?

bauen to build
dort there
Flasche (f) bottle
in der Nähe von near to
sich kümmern um to take care of, to concern ourselves about
Müll (m) rubbish, waste
Plastik (nt) plastic
Platz (m) space, room, square
retten to save, to rescue
sauber clean
scheinen to shine, to seem
Sonne (f) sun
Sonnenenergie (f) solar power
steigen to rise, to increase, to climb
Vergangenheit (f) past

9.1H Unsere Umwelt

achten auf to pay attention to
Ausstellung (f) exhibition
besitzen to possess, to own
eigentlich actual, real, actually, really
Einfluss (m) influence
ernst serious, seriously
etwas Gutes something good
Fabrik (f) factory
Folge (f) consequence
Grad (nt) degree (temperature)
Händewaschen (nt) handwashing
Haushalt (m) household
im Vergleich zu in comparison to
Kilo (nt) kilo
Klima (nt) climate
Klimawandel (m) climate change
Liter (m) litre
Lösung (f) solution
nutzen to use
öffentliche Verkehrsmittel (nt) public transport
Organisation (f) organisation
produzieren to produce
Schutz (m) protection
Sekunde (f) second
statt instead of
sterben to die
Temperatur (f) temperature
Tiernährung (f) animal feed
tun to do
Tüte (f) bag
überlegen to consider
unbedingt absolutely
Unternehmen (nt) company
Unterschied (m) difference
Verantwortung (f) responsibility
verschwenden to waste
verschwinden to disappear
versprechen to promise
wegwerfen to throw away
zeigen to show

9.2F Wie ist deine Gegend?

Bad (nt) bath, bathroom
Boden (m) ground, floor, bottom
einzig only, single
Imbiss (m) snack, snack bar
Keller (m) cellar
Küche (f) kitchen
laut loud, noisy
modern modern
Schwimmbad (nt) swimming baths
Stadion (nt) stadium
Tisch (m) table
Toilette (f) toilet

9.2H Hier wohne ich gern

Arbeitslosigkeit (f) unemployment
betrunken drunk
Einwohner (m) inhabitant
endlich finally
fallen to fall
Flüchtling (m) refugee
Gewalt (f) violence, force
Heimat (f) home, native country
kämpfen to fight
Krieg (m) war
Lärm (m) noise
Mehrheit (f) majority
sammeln to collect
Schulgebäude (nt) school building
stören to disturb
Syrien Syria
trotz despite
verändern to change
Veranstaltung (f) event
Verschmutzung (f) pollution
verursachen to cause
viel a lot
viele a lot, many
wegen beause of, due to
Wirtschaft (f) economy, economics

Kultur

Arktis (f) Arctic
Druckpresse (f) printing press
entdecken to discover
Entdecker (m), Entdeckerin (f) discoverer
erfinden to invent
Erfinder (m), Erfinderin (f) inventor
erforschen to research
Erforscher (m), Erforscherin (f) researcher
Europa Europe
Gleitflieger (m), Gleitfliegerin (f) glider pilot
Gummibärchen (nt) gummy bear
handeln von to be about
Kaffeefilter (m) coffee filter
Kontaktlinse (f) contact lens
Leistung (f) achievement
Manuskript (nt) manuscript
Meteorologie (f) meteorology
Pandemie (f) pandemic
Philosoph (m) philosopher
Physiker (m), Physikerin (f) physicist
plötzlich suddenly
profitabel profitable
Revolution (f) revolution
Teilnehmer (m), Teilnehmerin (f) participant
ungefähr about, approximately
Universität (f) university
unterwegs on the way
zugänglich available

Theme 3 — Test and revise: Higher Listening

1 🎧 **You hear four German tourists talking on the radio about problems they had on holiday. Which four problems do they mention? Choose the correct number (1–6) for each person.**

1	I felt unwell.
2	Our favourite restaurant was closed.
3	I was unable to go for a swim.
4	The weather was not so good.
5	The hotel was really noisy.
6	My camera went missing.

a Person A — 1 mark
b Person B — 1 mark
c Person C — 1 mark
d Person D — 1 mark

2 🎧 **Listen to five German friends talking about types of holiday. What opinions do they have? Write P if their opinion is positive, write N if it is negative and write P+N if it is positive and negative.**

a Person A — 1 mark
b Person B — 1 mark
c Person C — 1 mark
d Person D — 1 mark
e Person E — 1 mark

Tipp

With all listening questions, but especially this type, it is essential to listen carefully to the full recording before deciding on your answer. You may hear a positive opinion to start with, but the speaker may then give a negative viewpoint as well. It's best to decide on your answer only when you have heard the person's full statement, and to check it again on your second listen.

3 🎧 **You listen to Olga and Sebastian discussing social media. Answer the questions in English.**

a How does Olga feel about using social media? (**two** details) — 2 marks
b Why? — 1 mark
c What does Sebastian think of social media? — 1 mark
d What does he want to do? — 1 mark

Tipp

Read the questions very carefully to ensure you provide the necessary information. In this particular task, the first question asks you to give **two** details. You do not have to write in full sentences, but always check your answers to make sure that they make sense.

4 🎧 **Four German teenagers are discussing how they use technology. For each person, choose the correct option.**

a Karl … — 1 mark
  1 never shops online.
  2 likes going into shops.
  3 orders everything on the internet.

b Derya … — 1 mark
  1 cannot afford to visit her family.
  2 does not want to see her family.
  3 has no brothers or sisters.

c Most of all, Hassan likes to … — 1 mark
  1 go to the cinema.
  2 stream programmes on his phone.
  3 watch TV at home.

d Sabine likes to … — 1 mark
  1 watch TV.
  2 listen to music online.
  3 play a musical instrument.

Tipp

In this type of task, don't be tempted to choose one of the options based on a single word you hear. Often, each answer option contains a detail mentioned in the recording, but only one of them matches the exact meaning of what is said.

Communication and the world around us — Theme 3

5 🎧 **You hear a Swiss podcast about the environment. Answer the questions in English.**

  a What does the speaker say is the result of pollution? (**two** details)   **2 marks**

  b Who is threatened by today's crisis?   **1 mark**

  c What solution does the campaigner suggest? (**two** details)   **2 marks**

6 🎧 **Listen to Herr König talk about his town.**

Select the correct answers to complete the sentences.

6a

  a Herr König lives in a …   **1 mark**
    1 small town.
    2 large town.
    3 village.

  b Many people in his town are …   **1 mark**
    1 well-off.
    2 poor.
    3 homeless.

  c There is little …   **1 mark**
    1 unemployment.
    2 pollution.
    3 work.

  d Some people …   **1 mark**
    1 shop online.
    2 have cheap cars.
    3 have nowhere to sleep.

6b

  e Herr König says that the economy today is …   **1 mark**
    1 strong.
    2 weak.
    3 growing.

  f He says everyone should have …   **1 mark**
    1 a job.
    2 enough money.
    3 enough to eat.

  g He feels that people …   **1 mark**
    1 have a responsibility to help.
    2 are not generous enough.
    3 should think about themselves first.

7 🎧 **Dictation A**

You will hear **five** short sentences (a–e).

- Listen carefully and, using your knowledge of German sounds, write down in German exactly what you hear for each sentence.
- You will hear each sentence **three** times: the first time as a full sentence, the second time in short sections and the third time again as a full sentence.
- Use your knowledge of German sounds and grammar to make sure that what you have written makes sense. Check carefully that your spelling is accurate.

  a Sentence 1
  b Sentence 2
  c Sentence 3
  d Sentence 4
  e Sentence 5   **10 marks**

8 🎧 **Dictation B**

You will now hear **five** more sentences (a–e).

- Write down in German exactly what you hear for each sentence.

  a Sentence 1
  b Sentence 2
  c Sentence 3
  d Sentence 4
  e Sentence 5   **10 marks**

> **Tipp**
>
> If you change your mind and need to change your answer, don't worry. Cross out your first answer with one clear line, and write the correct answer clearly next to it.

hundertfünfundvierzig

Theme 3 — Test and revise: Higher Speaking

1 Role play

You are talking to your Austrian friend.
Your teacher will play the part of your friend and will speak first.
You should address your friend as *du*.
When you see this – **?** – you will have to ask a question.

> **In order to score full marks, you must include a verb in your response to each task**.
>
> 1 Say what tourists can do in your area. (Give **two** details.)
> 2 Say if you like living in your area and why / why not. (Give **one** opinion and one reason.)
> 3 Describe an environmental problem in your area. (Give **one** detail.)
> 4 **?** Ask your friend a question about the environment.
> 5 Say what you did to protect the environment last week. (Give **two** details.)

10 marks

Tipp

To give yourself the best chance in the role play task, read the instructions and bullet points carefully so you know exactly what you need to say. Make sure that you include an opinion if the bullet point asks for one, and that you ask the question from the card when needed.

2 Reading aloud

When your teacher asks you, read aloud the following text in **German**.

> Ich benutze mein Handy jeden Tag, um mit meinem Freund zu sprechen.
>
> Mein Laptop ist schon sechs Jahre alt und ganz langsam.
>
> Gestern Abend habe ich viele Nachrichten geschickt.
>
> Ich sehe gern Filme auf meinem neuen Tablet, weil es Spaß macht.
>
> Nächsten Monat hoffe ich, einen moderneren Computer zu bekommen.

You will then be asked four questions in **German** that relate to the topic of technology**.**
Make sure you **answer all four questions as fully as you can.**

15 marks

Tipp

It's fine to take your time when reading aloud. Remember the pronunciation rules you have learned. Pay particular attention to cognates or loan words like 'Computer', taking care to use the German pronunciation.

Communication and the world around us — Theme 3

3 Photo card

- During your preparation time, look at the two photos. You may make as many notes as you wish on an Additional Answer Sheet and use these notes during the test.
- Your teacher will ask you to talk about the content of these photos. The recommended time is approximately **one and a half minutes. You must say at least one thing about each photo.**
- After you have spoken about the content of the photos, your teacher will then ask you questions related to **any** of the topics within the theme of **Communication and the world around us.**

25 marks

Tipp

When describing the photos, you will need to mention at least one thing from each photo. The priority is to communicate your message clearly, so it's best to stick to language that you are familiar with, rather than complicated sentences that might lead you to make errors.

Photo 1

Photo 2

Theme 3 — Test and revise: Higher Reading

1 Six teenagers are talking about their summer holidays. What is the opinion of each teenager about their holiday? Write **P** for a positive opinion, **N** for a negative opinion and **P+N** for a positive and negative opinion.

Mika: Meine Eltern und ich haben die Ferien zu Hause verbracht. Wir sind sehr oft an die Küste gefahren, und es hat sehr viel Spaß gemacht!

Sandra: Wir sind letztes Jahr nach Spanien geflogen. Der Flug war eigentlich ganz toll und hat mir gut gefallen. Im Hotel hatten wir aber Probleme.

Marco: Ich war eine Woche auf einer kleinen Insel. Jeden Tag gab es schönes Wetter, und ich habe mich richtig entspannt. Leider hat der Urlaub nur eine Woche gedauert.

Nadia: Meine Freundin und ich wollten im August in den Bergen Rad fahren, aber das Wetter war so schlecht! Also mussten wir zu Hause bleiben.

Anton: Im Sommer sind wir in die USA geflogen. Der Flug war gar nicht angenehm, weil ich nicht genug Platz hatte, aber die Leute und das Essen in Amerika haben wir wunderbar gefunden.

Erin: Unsere Sommerferien waren toll. Wir sind nicht ins Ausland gefahren, sondern haben regelmäßig Tagesausflüge mit dem Auto gemacht.

a	Mika	1 mark
b	Sandra	1 mark
c	Marco	1 mark
d	Nadia	1 mark
e	Anton	1 mark
f	Erin	1 mark

2 You read Laura's blog about where she lives. Answer the questions in English.

> Mein Vater und ich wohnen seit sechs Jahren in einer alten Wohnung neben einem Bahnhof. Das Gebäude ist sehr hoch, und von meinem Zimmer aus gibt es einen Ausblick auf das Meer.
>
> Meiner Meinung nach ist es hier nicht so gut, weil ich nachts die Züge hören kann. Ein Vorteil aber ist, dass wir viele Geschäfte in der Nähe haben. Zum Beispiel gibt es eine gute Metzgerei in der Hauptstraße.

a	Where exactly does Laura live? (**two** details)	2 marks
b	What can she see from her room?	1 mark
c	Why can she not sleep at night?	1 mark
d	What is an advantage of where she lives?	1 mark
e	Read the last sentence again. A *Metzgerei* is a type of what? 1 café 2 school 3 shop	1 mark

Tipp

For comprehension questions, note the number of points required. If the question asks for **'two** details', then you must convey **two** separate points, even if they are part of the same sentence.

3 You read the following headlines in a German news app. Which headline (1–5) matches each topic (a–c)?

1. **Bürgermeister hilft Flüchtlingen in unserer Stadt**
2. Wegen Wirtschaftsprobleme bleiben mehr Leute zu Hause.
3. Einfluss von Influencer*innen in sozialen Medien steigt
4. Berühmtes Schloss bis nächstes Jahr geschlossen
5. **Jugendlicher ins Krankenhaus gebracht nach Straßenunfall im Dorf**

a	tourism	1 mark
b	immigration	1 mark
c	economy	1 mark

hundertachtundvierzig

Communication and the world around us — Theme 3

4 Three young people are discussing their use of technology. For each of the following statements, write **E** for **Eva**, **A** for **Aaron** and **M** for **Marion**.

> Ein Leben ohne mein Handy wäre einfach unmöglich. Ich brauche es, um mit Familie und Freunden zu sprechen, Nachrichten zu schicken und auch Sendungen zu streamen. Ich mag mein Handy, aber manchmal ist der Bildschirm ein bisschen zu klein für mich, wenn ich vielleicht ein eBook lesen will.   **Eva**

> Meiner Meinung nach ist ein Laptop besser als ein Handy oder ein Tablet. Er ist komplizierter zu benutzen, aber es ist leichter, Sachen anzusehen und zu bestellen, ohne in die Stadt fahren zu müssen und etwas in Geschäften zu suchen. Und ich kann dabei Geld sparen.   **Aaron**

> Gestern bin ich spät aufgestanden. Ich wollte mein Handy aus meinem Zimmer holen, aber dann merkte ich, dass das Ladekabel nicht angeschlossen war. Mein Handy war tot, und ich musste sofort zur Arbeit gehen! Glücklicherweise konnte ich das Handy unterwegs im Bus aufladen.   **Marlon**

der Bildschirm — screen
das Ladekabel — charger

Who …
a forgot to charge their phone? 1 mark
b thinks their phone is too small? 1 mark
c was in a hurry to get to work? 1 mark
d prefers online shopping? 1 mark
e uses the phone for watching programmes online? 1 mark
f sometimes likes to read books? 1 mark
g got up late the day before? 1 mark
h doesn't think a mobile phone is as good as a laptop? 1 mark

Tipp

With questions like these where you have to choose a letter, never leave a blank if you are unsure of the answer. Always make a guess; there is a chance you may be right.

5 Translate these sentences into **English**.
a Mein Onkel ist letzten Herbst nach Österreich gefahren.
b Ihr Vater hat gesagt, sie muss immer ihr Handy mitnehmen.
c Man sollte alles recyceln, um die Umwelt zu schützen.
d Nach der langen Reise wollte er sich nur entspannen.
e Wenn ich genug Geld habe, werde ich ein neues Tablet kaufen.

10 marks

6 Translate these sentences into **English**.
a Während der Sommerferien sind wir nach Berlin gefahren.
b Nächsten Oktober hoffe ich, in die Türkei zu fliegen.
c Ich wohne gern auf dem Land, da es so ruhig ist.
d Ich versuche, zu Fuß zu gehen, statt mit dem Auto zu fahren.
e Im Juli wird mein Bruder das berühmte Museum besuchen.

10 marks

Tipp

You will come across verbs in various tenses in the translation sentences. Before you translate each sentence, take your time to look at the verb endings and the stems to help you identify what tense each verb is in.

Theme 3 — Test and revise: Higher Writing

1 **Translate the sentences into German.**

   a I would like to go cycling every morning.
   b In the summer, I'll fly to Spain.
   c It is important that one cleans the beach.
   d I watch TV when I am at home with my sister.
   e I tried to buy a cheap laptop in order to do my homework.   **10 marks**

Tipp

Once you have completed your translations, check that they make sense and that your grammar, punctuation and spelling are accurate. Remember that a good translation is not always done word for word, but you must convey the full meaning of the original sentence.

EITHER Question **2.1** OR Question **2.2**:

2.1 **You are emailing your Swiss friend about using technology.**

Write approximately **90** words in **German**.

You must write something about each bullet point.

Describe:
- what sort of devices you have
- how you used technology recently
- what you will do on social media at the weekend.   **15 marks**

Or:

2.2 **You write an email to attract Austrian tourists to your town.**

Write approximately **90** words in **German**.

You must write something about each bullet point.

Describe:
- what there is to do in your area
- what place of interest you visited recently
- a future event in your area.   **15 marks**

Tipp

Remember that when covering all of the bullet points, you do not have to tell the truth! For instance, for activity 2b, if you haven't visited a place of interest recently, just make it up. As long as your German is good and you give the information required, no one is going to check.

Communication and the world around us

Theme 3

EITHER Question 3.1 OR Question 3b:

3.1 **You are writing a post for a German environmental website.**

Your post is about helping the environment.

Write approximately **150** words in **German**.

You must write something about both bullet points.

Describe:
- the importance of protecting the environment
- how you will help the environment in the future.

25 marks

> **Tipp**
>
> You can showcase more complex language with: a range of tenses; a range of verbs and verb forms; and longer sentences linked with *weil*, *denn*, *und* and *aber*.

Or:

3.2 **You are writing an article for a website for young people in Austria about travel.**

Your post is about travel abroad.

Write approximately **150** words in **German**.

You must write something about both bullet points.

Describe:
- the advantages and disadvantages of going abroad
- where you spent your holiday last year.

25 marks

hunderteinundfünfzig

All themes
Test and revise: Higher Listening

1 🎧 **Carla is talking about a recent concert. Decide whether her opinions on the following topics are positive (P) or negative (N).**

a	ticket price	1 mark
b	seats	1 mark
c	singer's voice	1 mark
d	atmosphere	1 mark

> **Tipp**
>
> When you are listening out for specific information, use the preparation time to think about which words you might hear.

2 **Layla and Gustav are talking about their career plans. Answer the questions in English.**

2.1

a	Why did Gustav find last year difficult?	1 mark
b	What does Gustav plan on doing next year? (**two** details)	2 marks
c	Why does he want to do this? (**two** reasons)	2 marks

2.2

d	What company did Layla work for last year?	1 mark
e	How did she find it?	1 mark
f	Where will Layla go next year?	1 mark

> **Tipp**
>
> In this task, you will need to understand which things happened in the past, and which things are future plans. To help you with recognising different time frames, listen carefully for time indicators such as *letztes Jahr* and *nächstes Jahr*. Remind yourself of other ways to distinguish between past and future tense forms of verbs you may hear.

3 🎧 **Listen to Heike talk about her relationship with Lars and their wedding plans. Answer the questions in English.**

Who …

a	wants to get married abroad?	1 mark
b	finds white dresses boring?	1 mark
c	thinks tradition is important?	1 mark
b	expects the wedding to take place in a church?	1 mark

4 **Giovanni is talking about his use of technology. Choose the correct option to complete each sentence.**

a Giovanni uses his phone … a day.
  1 one hour
  2 two hours
  3 four hours — 1 mark

b He uses his phone …
  1 only to make calls and to send text messages.
  2 to call, text, listen to music and find information.
  3 to play games and use social media. — 1 mark

c He often shares photos …
  1 on social media.
  2 with his family.
  3 with his friends. — 1 mark

d He complains about …
  1 his phone being old.
  2 the phone bill.
  3 the battery life. — 1 mark

> **Tipp**
>
> Especially when doing multiple choice tasks, it is important to listen carefully to each sentence as a whole. Try not to jump to a conclusion about the correct answer based on a key word. You are likely to hear words from each option, so context is important.

All themes

5 🎧 **Jens and Kiana are talking about their last holiday. For each person, say what they liked and disliked most about it.**

a	Jens liked ___ .	**1 mark**
b	Jens disliked ___ . (**two** details)	**2 marks**
c	Kiana liked ___ .	**1 mark**
b	Kiana disliked ___ .	**1 mark**

6 🎧 **Paul and Antonia are discussing the next school year. Complete the sentences in English.**

a	Paul is worried that he has forgotten his ___ .	**1 mark**
b	According to Paul's brother, his English teacher ___ .	**1 mark**
c	Antonia is worried she won't have ___ .	**1 mark**
d	Antonia wants to get good marks because she wants ___ . (**two** details)	**2 marks**

Tipp

Often, a listening extract includes information that you do not need. Therefore, it's important to focus carefully on what the question is asking for and not to give information that is not needed.

7 🎧 **Dictation A**

You will hear **five** short sentences.

Listen carefully and, using your knowledge of German sounds, write down in **German** exactly what you hear for each sentence.

You will hear each sentence **three** times: the first time as a full sentence, the second time in short sections and the third time again as a full sentence.

Use your knowledge of German sounds and grammar to make sure that what you have written makes sense. Check carefully that your spelling is accurate.

10 marks

8 🎧 **Dictation B**

You will now hear **five** more sentences.

Write down in **German** exactly what you hear for each sentence.

10 marks

All themes

Test and revise: Higher Speaking

1 Role play

You are talking to a young German visitor to your town.

Your teacher will play the part of the young German and will speak first.

You should address the visitor as *du*.

When you see this – **?** – you will have to ask a question.

> **In order to score full marks, you must include a verb in your response to each task.**
>
> 1 Say what you like about your town and why. (Give **one** detail and **one** reason.)
>
> 2 Give **two details** of environmental problems in the town.
>
> 3 Say what you do to protect the environment. (Give **two** details.)
>
> 4 Say where you would like to live in the future and why. (Give **one** detail and **one** reason.)
>
> 5 **?** Ask the young German a question about the environment in their town.

10 marks

Tipp

The role play should usually last one to one and a half minutes. There are two marks for each task (1–5) on the role play card. Try to make sure you use a conjugated verb in each one. Read each task on the card carefully to identify whether it is about the present, past or future. Prepare what to say in the correct time frame. Be careful about the number of details that each task asks for; cover all the information needed.

2 Reading aloud

When your teacher asks you, read aloud the following text **in German**.

> Ich versuche, mich gesund zu ernähren, um fit zu sein.
>
> Deshalb würde ich nie rauchen oder Alkohol trinken.
>
> Ich finde das total blöd, weil es krank macht.
>
> Es ist auch wichtig, dass man oft Sport treibt.
>
> Jugendliche sollen mindestens acht Stunden schlafen und dann ein gutes Frühstück essen.

You will then be asked four questions in **German** that relate to the topic of **Healthy living and lifestyle**.

Make sure you **answer all four questions as fully as you can.**

15 marks

Tipp

The reading aloud task and follow-up questions should usually last three to three and a half minutes in total.

When reading the text aloud, focus carefully on your pronunciation, particularly verb and noun endings and vowel sounds, especially those with an umlaut. It's important to avoid any pronunciation mistakes that could affect communication and clarity.

Listen to the follow-up questions carefully and use the vocabulary from the questions to help you formulate your answers.

All themes

3 **Photo card**

- During your preparation time, look at the two photos. You may make as many notes as you wish on an Additional Answer Sheet and use these notes during the task.
- Your teacher will ask you to talk about the content of these photos. The recommended time is approximately **one minute**. You must **say at least one thing about each photo.**
- After you have spoken about the content of the photos, your teacher will then ask you questions related to **any** of the topics within the theme of **Popular culture**.

25 marks

> **Tipp**
>
> In the photo card task, your description of the two photos should last about one and a half minutes and include something about both photos. The follow-up conversation should last four and a half to five and a half minutes.
>
> Listen carefully to the tense of the follow-up questions before answering. If the question asks you for an opinion, make sure you include one in your answer.

Photo 1

Photo 2

hundertfünfundfünfzig 155

All themes
Test and revise: Higher Reading

1 You see some headlines in an Austrian newspaper. Match each of the topics (a–d) to one of the headlines (1–6).

1	11.000 bis 58.000 Tierarten verschwinden jedes Jahr.
2	Zahl der Flüchtlinge steigt in der Schweiz.
3	Erfolgreiche Fußballspieler*innen sind wichtige Vorbilder.
4	Junge Ärzt*innen verdienen höheres Gehalt.
5	Bewegung nötig für einen gesunden Körper.
6	Wegen Krankheit findet Veranstaltung nicht statt.

a immigration — **1 mark**
b healthy lifestyle — **1 mark**
c celebrity — **1 mark**
d climate change — **1 mark**

Tipp
For this type of question, read the headlines carefully, but don't panic if you cannot understand every single word. Try to get a general idea of what each headline is about, then look at the answer options and see which one fits best.

2 Two German teenagers are discussing relationships online. Answer the questions in English. Write **A** for Ahmed, **R** for Romy and **A+R** for Ahmed and Romy.

Ahmed
Ich verstehe mich sehr gut mit meiner Mutter, aber mit meinem Stiefvater komme ich nicht so gut aus. Meiner Meinung nach unterstützt er mich nicht. Wenn ich Schwierigkeiten mit Hausaufgaben oder persönlichen Beziehungen habe, will er mir nicht helfen. Er glaubt, dass ich meine eigenen Probleme lösen sollte. Als ich letzte Woche meinen neuen Freund nach Hause gebracht und ihn vorgestellt habe, hat sich meine Mutter darüber gefreut, aber mein Stiefvater wollte nichts davon wissen.

Romy
Meine Mutter ist vor sechs Jahren gestorben, also wohne ich mit meiner älteren Schwester und meinem Vater. Weil er Sänger in einer berühmten Gruppe ist, ist er oft unterwegs. Deswegen ist es toll, dass unsere Tante in der Nähe wohnt und sich um uns kümmern kann. Obwohl meine Schwester manchmal ärgerlich ist, finde ich sie sehr nett, da sie viel im Haus und in unserem Garten hilft, wo wir einen großen Teich mit Pflanzen und Fischen darin haben!

Who …
a is no longer living with both original parents? **1 mark**
b has a difficult relationship at home? **1 mark**
c has a famous parent? **1 mark**
d has a relative helping the family? **1 mark**
e has a parent who wants them to be independent? **1 mark**
f has a positive relationship at home? **1 mark**
g Read the last sentence again. What is the meaning of *Teich*?
   1 pond   2 shed   3 greenhouse   **1 mark**

Tipp
The final question in this task asks you for the meaning of a word that you might not have encountered before. Remember that the key is to look at what the rest of the sentence means and to work out which of the three answer options fits the context best.

All themes

3 Read this article about the environment. Answer the questions in **English**.

Überbevölkerung – ein Umweltproblem?

Die Überbevölkerung der Erde ist kein direktes Umweltproblem – aber es ist trotzdem ein Problem für die Umwelt. Vor 100 Jahren lebten etwa 1,6 Mrd. Menschen auf der Erde. Ein halbes Jahrhundert später waren es schon, 2,5 Mrd, und bis heute ist die Anzahl der Weltbevölkerung auf fast 8 Mrd. Menschen angestiegen.

Natürlich hat das Folgen für unsere Gesellschaft und ganz besonders die Umwelt. Jeder zusätzliche Einwohner hinterlässt Müll, braucht Energie, viel Wasser und muss ja auch irgendetwas essen. Um den steigenden Bedarf nach Essen zu decken, braucht man mehr Ackerland. Das bedeutet, dass wir mehr Wälder verlieren müssen. Außer Klimawandel sind die Folgen davon Bodenerosion und das Artensterben.

die Überbevölkerung	overpopulation
Milliarden (Mrd.) (pl)	billions
der Bedarf	need, demand
das Ackerland	farmland

a   What is mentioned in the first paragraph as being a problem for the environment?   **1 mark**

b   What is the global population now, according to the article?   **1 mark**

c   What is affected by having so many inhabitants? (**two** details)   **2 marks**

d   Apart from climate change, what two consequences of losing woodland are mentioned? (**two** details)   **2 marks**

Tipp

In longer texts, you may come across words which you have not seen before. Look at the end of the text, where the translation of the word(s) might be given to you in a glossary.

4 Translate these sentences into **English**.

a   Sie ist im März mit dem Zug nach Frankreich gefahren.

b   Meine Eltern möchten einen Tagesausflug in die Berge machen.

c   Sein Freund plant, nächstes Jahr auf die Uni zu gehen.

d   Er wollte gestern seiner Freundin eine Nachricht schicken.

e   In den Herbstferien werden wir eine Woche an der Ostsee verbringen.

10 marks

5 Translate these phrases into **English**.

a   Meine Freund*innen und ich sind letzten Freitag ins Kino gegangen.

b   Ihr Bruder möchte in der Zukunft im Ausland wohnen.

c   Um eine gute Stelle zu bekommen, muss ich meine Prüfungen bestehen.

d   Vor drei Jahren hat sie ihren Mann am Strand geheiratet.

e   Am Donnerstag wird er seinen Opa im Krankenhaus besuchen.

10 marks

Tipp

For the translation question, make sure that you translate everything. Check your work carefully at the end to make sure that all of the information is included.

hundertsiebenundfünfzig

All themes

Test and revise: Higher Writing

1 Translate the following sentences into German.

a I get on well with my brother.
b Our English teacher is too strict, and the lessons are boring.
c When I am older I would like to be a journalist.
d There is an old church in the village, which tourists like to visit.
e We went into town by bus to buy new clothes.

10 marks

EITHER Question 2.1 OR Question 2.2:

2.1 You write an email to a German friend about school life.

Write approximately 90 words in **German**.

You must write something about each bullet point.

Describe:
- your school day
- a recent school trip
- your study or work plans for the future.

15 marks

Or:

2.2 You are writing to your Swiss friend about holidays.

Write approximately 90 words in **German**.

You must write something about each bullet point.

Describe:
- what you usually do in the summer holidays
- something you did in the last holidays
- your plans for next year's summer holidays.

15 marks

Tipp

When translating into German, remember that you need to convey the message clearly in each sentence. Using the correct pronoun and verb form is very important, so check the tense required and conjugate your verb correctly. Try not to leave any gaps and use a synonym (something with the same meaning) if you don't know the exact word.

Tipp

For this task, write something about all the bullet points, but remember that you don't need to cover them equally. You can make up the information you give, as long as it is relevant to the bullet points and conveys your message accurately. Remember to develop your ideas by adding further detail. Try to use varied vocabulary, a range of grammatical structures and to refer to all three time frames.

All themes

EITHER Question 3.1 OR Question 3.2:

3.1 You are writing a post on a German forum for young people.
Your post is about technology and social media.
Write approximately 150 words in **German**.
You must write something about both bullet points.
Describe:
- the positive **and** negative aspects of technology or social media
- how you have used technology recently.

25 marks

Tipp

Although you will need to write something relevant to both bullet points in this task, remember that you can write in more detail about one and cover the other less fully. Check which tense is required for each bullet point, as one will target a time frame other than the present.
Develop your ideas as much as possible, and try to use some longer sentences, with complex and varied language.

Or:

3.2 You are writing a post for an Austrian online forum.
Your post is about celebrity culture and events.
Write approximately 150 words in **German**.
You must write something about both bullet points.
Describe:
- the advantages **and** disadvantages of being a celebrity
- a celebrity event you would like to attend in the future.

25 marks

hundertneunundfünfzig

Grammar

Contents

1. **Number and gender**

    Number

    Gender

    Article
    - The definite article: *der, die, das, die*
    - The indefinite article: *ein, eine, ein*
    - The negative article: *kein, keine, kein, keine*

    Nouns

    Plurals of nouns

    Weak nouns

    Nominalisation
    - Verb to noun
    - Adjective to nouns

    Compound nouns

    Possessive adjectives

    Demonstrative adjectives and quantifiers

    Interrogative adjectives

2. **Case**

    The nominative

    The accusative

    The dative

    The genitive

3. **Other parts of a German sentence**

    Prepositions
    - Prepositions + dative
    - Prepositions + accusative
    - Prepositions + dative or accusative
    - Prepositions + genitive

    Adjectives
    - Adjectives as nouns
    - Adjectives after *etwas / nichts*, etc.
    - Comparative and superlative adjectives

    Adverbs
    - Comparative and superlative adverbs
    - Adverbs of time and place
    - Adverbs of degree (quantifiers/intensifiers)
    - Interrogative adverbs
    - Adverbial phrases

    Pronouns
    - Words for 'you'
    - Words for 'it'
    - Subject pronouns
    - Object pronouns
    - Reflexive pronouns
    - Relative pronouns and clauses
    - Interrogative pronouns
      Words for 'who' and 'whom'
      Words for 'when'

4. **Verb**

    The present tense
    - Regular verbs
    - Irregular verbs
      Haben
      Sein
    - Modal verbs
    - Separable verbs
    - Inseparable verbs

    The perfect tense
    - The perfect tense with *haben*
    - Irregular past participles
    - The perfect tense with *sein*

    The imperfect tense
    - Regular verbs
    - Irregular verbs
    - Modal verbs

    The pluperfect tense

    The future tense
    - Present tense with future meaning
    - Future tense with *werden*

Grammar

The conditional tense

Impersonal verbs

Infinitive constructions
- *Um … zu, ohne … zu, anstatt … zu*
- *Zu* + infinitive

Nicht

Other negatives

Gern

Giving instructions (the imperative)

Seit with the present tense

Seit with the imperfect tense

5 Word order

Basic word order
- Verb as second idea

- Subordinate clauses
- Time – manner – place

Conjunctions
- Coordinating conjunctions
- Subordinating conjunctions

6 Asking questions

Verb first

Interrogatives (question words)

7 Numbers and time

Numbers
- Cardinal numbers
- Ordinal numbers

The time

8 Verb tables

Glossary of terms

Adjectives *die Adjektive*
Words that describe somebody or something:
   groß big *blau* blue

Adverbs *die Adverbien*
Words that describe an action:
   Ich laufe schnell.   I run fast.

Articles (definite and indefinite) *die Artikel*
The words 'the' and 'a':
   der, die, das   the
   ein, eine, ein   a

Cases
They tell you what words are doing in the sentence.
The nominative case is used for the subject:
   Der Junge *spielt Klavier.*

The accusative case is used for the object and after some prepositions:
   *Amelie kauft **einen Kuli**.*
   *Ich fahre durch **die Stadt**.*

The dative case is used for the indirect object and after some prepositions:
   *Ich gebe **dem Kind** einen Apfel.*
   *Die Katze ist neben **der Lampe**.*

The genitive case is used to indicate possession:
   *Hier ist das Auto **meiner Mutter**.*

Infinitive *der Infinitiv*
The name of the verb as listed in the dictionary and always ends in *-en*:
   spielen   to play
   gehen   to go
   haben   to have
   sein   to be

Nouns *die Nomen*
Words for somebody or something:
   *das **Haus***
   *der **Bruder***
   *die **Tür***
   Susanne

Object *das Objekt*
A person or thing affected by the verb:
   *Ich esse **einen Apfel**.*
   *Ich spiele **Tennis**.*

Prepositions *die Präpositionen*
Words used with nouns to give information about where, when, how, with whom:
mit, aus, nach, zu, in, …

Grammar

Pronouns *die Pronomen*

Short words used instead of a noun or name:
- ich   I
- du   you
- er   he / it
- sie   she / it
- es   it

Singular and plural

Singular refers to just one thing or person:
  Hund, Bruder

Plural refers to more than one thing or person:
  Hunde, Brüder

Subject *das Subjekt*

A person or thing 'doing' the verb:
- **Martina** lernt Deutsch.
- **Ich** gehe ins Kino.
- **Mein Haus** hat zwei Schlafzimmer.

Verbs *die Verben*

They express an action or state:
- ich wohne   I live
- ich habe   I have
- ich bin   I am
- ich mag   I like

1 Number and gender

Number

Many words in German change according to whether they are singular or plural. You use the singular when there is only one of something or someone. You use the plural when there is more than one of something or someone:

- das Auto   the car   die Autos   the cars
- ich wohne   I live   wir wohnen   we live

Gender

Many words in German also change according to whether they are masculine, feminine or neuter. This is called grammatical gender. It does not exist in English, but it does in most other languages.

The grammatical gender of something has nothing to do with its sex or gender in real life. For instance, in German, 'table' is masculine but 'girl' is neuter!

Articles

Articles are words like 'the' and 'a', and are usually used with nouns. There are three kinds of article in German: definite (the), indefinite (a) and negative (not a).
The gender of an article must match the gender of the word(s) it is with. Its number must match the number of the word(s) it is with. In the plural, all genders have the same article.

The definite article: *der, die, das, die*

The definite article means 'the'.

masculine	feminine	neuter	plural
der	die	das	die

Das ist **der** Tisch.   That is the table.

The indefinite article: *ein, eine, ein*

The indefinite article means 'a' or 'an'. There is no plural because 'a' has no plural!

masculine	feminine	neuter
ein	eine	ein

Das ist **ein** Tisch.   That is a table.

You do not use the indefinite article in German if you are talking about what job someone does or what nationality they are, or for ailments:
- Ich bin Lehrerin.   I'm **a** teacher.
- Er ist Deutscher.   He's **a** German.
- Sie hat Halsschmerzen.   She has **a** sore throat.

The negative article: *kein, keine, kein, keine*

The negative article means 'not a', 'not any' or 'no'.

masculine	feminine	neuter	plural
kein	keine	kein	keine

Das ist **kein** Tisch.   That is not a table. / That isn't a table.

Nouns

A noun is a word used to name something. Nouns are objects or things, but not all nouns are things that can be touched (e.g. laughter). A good test of a noun is whether or not you can put 'the' in front of it (e.g. the book ✓; the have ✗).

All German nouns are either masculine, feminine or neuter, and either singular or plural. When you see a noun, you can often work out its gender or number from its article.

masculine	feminine	neuter	plural
der Tisch	die Tasche	das Heft	die Hefte

hundertzweiundsechzig

Grammar

Plurals of nouns

There are different ways of making nouns plural in German, just as in English. Unfortunately, there isn't really a quick rule – you just have to get the feel of them!

- Feminine nouns which end in -e usually just add -n: eine Katze – zwei Katze**n**, eine Schule – drei Schule**n**

  Feminine nouns not ending in -e usually add -en: eine Frau – viele Frau**en**, die Freiheit – die Freiheit**en**, die Gesellschaft – die Gesellschaft**en**

  Some mostly single-syllable feminine nouns add -e (with or without umlaut on the vowel ä/ö/ü): die Hand – die H**ä**nd**e**, die Nacht – die N**ä**cht**e**, die Stadt – die St**ä**dt**e**

  Feminine nouns to do with occupation which end in -in have -nen added to make it plural: die Autorin – die Autor**innen**, die Ärztin – die Ärzt**innen**

- Some nouns stay the same in the plural: ein Hamster – drei Hamster

- Some nouns (mainly those borrowed from English) just add -s, as in English: ein Auto – zwei Auto**s**

- Most masculine and neuter nouns add -e: ein Hund – drei Hund**e**, das Jahr – die Jahr**e**

- Some nouns add -e, but also take an umlaut (¨) on the first vowel: eine Maus – hundert M**äu**s**e**

- A few nouns add -er: ein Ei – sechs Ei**er**

- Some masculine and neuter nouns add -er and take an umlaut on the first vowel: ein Mann – zwei M**ä**nn**er**

- Some neuter nouns add -(e)n: das Thema – die Them**en**, das Museum – die Muse**en**

- For many nouns ending in -el/-en/-er, only the definite article changes to indicate a plural form: das Mädchen – **die** Mädchen, der Onkel – **die** Onkel, der Lehrer – **die** Lehrer

- The plurals of nouns in the dative case add -n: mit Freund**en**

- Feminine and neuter nouns ending in -nis add -se in the plural form: die Kenntnis – die Kenntnis**se**, das Erlebnis – die Erlebnis**se**

Weak nouns

There is a small group of nouns that are called weak nouns. They add an –(e)n ending in the accusative, dative and genitive singular and all plural forms.

	singular	plural
nominative	der Junge	die Jung**en**
accusative	den Jung**en**	die Jung**en**
genitive	des Jung**en**	der Jung**en**
dative	dem Jung**en**	den Jung**en**

Nominalisation

Verb to noun

You can make a noun from the infinitive of the verb by capitalising the beginning of the verb. The gender of these nouns is neuter.

schwimmen → (das) Schwimmen
wandern → (das) Wandern

Adjective to nouns

You can also make uninflected adjectives into nouns for languages using the same rule as above.

englisch → (das) Englisch

Compound nouns

- By combining two or more words, you can create a noun.

  Vor + Name → Vorname — forename
  Mathe + Stunde → Mathestunde — mathematics lesson

- However, note that some compound nouns add -e, -s/es:

  Arbeit + Platz → Arbeitsplatz — workplace
  Jahr + Zeit → Jahreszeit — season

- or -n/-en/-ens:

  Klasse + Arbeit → Klassenarbeit — classwork

- Letters can also be omitted from the formation of compound nouns:

  Wohnen + Zimmer → Wohnzimmer — living room
  Schule + Buch → Schulbuch — school book
  Spazieren + Gang → Spaziergang — walk

Possessive adjectives

Possessive adjectives are words like 'my', 'your', 'his' and 'her'. Their gender and number must match (or 'agree with') the noun they refer to and their endings change (just like der, ein, etc.).

Their endings follow the same pattern as kein (see page 162).

	masculine	feminine	neuter	plural
my	mein	meine	mein	meine
your	dein	deine	dein	deine
his	sein	seine	sein	seine
her	ihr	ihre	ihr	ihre
our	unser	unsere	unser	unsere
your	euer	eure	euer	eure
their	ihr	ihre	ihr	ihre

Grammar

mein Bruder	my brother
deine Schwester	your sister
sein Vater	his father
ihre Schwestern	her sisters

Demonstrative adjectives

Demonstrative adjectives are words like 'this' or 'that' and quantifiers are words like 'each' or 'every'. You use them in sentences such as these:

Diese Hose ist schön.   These trousers are nice.

masculine	feminine	neuter	plural
dies**er** Mann	dies**e** Frau	dies**es** Kleid	dies**e** Röcke

Indefinite adjectives

masculine	feminine	neuter	plural
jeder Mann	jede Frau	jedes Kleid	-
letzter Tag	letzte Woche	letztes Jahr	letzte Tage
nächster Schritt	nächste Station	nächstes Ziel	nächste Tage

Interrogative adjectives

The interrogative adjective 'which' is used in questions.

Welcher Pullover ist zu klein?   Which pullover is too small?

masculine	feminine	neuter	plural
welch**er** Mann	welch**e** Frau	welch**es** Kleid	welch**e** Röcke

Other quantifiers

There are uncountable quantifiers which have a singular form only: *viel* and *wenig*.

viel Geld, wenig Zeit

And then there are plural forms: *viele, wenige, alle, einige*

2 Case

Besides number and gender, German nouns and the words that go with them have a case. The way cases work is quite complex, but they tell you certain simple things about the noun.

The nominative

A word is in the nominative if it is the **subject** or 'doer' of an action (and actions include words like 'is').

Der Tisch ist braun.   The table is brown.
Mein Bruder wohnt in London.   My brother lives in London.
Diese Katze ist launisch.   This cat is moody.

	masculine	feminine	neuter	plural
the	der	die	das	die
a	ein	eine	ein	–
not a	kein	keine	kein	keine
my	mein	meine	mein	meine
this	dieser	diese	dieses	diese
each	jeder	jede	jedes	–
which	welcher	welche	welches	welche

The accusative

For the object of most verbs (like *haben* or *es gibt*), and after some prepositions, you use the accusative.

Der, ein, mein, etc. are different in the accusative – but only in the masculine form.

Ich habe **einen** Bruder.   I have a brother.
Er hat **keinen** Stuhl.   He hasn't got a chair.
Es gibt **einen** Supermarkt.   There's a supermarket.
Er geht in **den** Park.   He goes into the park.

	masculine	feminine	neuter	plural
the	den	die	das	die
a	einen	eine	ein	–
not a	keinen	keine	kein	keine
my	meinen	meine	mein	meine
this	diesen	diese	dieses	diese
each	jeden	jede	jedes	–
which	welchen	welche	welches	welche

The dative

After some prepositions (e.g. *zu, mit*) you use the dative. Words like *ein, mein*, etc. are different in the dative. You will have to learn them.

mit **dem** Mann   with the man
mit **meinem** Bruder   with my brother

	masculine	feminine	neuter	plural
the	dem	der	dem	den
a	einem	einer	einem	–
not a	keinem	keiner	keinem	keinen
my	meinem	meiner	meinem	meinen
this	diesem	dieser	diesem	diesen
each	jedem	jeder	jedem	–
which	welchem	welcher	welchem	welchen

Grammar

In the plural, an extra **-(e)n** is added to the end of the noun.

*Ich komme mit meinen Brüder**n**.*
I am coming with my brothers.

Some prepositions combine with *dem, der, dem* to make shortened forms (see Section 3).

The genitive

You use the genitive to indicate possession (and with certain prepositions). Words like *ein* and *mein* are different in the genitive. You will have to learn them.

In English, we say 'my brother's room' but in German you have to say 'the room of my brother'. The 'of my' part is incorporated into one word – *meines / meiner*.

*Das Zimmer mein**es** Bruder**s** …*
*Das Zimmer mein**er** Schwester …*
*Das Zimmer mein**es** Kind**es** …*

Note the extra -(e)s on the end of masculine and neuter nouns.

	masculine	feminine	neuter	plural
the	des Bruders	der Schwester	des Kindes	der Kinder
a	eines Bruders	einer Schwester	eines Kindes	–
not a	keines Bruders	keiner Schwester	keines Kindes	keiner Kinder
my	meines Bruders	meiner Schwester	meines Kindes	meiner Kinder
this	dieses Bruders	dieser Schwester	dieses Kindes	dieser Kinder
each	jedes Bruders	jeder Schwester	jedes Kindes	–
which	welches Bruders	welcher Schwester	welches Kindes	welcher Kinder

3 Other parts of a German sentence

Prepositions

Prepositions are words that tell you where things are (or their 'position'), for example 'on', 'under', 'by', 'at', 'with'.

Prepositions + dative

These prepositions are always followed by the dative:

ab	from (time)
aus	from, out of
bei	at the house of, with
gegenüber	opposite
mit	with, by (transport)
nach	after, to
seit	since, for (a period of time)
von	from, by, of
zu	to
gegenüber **dem** Haus	opposite the house
bei **ihnen**	at their house

Shortened forms

zu dem → zum		bei dem → beim	
zu der → zur		von dem → vom	
zur Schule	to school		

Prepositions + accusative

These prepositions are always followed by the accusative:

bis	until
durch	through
für	for
gegen	against
ohne	without
um	around
für **meine** Freundin	for my friend
um **die** Ecke	around the corner
ohne **die** Geschenke	without the gifts
durch **den** Tunnel	through the tunnel

Prepositions + dative or accusative

Most of the prepositions you have met are sometimes followed by the dative and sometimes (but not as often) by the accusative. Here is a list of them with their meaning when followed by the dative:

an	at, on (vertical)
auf	on (horizontal)
hinter	behind
in	in
neben	near, next to
über	over, above
unter	under, underneath
vor	in front of
zwischen	between
an **der** Wand	on the wall
auf **einem** Tisch	on a table
in **seiner** Tasche	in his pocket
unter **dem** Bett	under the bed

Grammar

Usually when there is movement involved (e.g. 'into' rather than 'in'), these same prepositions are followed by the accusative.

an	up to, over to
über	(go) over, across
auf	onto
hinter	(go) behind
in	into
neben	(go) next to
unter	(go) under
vor	(go) in front of
zwischen	(go) between

Shortened forms

in das → **ins**
an das → **ans**
in dem → **im**
an dem → **am**

in **die** Schule
   into school
ins Schwimmbad
   into the swimming pool
auf **den** Tisch
   on to the table
*Die Katze geht unter **den** Stuhl.*
   The cat goes under the chair.
*Der Hund springt über **die** CDs.*
   The dog jumps over the CDs.

Prepositions + genitive

These prepositions are always followed by the genitive:

(an)statt	instead of
außerhalb	outside of, excluding
innerhalb	inside of, within
trotz	in spite of
während	during
wegen	because of

wegen **des** Wetters
   because of the weather
außerhalb **der** Stadt
   outside of the town
während **der** Reise
   during the journey

Adjectives

Adjectives are words that describe nouns. When adjectives come after the noun, they work just like English adjectives.
   *Die Blume ist **schön**.* The flower is pretty.
   *Das Haus ist **rot**.* The house is red.

However, when adjectives come before the noun, you have to give them an ending.

Here are the adjective endings for nominative, accusative, dative, genitive and plural nouns after *der / die / das / die*.

	masculine	feminine	neuter	plural
nominative	der schön**e** Park	die schön**e** Stadt	das schön**e** Haus	die schön**en** Blumen
accusative	den schön**en** Park	die schön**e** Stadt	das schön**e** Haus	die schön**en** Blumen
genitive	des schön**en** Parkes	der schön**en** Stadt	des schön**en** Hauses	der schön**en** Blumen
dative	dem schön**en** Park	der schön**en** Stadt	dem schön**en** Haus	den schön**en** Blumen

Here are the adjective endings for nominative, accusative, dative and genitive nouns after *ein / eine / ein*. The same endings are used after *kein / keine / kein* and *keine* (plural).

Note that the genitive and dative adjective endings are all *-en*.

	masculine	feminine	neuter	plural
nominative	ein schön**er** Park	eine schön**e** Stadt	ein schön**es** Haus	keine schön**en** Blumen
accusative	einen schön**en** Park	eine schön**e** Stadt	ein schön**es** Haus	keine schön**en** Blumen
genitive	eines schön**en** Parkes	einer schön**en** Stadt	eines schön**en** Hauses	keiner schön**en** Blumen
dative	einem schön**en** Park	einer schön**en** Stadt	einem schön**en** Haus	keinen schön**en** Blumen

Adjectives as nouns

Adjectives can be used as nouns by giving them a capital letter and adding the correct adjective ending. This is most common when using an adjective of nationality to talk about a person:

deutsch	German
der Deutsche / ein Deutscher	the / a German (m)
die Deutsche / eine Deutsche	the / a German (f)

The noun behaves like an adjective, as if another noun were to follow it.

Grammar

Adjectives after *etwas* **/** *nichts***, etc.**

After the following words, an adjective changes its form: *etwas* (something), *nichts* (nothing), *viel* (much), *wenig* (little), *alles* (all).

If you want to say 'something interesting' or 'nothing new', for example, the adjective gains a capital letter (becomes a noun) and you add *-es* to the end of it:
- *etwas* **I**nteressant**es**
- *nichts* **N**eu**es**

After *alles* (everything), you just add *-e* to the adjective. You may already be familiar with the form *Alles Gute* (all the best) at the end of informal cards or letters.

Comparative and superlative adjectives

Comparative

When comparing two things in English, we usually add *-er*, for example 'quick – quicker'. This applies in German as well.
- *schnell* → *schnell***er**

There are some exceptions, however, where an umlaut (¨) is added to the vowel. Some common ones are:
- *alt* → **ä***lter*
- *jung* → *j***ü***nger*
- *groß* → *gr***ö***ßer*
- *kalt* → *k***ä***lter*

In English, we stop adding *-er* to longer adjectives and use 'more', e.g. 'more interesting'. In German, though, *-er* is added to all adjectives:
- *interessant* → *interessant***er**

To say 'than' when making a comparison, use *als*.
- *Mein Haus ist größer* **als** *deine Wohnung*.
- My house is bigger than your flat.

Superlative

When talking about 'the youngest', 'the quickest', etc., add *-st* to the adjective, plus the usual adjective endings. Add an umlaut if there is one in the comparative form.
- *Lisa ist das j***ü***ng***ste** *Mädchen*. Lisa is the youngest girl.

To make the superlative adjective into a noun, give the superlative form a capital letter and add the correct adjective ending.
- *der Jüngst***e**   *die Jüngst***e**
- *das Jüngst***e**   *die* **Jüngsten**
- *Max ist* **der Jüngste** *in der Klasse.* Max is the youngest in the class.

Adverbs

Adverbs are used to qualify the action of the verb.
- *Der Bus ist* **langsam**.
  The bus is slow. (adjective)
- *Ich gehe* **langsam** *in die Schule.*
  I walk to school slowly. (adverb)

In English we add -ly to make the adverb, but in German the adjective and adverb forms are the same.

Comparative and superlative adverb s

You form the comparative of adverbs by adding *-er* (and an umlaut for some adverbs). Use *als* to compare.
- *Ich laufe schnell***er als** *mein Bruder*.
  I run faster than my brother.

For the superlative form, use am before the adverb and add *-sten* to the end. (And add an umlaut if there is one in the comparative form.)
- *Ich laufe* **am** *schnell***sten**.   I run the fastest.

Adverbs of time and place

immer	always
manchmal	sometimes
selten	rarely
nie	never
normalerweise	normally
oft	often
draußen	outside
dort	there
hier	here

Adverbs of degree (quantifiers / intensifiers)

Adverbs of degree qualify other adverbs and adjectives.

sehr	very
ein bisschen	a little, a bit
ziemlich	fairly
zu	too
ganz	quite, rather
fast	almost
Du isst **zu** *schnell*.	You eat too quickly.

hundertsiebenundsechzig **167**

Grammar

Interrogative adverbs

Interrogative adverbs are used when asking questions and need to be learnt.

Wann?	When?
Wie viel?	How much?
Warum?	Why?
Wer?	Who?
Wo?	Where?
Was?	What?
Wie?	How?

Adverbial phrases

Adverbial phrases give additional information about when, where or how an action takes place. Examples are:

nach dem Essen	after the meal
vor der Schule	before school
jeden Tag	every day
ab und zu	now and again
letzte Woche	last week
nächstes Wochenende	next weekend
so bald wie möglich	as soon as possible

If an adverbial phrase is used at the beginning of a sentence, remember to adjust the word order and to return the verb to its second idea position by swapping around the verb and subject.

Pronouns

Words for 'you'

There are three German words for 'you', depending on the number of people and your relationship to them.

- **du** Informal singular – for talking to one young person or friend: *Kommst du mit?*
- **ihr** Informal plural – for talking to more than one young person or friend: *Kommt ihr mit?*
- **Sie** Formal singular or plural – for talking to one or more than one older person or stranger: *Kommen Sie mit?*

Words for 'it'

The German word for 'it' is not always *es*! It depends on the gender of the noun 'it' refers to. For the nominative case, you use *er* (m), *sie* (f) and *es* (n). So *das Buch* is *es*, but *die Banane* is *sie*. Don't be put off by the fact that *er* and *sie* also mean 'he' and 'she' – it should be clear from the context what the particular meaning is.

Ich habe einen Apfel. **Er** *ist lecker.*
I have an apple. It is delicious.

Subject pronouns

Subject pronouns are words like 'I', 'you', 'he', etc. They are usually used with a verb.

ich	I	wir	we
du	you (informal singular)	ihr	you (informal plural)
er	he	Sie	you (formal singular or plural)
sie	she	sie	they
es	it		
man	one, people, you (non-specific)		

The subject pronoun *man* is used when you are not talking about anyone in particular. It is used to say 'one', 'people', 'you', 'they' or 'we'.

Man *darf nicht rauchen.* You're not allowed to smoke.

Man *muss eine Uniform tragen.* We have to wear a uniform

Object pronouns

Object pronouns are used to replace the object in a sentence. **Direct objects** are in the **accusative** and **indirect objects** in the **dative**.

	accusative	dative
me	mich	mir
you (inf sing)	dich	dir
him / her / it	ihn / sie / es	ihm / ihr / ihm
us	uns	uns
you (inf pl)	euch	euch
them / you (form)	sie / Sie	ihnen / Ihnen

Nimmst du Toby mit nach Köln? Ja, ich nehme **ihn** *mit nach Köln.* (direct object)

Gibst du **mir** *bitte ein Eis? Ja, ich gebe* **dir** *ein Eis.* (indirect object)

Reflexive pronouns

Reflexive pronouns are used with reflexive verbs, which are listed in the infinitive with *sich*, e.g. *sich fühlen, sich waschen, sich treffen*. The reflexive pronoun usually changes as follows:

ich fühle **mich**	wir fühlen **uns**
du fühlst **dich**	ihr fühlt **euch**
er / sie / es / man fühlt **sich**	sie / Sie fühlen **sich**

Grammar

Some reflexive verbs use *mir* and *dir* etc. (dative reflexive pronouns) instead of *mich* and *dich* etc. (accusative reflexive pronouns).

    *Ich wasche **mich**.*   I wash. (lit. I wash myself.)

This is the usual accusative reflexive pronoun.

    *Ich putze **mir** die Zähne.*   I brush my teeth. (lit. I clean the teeth to me.)
    *Du bürstest **dir** die Haare.*   You brush your hair. (lit. You brush the hair to you.)

These last two examples use dative reflexive pronouns.

Relative pronouns and clauses

Relative pronouns (who, whom, which, that) are used to introduce a relative clause. In German, they vary according to the gender and number of the word they refer back to, and their case depends on their function in the relative clause. The verb in the relative clause goes to the end.

These examples show the nominative form for each gender:

    *Das ist mein Bruder, **der** Jürgen **heißt**.*
    This is my brother, who is called Jürgen.
    *Ingrid, **die** sehr schön **ist**, kommt heute.*
    Ingrid, who is very beautiful, is coming today.
    *Das Meerschweinchen, **das** sehr klein **ist**, ist schwarz.*
    The guinea pig, which is very small, is black.

Relative clauses can also be introduced by question words such as 'where' and 'why'.

    *Meine Schule hat ein Sprachlabor, **wo** ich Französisch lerne.*
    My school has a language lab where I learn **French**.

Here are the relative pronouns in all the cases.

	masculine	feminine	neuter	plural
nominative	der	die	das	die
accusative	den	die	das	die
genitive	dessen	deren	dessen	deren
dative	dem	der	dem	denen

    *Das ist der Junge, **den** ich gesehen **habe**.*
    That's the boy (whom) I saw.
    *Der Mann, mit **dem** ich gesprochen **habe**, ist obdachlos.*
    The man with whom I spoke is homeless.
    *Hier ist die Dame, **deren** Handtasche ich gefunden **habe**.*
    Here is the lady whose handbag I found.

Was can be used as a relative prounoun, meaning 'that' or 'which'. Use it when the relative pronoun doesn't refer to a noun or after *alles, etwas, vieles* or *nichts*.

    *Ludo ist mitgekommen, **was** echt toll war!*
    Ludo came with us, which was really great!
    *Alles, **was** du mir sagst, ist interessant.*
    Everything (which / that) you say to me is interesting.

Interrogative pronouns

Words for 'who' and 'whom'

When you're using 'who' in a question, use *wer*.

    ***Wer** ist dein Chemielehrer?*   Who is your chemistry teacher?

If you're asking 'what kind of' in a question, use *was für*.

    ***Was für** einen Hund hast du?*   What kind of a dog have you got?

In German, there are two words for 'whom': *wen* and *wem*. Use *wen* after prepositions taking the accusative and *wem* after prepositions taking the dative.

    *Für **wen** hatte er das Buch gekauft?*
    For whom had he bought the book? (or more commonly you might say 'Who had he bought the book for?')
    *Mit **wem** hast du gegessen?*
    With whom did you eat? or Who did you eat with?

Words for 'when'

Wenn means 'when', 'if' or 'whenever' and is used to refer to the present, future or a habitual action in the past.

    ***Wenn** ich nach Deutschland fuhr, habe ich immer bei meinem Brieffreund gewohnt.*
    When I used to go to Germany, I always stayed with my penfriend.

Als means 'when' and refers to a particular event in the past.

    ***Als** ich in Deutschland war, habe ich bei meinem Freund gewohnt.*
    When I was in Germany (one occasion), I stayed with my friend.

Wann introduces a 'when' question, in any tense.

    ***Wann** hast du bei deinem Brieffreund gewohnt?*
    When did you stay with your penfriend?

Grammar

4 Verbs

The present tense

Verbs are 'doing words' – they describe actions. You use a **noun** (e.g. *mein Bruder*) or a **pronoun** (*ich*, *du*, etc.) as the **subject** or doer of the action. For each different person or pronoun, you need to use the correct verb ending.

Regular verbs

In the present tense, regular (or weak) verbs (verbs which follow the usual pattern) have the following endings:

ich spiel**e**	I play, I'm playing
du spiel**st***	you play, you're playing
er spiel**t**	he plays, he's playing
sie spiel**t**	she plays, she's playing
es spiel**t**	it plays, it's playing
man spiel**t**	one plays, one's playing
wir spiel**en**	we play, we're playing
ihr spiel**t***	you play, you're playing
sie spiel**en**	they play, they're playing
Sie spiel**en***	you play, you're playing

*For *du / ihr / Sie* ('you') see Words for 'you', page 168.

Ich spiele Tennis.	I play tennis.
Mein Onkel spielt gern Fußball.	My uncle likes playing football.
Sie spielen Schach.	They're playing chess.

Other verbs that work like this are:

machen	to do
kochen	to cook
kaufen	to buy
wohnen	to live (location)

Regular verbs which end in *-ten* (e.g. *antworten* – to answer) add *-est* in the *du* form and *-et* in the *er / sie / es / man* form.

Warum antwortest du nicht?   Why don't you answer?

Irregular verbs

Irregular (or strong) verbs use the same endings as regular verbs, but there is a difference: the first vowel usually changes in the *du* and *er / sie / es* forms.

laufen (to run, to walk)

ich laufe	wir laufen
du l**äu**fst	ihr lauft
er / sie / es / man l**äu**ft	sie / Sie laufen

essen (to eat)

ich esse	wir essen
du **i**sst	ihr esst
er / sie / es / man **i**sst	sie / Sie essen

Other common verbs in this category are: *fallen, fahren, helfen, schlafen, geben, tragen* and *treffen*.

Some irregular verbs change their vowel sound more radically, such as *lesen* and *sehen*.

lesen (to read)

ich lese	wir lesen
du l**ie**st	ihr lest
er / sie / es / man l**ie**st	sie / Sie lesen

haben (to have)

Another important irregular verb is *haben* (to have) which drops the *b* in the *du* and *er / sie / es* forms.

ich habe	wir haben
du ha**st**	ihr habt
er / sie / es / man ha**t**	sie / Sie haben

sein (to be)

The verb *sein* (to be) is totally different and must be learnt!

ich bin	wir sind
du bist	ihr seid
er / sie / es / man ist	sie / Sie sind

Modal verbs

These are verbs like 'will', 'must', 'can' and 'could', and they usually have to be used with another verb, which is in the infinitive and goes to the end of the sentence.

Usually, the singular forms of modal verbs are different from others because the vowel changes. An exception to this is *sollen* (should, ought to). For all modal verbs there is no *-e* ending for the first person singular.

müssen (must, to have to)	**mögen (to like)**
ich **muss**	ich **mag**
du **musst**	du **magst**
er / sie / es / man **muss**	er / sie / es /man **mag**
wir **müssen**	wir **mögen**
ihr **müsst**	ihr **mögt**
sie / Sie **müssen**	sie / Sie **mögen**

wollen (to want to)	**können (can, to be able to)**
ich **will**	ich **kann**
du **willst**	du **kannst**
er / sie / es / man **will**	er / sie / es / man **kann**
wir **wollen**	wir **können**
ihr **wollt**	ihr **könnt**
sie / Sie **wollen**	sie / Sie **können**

Grammar

dürfen (may, to be allowed to)
ich **darf**
du **darfst**
er / sie / es / man **darf**
wir **dürfen**
ihr **dürft**
sie / Sie **dürfen**

sollen (to be supposed to, should)
ich **soll**
du **sollst**
er / sie / es / man **soll**
wir **sollen**
ihr **sollt**
sie / Sie **sollen**

Ich **will** mein Geld nicht verschwenden.
I don't want to waste my money
Sie **soll** das Rauchen aufgeben.
She is supposed to give up smoking.

Separable verbs

Some verbs are in **two parts**. They consist of the **normal verb** and a **separable prefix**.

The normal verb goes in the usual place (see Verb as second idea, page 175), but the prefix goes at the end of the sentence. When listed in a dictionary or glossary, the separable prefix is always listed first.

Here is a separable verb, *einkaufen* (to shop), in full:
ich **kaufe ein**
du **kaufst ein**
er / sie / es / man **kauft ein**
wir **kaufen ein**
ihr **kauft ein**
sie / Sie **kaufen ein**

Ich **kaufe** am Montag **ein**. — I go shopping on Monday.
Er **kauft** mit seiner Mutter **ein**. — He goes shopping with his mother.
Sie **kaufen** in Berlin **ein**. — They go shopping in Berlin.

These are some other separable verbs you have met:
abwaschen (ich **wasche ab**) — to wash up
aufräumen (ich **räume auf**) — to tidy up
aufstehen (ich **stehe auf**) — to get up
ausgeben (ich **gebe aus**) — to spend (money)
aufmachen (ich **mache auf**) — to open
ansehen (ich **sehe an**) — to look at
fernsehen (ich **sehe fern**) — to watch TV

Inseparable verbs

Some verbs look like they might have a separable prefix at the front but are in fact inseparable. These include any verbs starting with: be-, emp-, ent-, er-, ge-, miss-, ver- or zer-, e.g. *benutzen* (to use), *empfehlen* (to recommend), *enthalten* (to contain), *erzählen* (to tell), *gewinnen* (to win), *versuchen* (to try), *zerstören* (to destroy).

So these verbs don't split up like separable verbs and are formed in the normal way in the present tense.

The perfect tense

The perfect tense is used to talk about things that happened in the past.

It is made up of two parts: the **auxiliary** (or 'helping' verb) and the **past participle**. The auxiliary verb goes in the usual place (second): it is usually *haben*. The past participle goes at the end of the sentence.

The perfect tense with *haben*

To form the past participle, you take the *-en* off the infinitive of the verb. Then you (usually) add *ge-* to the beginning of the word and *-t* to the end.

ich **habe gespielt** — I played, I have played
du **hast gemacht** — you did, you have done
er / sie / es / man **hat gekauft** — he / she / it bought, he / she / it has bought
wir **haben gespielt** — we played, we have played
ihr **habt gemacht** — you did, you have done
sie / Sie **haben gekauft** — they / you bought, they / you have bought

Verbs which begin with *ver-* and *be-* and verbs which end in *-ieren* do not add the *ge-* to the beginning.
Ich **habe versucht**. — I tried.
Ich **habe** Gabi **besucht**. — I visited Gabi.
Hast du dich **amüsiert**? — Did you enjoy yourself?

With separable verbs, the *ge-* goes after the separable prefix.
Ich **habe** in der Stadt **eingekauft**. — I went shopping in town.

Irregular past participles

Some verbs are irregular in the perfect tense. They still make their perfect tense with *haben*, but the past participle is formed differently. You (usually) change the **vowel** in the participle and keep the *-en* from the infinitive on the end:

essen (to eat) — **gegessen**
lesen (to read) — **gelesen**
sehen (to see) — **gesehen**
finden (to find) — **gefunden**
trinken (to drink) — **getrunken**
nehmen (to take) — **genommen**
schreiben (to write) — **geschrieben**
treffen (to meet) — **getroffen**
abwaschen (to wash up) — **abgewaschen**
anfangen (to begin) — **angefangen**
ansehen (to look at) — **angesehen**
fernsehen (to watch TV) — **ferngesehen**

hunderteinundsiebzig

Grammar

Again, verbs which begin with *be-*, *emp-*, *ent-*, *er-*, *ge-*, *miss-*, *ver-* or *zer-* do not add the ge- to the beginning of the verb.

    Ich **habe begonnen**.   I began.
    Ich **habe vergessen**.   I forgot.

The perfect tense with *sein*

Another group of verbs form their perfect tense with *sein* (to be). These are usually verbs of movement. As with the other verbs, the auxiliary (*sein*) is in second place and the participle is at the end of the sentence.

Here are the ones you have learnt so far:

fahren → ich bin gefahren	I went / drove, I have gone / driven
gehen → ich bin gegangen	I went / walked, I have gone / walked
kommen → ich bin gekommen	I came, I have come
fliegen → ich bin geflogen	I flew, I have flown
fallen → ich bin gefallen	I fell, I have fallen
laufen → ich bin gelaufen	I ran, I have run ich bin gefahren

    du **bist gegangen**
    er / sie / es / man **ist gekommen**
    wir **sind geflogen**
    ihr **seid gefahren**
    sie / Sie **sind gekommen**

With separable verbs, the *ge-* goes after the separable prefix.
    Ich **bin** um 7 Uhr **aufgestanden**.

The imperfect tense

Regular verbs

The imperfect tense is another way of talking about the past, but is not usually used in speech.

To form the imperfect tense, take the infinitive of the verb, remove the *-en* and add the endings as follows:

    ich spiel**te**   wir spiel**ten**
    du spiel**test**   ihr spiel**tet**
    er / sie / es / man spiel**te**   sie / Sie spiel**ten**

Irregular verbs

Irregular (strong) verbs have set stems to which the following endings are added. Note that nothing is added in the *ich* and *er / sie / es / man* forms. This example shows the endings for *fahren* (to travel, to drive):

    ich fuhr   wir fuhr**en**
    du fuhr**st**   ihr fuhr**t**
    er / sie / es / man fuhr   sie / Sie fuhr**en**

Some common stems are as follows:

beginnen (to begin)	begann
essen (to eat)	aß
gehen (to go)	ging
lesen (to read)	las
sehen (to see)	sah
trinken (to drink)	trank

Some verbs are mixed verbs and have set stems but add regular endings, e.g. *bringen*.

ich brach**te**	wir brach**ten**
du brach**test**	ihr brach**tet**
er / sie / es brach**te**	sie / Sie brach**ten**

Other examples are:

denken (to think)	dachte
kennen (to know)	kannte

The most common irregular forms used, and ones to learn, are:

sein (to be)	**haben (to have)**
ich **war**	ich **hatte**
du **warst**	du **hattest**
er / sie / es / man **war**	er / sie / es / man **hatte**
wir **waren**	wir **hatten**
ihr **wart**	ihr **hattet**
sie / Sie **waren**	sie / Sie **hatten**

It's also useful to remember the imperfect tense for *es gibt* (there is / are): *es gab* (there was / were).

Modal verbs

These are the imperfect tense forms for the modal verbs you have encountered.

***müssen* (must, to have to)**	***mögen* (to like)**
ich **musste**	ich **mochte**
du **musstest**	du **mochtest**
er / sie / es / man **musste**	er / sie / es / man **mochte**
wir **mussten**	wir **mochten**
ihr **musstet**	ihr **mochtet**
sie / Sie **mussten**	sie / Sie **mochten**

***wollen* (to want to)**	***können* (can, to be able to)**
ich **wollte**	ich **konnte**
du **wolltest**	du **konntest**
er / sie / es / man **wollte**	er / sie / es / man **konnte**
wir **wollten**	wir **konnten**
ihr **wolltet**	ihr **konntet**
sie / Sie **wollten**	sie / Sie **konnten**

dürfen (may, to be allowed to)
ich **durfte**
du **durftest**
er / sie / es / man **durfte**
wir **durften**
ihr **durftet**
sie / Sie **durften**

sollen (should, ought to)
ich **sollte**
du **solltest**
er / sie / es / man **sollte**
wir **sollten**
ihr **solltet**
sie / Sie **sollten**

The pluperfect tense

The pluperfect tense conveys a moment **further back** in time than the perfect tense and is formed with 'had' in English, e.g. 'By the time I was 16, I had moved house three times.' For verbs which form their perfect tense with *haben*, use the correct form of *haben* in the imperfect tense (*hatte*, etc.) plus the past participle.

ich **hatte gekauft** (I had bought)   wir **hatten gekauft**
du **hattest gekauft**   ihr **hattet gekauft**
er / sie / es / man **hatte gekauft**   sie / Sie **hatten gekauft**

For verbs which form their perfect tense with *sein*, use the correct form of *sein* in the imperfect tense (*war*, etc.) plus the past participle.

ich war gegangen (I had gone)   wir waren gegangen
du warst gegangen   ihr wart gegangen
er / sie / es / man war gegangen   sie / Sie waren gegangen

The future tense

Present tense with future meaning

As in English, the present tense can be used to convey a future meaning if a future time indicator is used.

Nächstes Jahr gehe ich auf die Uni.
I'm going to university next year.

Future tense with werden

To form the future tense, use the correct present tense form of the verb *werden* plus the infinitive.

Ich **werde** nach Berlin **fahren**.   I will travel to Berlin.*
ich **werde**   wir **werden**
du **wirst**   ihr **werdet**
er / sie / es / man **wird**   sie / Sie **werden**

*Remember that ich will doesn't mean 'I will', but 'I want to'.

The conditional tense

The conditional tense (strictly speaking, the conditional 'mood') uses 'would' and is used to talk about actions that are dependent on certain conditions being fulfilled. The easiest way of translating 'would like' into German is to use the following forms of *mögen*: *möchte / möchtest / möchten* (would like) with the infinitive of the second verb at the end of the sentence or clause.

Ich **möchte heiraten** und Kinder **haben**.
I'd like to get married and have children.

To form the standard conditional tense, use *ich würde, du würdest, er / sie / es / man würde, wir würden*, etc., plus the infinitive.

Was **würdest** du mit einem Lottogewinn **machen**?
What would you do with a lottery win?
Ich **würde** um die Welt **fahren**.   I would travel around the world.

The conditional (*würde* + infinitive) is often used with a *wenn* clause.

Wenn ich reich wäre, würde ich ein Flugzeug kaufen.
Note that würde haben und würde sein are normally replaced by **wäre** und **hätte**.
Wenn ich reich wäre, würde ich ein Flugzeug haben. →
Wenn ich reich wäre, **hätte** ich ein Flugzeug.
Wenn ich reich wäre, würde ich glücklich sein. →
Wenn ich reich wäre, **wäre** ich glücklich.

Wäre und *hätte* are known as **imperfect subjunctive forms**.

The verb in the wenn clause is also the imperfect subjunctive.

Wenn ich reich **wäre**, …

The most common imperfect subjunctive forms you'll come across are:

wäre (would be), **hätte** (would have), **könnte** (could), **würde** (would), **möchte** (would like), **sollte** (ought to – This form is the same as the imperfect of *sollen*!).

You do not need to learn about subjunctive forms in detail at this stage, but you may want to find out more about them as you progress in your studies.

Grammar

Impersonal verbs

Some verbs are 'impersonal', which means they do not have a subject like *ich* or *du*. They are used with the impersonal subject *es* (it).

If you want to say 'there is' or 'there are', you use *es gibt* with the accusative case.

Es gibt einen Supermarkt.   There is a supermarket.

If you want to say 'there is no' or 'there are no', use *es gibt* + *kein(e)(n)* + accusative case.

Es gibt kein Schwimmbad.   There is no swimming pool.

Other examples of impersonal verbs are:
- Es tut mir leid.   I'm sorry.
- Es geht.   It's OK.
- Wie geht es dir?   How are you?
- Mir geht's gut.   I'm well.
- Es tut weh.   It hurts.

Infinitive constructions

Um … zu, ohne … zu, anstatt … zu

To say 'in order to', you use the construction *um … zu* plus the infinitive at the end of the clause. Note the comma before *um*.

Ich treibe Sport, **um** gesund **zu** bleiben.
I do sport in order to stay healthy.

Ohne … zu (without doing something) and *anstatt … zu* (instead of doing something) work in a similar way.

Ich werde nach Amerika fliegen, **ohne** viel Geld aus**zu**geben.*
I will fly to America without spending a lot of auszugeben.
Ich werde in den Osterferien Ski fahren, **anstatt** auf meine meine Prüfungen **zu** lernen.
I will go skiing in the Easter holidays instead of studying for my exams.

*Note that with separable verbs such as *ausgeben*, *zu* goes after the prefix.

Zu + infinitive

After modal verbs, you do not need *zu* (*Ich will mit dem Bus* **fahren**.), but after some verbs, the use of *zu* is required. Here are some of them:

beginnen	to begin
beschließen	to decide
helfen	to help
hoffen	to hope
vergessen	to forget
versuchen	to try
vorhaben	to intend

Ich **versuche**, Energie **zu** sparen.   I'm trying to save energy

Nicht

Nicht means 'not' and it usually comes after the verb.
Ich bin **nicht** doof.   I am not stupid.

However, when there is an object in the sentence, *nicht* comes after the object.
Lena mag Englisch **nicht**.   Lena doesn't like English.

(Don't forget that you use *kein* to say 'not a'. See page 162.)

Other negatives

nie(mals)	never
Ich gehe **nie** in die Stadt.	I never go into town.
nicht mehr	no longer
Er lernt **nicht mehr** Italienisch.	He's no longer learning Italian.
niemand	no one
Er hat **niemanden** bei ihr gesehen.	He saw no one at her house / accompanying her.

And *niemand*'s opposite, *jemand* (meaning someone), is also a good one to know.

Jemand ist in diesem Zimmer gewesen.
Someone has been in this room.

Gern

When you want to say that you 'like doing' something, you use *gern*. It comes after the verb.
Ich gehe **gern** einkaufen.   I like going shopping.

When you want to say that you 'don't like' doing something, you use *nicht gern*.
Ich gehe **nicht gern** einkaufen.   I don't like going shopping.

Giving instructions (the imperative)

When you give someone instructions (e.g. 'Turn right!') you use a particular form of the verb called the **imperative**.

- With teachers or adults you don't know very well, use the *Sie* form. The verb goes first, with *Sie* after.
  Sie machen das Licht aus. → **Machen Sie** das Licht aus!
  Turn the light out!

- With one friend or family member, use the *du* form without the **-st** ending. Put the verb first and omit *du*.
  Du **machst** das Licht aus. → **Mach** das Licht aus!
  Turn the light out!

hundertvierundsiebzig

Grammar

- With more than one friend or family member, use the *ihr* form without the pronoun *ihr*.
  *Ihr **macht** das Licht aus.* → ***Macht** das Licht aus!*
  Turn the light out!

Seit with the present tense

Seit means 'since' and is usually used with the present tense in German.
  *Ich bin **seit** 9 Uhr hier.*   I've been here since 9 o'clock.

It is also used to mean 'for', again with the present tense.
  *Ich lerne **seit** vier Jahren Deutsch.*   I have been learning German for four years.

(Note that *seit* takes the dative, which is why *Jahren* has an *-n* at the end.)

Seit with the imperfect tense

You can also use *seit* with the imperfect tense in German to imply the pluperfect ('had done') tense.
  *Ich **wohnte seit** vier Jahren in München, als meine Tante starb.*
  I'd been living in Munich for four years when my aunt died.
  ***Seit** der Hochzeit **war** er sehr froh.*
  He'd been very happy since the wedding.

5 Word order

Basic word order

Here is the basic word order in a German sentence:

subject	verb	rest of the sentence
Ich	spiele	Gitarre.
Lukas	geht	in die Stadt.

Verb as second idea

In German, the verb is always in second place in a sentence or clause. It's not always the second word, because you can't separate a phrase like *in meinem Zimmer*, but the verb must be the second idea or concept in the sentence.

1	2	3	4
<u>Ich</u>	**lese**	oft	in meinem Zimmer.
Oft	**lese**	<u>ich</u>	in meinem Zimmer
In meinem Zimmer	**lese**	<u>ich</u>	oft.

Changing a sentence so that the first idea is no longer the subject is called using inversion.

Subordinate clauses

A subordinate clause is dependent on a main clause and does not make sense on its own, e.g. *weil es 11 Uhr ist* (because it is 11 o'clock).

- The conjunctions *weil*, *dass*, *da*, *obwohl*, *als* and *wenn* send the verb to the end of the subordinate clause which they introduce.
  *Ich kann nicht gut schlafen, **weil** ich Angst **habe**.*
  I can't sleep well because I'm afraid.
  *Ich weiß, **dass** er obdachlos **ist**.* I know that he's homeless.
  *Er ist ungesund, **da** er Zigaretten **raucht**.*
  He is unhealthy, as he smokes cigarettes.
  *Ich will eine Karriere haben, **obwohl** meine Eltern reich **sind**.*
  I want to have a career, even though my parents are rich.
  *Er sah fern, **als** seine Mutti wieder nach Hause **kam**.*
  He was watching TV when his mum came back home.
  *Ich gehe zum Strand, **wenn** die Sonne **scheint**.*
  I go to the beach when the sun shines.

- If two verbs appear in a subordinate clause, the **finite verb** (not the infinitive or past participle) is sent to the end of the clause. The finite verb is often an auxiliary verb (*haben*, *sein*) or a modal verb (e.g. *können*, *müssen*).
  Ich kann im Meer schwimmen. → *Ich gehe gern zum Strand, **weil** ich im Meer schwimmen **kann**.*
  Ich bin im Meer geschwommen. → *Der Urlaub war toll, **weil** ich im Meer geschwommen **bin**.*

- If a sentence begins with the subordinate clause, the verbs meet in the middle, separated by a comma.
  ***Wenn** die Sonne **scheint**, **gehe** ich zum Strand.*
  When the sun shines, I go to the beach.

- Other subordinate clauses are introduced by *damit*, *sodass*, *ob* and *als*.
  *Ich schreibe schnell, **damit** ich bald fertig **bin**.*
  I'm writing fast, so that (in order that) I finish quickly.
  *Ich esse viel Obst, **sodass** ich gesund **bleibe**.*
  I eat lots of fruit, so that (as a result) I stay healthy.
  *Ich weiß nicht, **ob** er **kommt**.*
  I don't know whether he is coming.
  ***Als** das Wetter gut **war**, **bin** ich zum Strand gegangen.*
  When the weather was good, I went to the beach.

Grammar

Time – manner – place

When you mention when (time), how (manner) and where (place) you do something, you give the time first, then the manner and then the place.

	Time	Manner	Place
Ich fahre	am Wochenende	mit dem Auto	nach Paris.
Er fährt	-	mit dem Zug	nach Berlin.
Wir wohnen	seit Januar	-	in Leipzig.

Conjunctions

Conjunctions are words that join together sentences (or clauses, which are parts of sentences).

Coordinating conjunctions

Common conjunctions are *und* (and), *oder* (or) and *aber* (but). They do not affect the word order in a sentence.

> *Er hat kein Geld. Er kann die Sprache nicht verstehen.* → *Er hat kein Geld **und** er kann die Sprache nicht verstehen.*
> He has no money. He can't understand the language. → He has no money and he can't understand the language.
>
> *Ich kenne ein paar Leute. Wir sind keine richtigen Freunde.* → *Ich kenne ein paar Leute, **aber** wir sind keine richtigen Freunde.**
> I know a few people. We aren't really friends. → I know a few people but we aren't really friends.

*When using *aber* or *denn*, put a comma before it.

You might like to use some of the following, less common, coordinating conjunctions in your work:

denn	because
*Ich mag ihn, **denn** er ist klug.*	I like him because he's clever.*
sondern	but (only used after a negative)
*Er hat **nicht** drei, **sondern** vier Katzen.*	He doesn't have three but four cats.*

*Both *denn* and *sondern* need a comma before them.

Subordinating conjunctions

Some conjunctions including *weil*, *dass*, *da*, *obwohl*, *als* and *wenn* send the verb in the clause they introduce right to the end (see Subordinate clauses, page 175).

6 Asking questions

Verb first

You can ask questions by putting the verb first in the sentence.

> ***Du hörst** Musik.* → ***Hörst** du Musik?*
> You are listening to music. → Are you listening to music?
>
> ***Birgit ist** sportlich.* → ***Ist** Birgit sportlich?*
> Birgit is sporty. → Is Birgit sporty?

Interrogatives (question words)

You can ask a question by starting with a question word or interrogative. Most German question words start with *w*.

Wer?	Who?
Wie lange?	How long?
Wann?	When?
Wo?	Where?
Was?	What?
Wohin?	Where to?
Welche(r / s)?	Which?
Woher?	Where from?
Wie?	How?
Womit?	What with?
Warum?	Why?
Wie viel(e)?	How much / many?
Wozu?	What for? / Why?

Most of these are pronouns or adverbs (see Interrogative adverbs, page 167) and are immediately followed by a verb.

> *Wer **kommt mit**?* Who's coming with us?
> *Wann **kommt sie**?* When is she coming?
> *Wohin **fahren wir**?* Where are we going (to)?

Welche(r / s) and *wie viel(e)* can be used as adjectives and followed by a noun (see Interrogative adjectives, page 164).

> ***Wie viel** Taschengeld bekommst du?*
> How much pocket money do you get?

176 hundertsechsundsiebzig

Grammar

Numbers

Cardinal numbers

1	eins	23	dreiunzwanzig
2	zwei	24	vierundzwanzig
3	drei	25	fünfundzwanzig
4	vier	30	dreißig
5	fünf	40	vierzig
6	sechs	50	fünfzig
7	sieben	60	sechzig
8	acht	70	siebzig
9	neun	80	achtzig
10	zehn	90	neunzig
11	elf	100	hundert
12	zwölf	35	fünfunddreißg
13	dreizehn	45	fünfundvierßig
14	vierzehn	55	fünfundfünfzig
15	fünfzehn	65	fünfundsechzig
16	sechzehn	75	fünfundsiebzig
17	siebzehn	85	fünfundachtzig
18	achtzehn	95	fünfundneunzig
19	neunzehn	200	zweihundert
20	zwanzig	305	dreihundertfünf
21	einundzwanzig	411	vierhundertelf
22	zweiundzwanzig		

525	fünfhundertfünfundzwanzig
1000	tausend
2500	zweitausendfünfhundert
1984	neunzehnhundertvierundachtzig (in dates)

Ordinal numbers

To make the ordinal numbers (first, second, etc.) up to 19th, you add **-te** to the cardinal number. There are a few exceptions: first (*erste*), third (*dritte*), seventh (*siebte*) and eighth (*achte*).

1st	erste	11th	elfte
2nd	zweite	12th	zwölfte
3rd	dritte	13th	dreizehnte
4th	vierte	14th	vierzehnte
5th	fünfte	15th	fünfzehnte
6th	sechste	16th	sechzehnte
7th	siebte	17th	siebzehnte
8th	achte	18th	achtzehnte
9th	neunte	19th	neunzehnte
10th	zehnte	20th	zwanzigste

To make the ordinal numbers from 20th upwards you add **-ste** to the cardinal number.
*Ich bin auf **den zwanzigsten** Platz gekommen.*
I came in twentieth place.

When giving dates, use the dative: use *am* before the ordinal number and add **-n**.
*Ich habe **am zwölften** Dezember Geburtstag.*
My birthday is on the twelfth of December.

Verb tables

8 Verb tables

infinitive	present	imperfect	perfect	English
beginnen	beginnt	begann	begonnen	to begin
beißen	beißt	biss	gebissen	to bite
bewegen	bewegt	bewog	bewogen	to move
biegen	biegt	bog	gebogen	to bend
bieten	bietet	bot	geboten	to offer
binden	bindet	band	gebunden	to tie
bitten	bittet	bat	gebeten	to ask
blasen	bläst	blies	geblasen	to blow
bleiben	bleibt	blieb	geblieben*	to stay
brechen	bricht	brach	gebrochen	to break
brennen	brennt	brannte	gebrannt	to burn
bringen	bringt	brachte	gebracht	to bring
denken	denkt	dachte	gedacht	to think
dürfen	darf	durfte	gedurft	to be allowed to
empfehlen	empfiehlt	empfahl	empfohlen	to recommend
essen	isst	aß	gegessen	to eat
fahren	fährt	fuhr	gefahren*	to go, to travel
fallen	fällt	fiel	gefallen*	to fall
fangen	fängt	fing	gefangen	to catch
finden	findet	fand	gefunden	to find
fliegen	fliegt	flog	geflogen*	to fly
fliehen	flieht	floh	geflohen*	to flee
fließen	fließt	floss	geflossen*	to flow
frieren	friert	fror	gefroren	to freeze
geben	gibt	gab	gegeben	to give
gehen	geht	ging	gegangen*	to go
gelingen	gelingt	gelang	gelungen*	to succeed
genießen	genießt	genoss	genossen	to enjoy
geschehen	geschieht	geschah	geschehen*	to happen
gewinnen	gewinnt	gewann	gewonnen	to win
graben	gräbt	grub	gegraben	to dig
greifen	greift	griff	gegriffen	to grasp
haben	hat	hatte	gehabt	to have
halten	hält	hielt	gehalten	to stop
hängen	hängt	hing	gehangen	to hang
heben	hebt	hob	gehoben	to lift
heißen	heißt	hieß	geheißen	to be called
helfen	hilft	half	geholfen	to help
kennen	kennt	kannte	gekannt	to know

Verb tables

infinitive	present	imperfect	perfect	English
kommen	kommt	kam	gekommen*	to come
können	kann	konnte	gekonnt	to be able to
laden	lädt	lud	geladen	to load
lassen	lässt	ließ	gelassen	to allow
laufen	läuft	lief	gelaufen*	to run
leiden	leidet	litt	gelitten	to suffer
leihen	leiht	lieh	geliehen	to lend
lesen	liest	las	gelesen	to read
liegen	liegt	lag	gelegen	to lie
lügen	lügt	log	gelogen	to tell a lie
meiden	meidet	mied	gemieden	to avoid
misslingen	misslingt	misslang	misslungen*	to fail
mögen	mag	mochte	gemocht	to like
müssen	muss	musste	gemusst	to have to
nehmen	nimmt	nahm	genommen	to take
nennen	nennt	nannte	genannt	to name
raten	rät	riet	geraten	to guess
reißen	reißt	riss	gerissen	to rip
reiten	reitet	ritt	geritten	to ride
rennen	rennt	rannte	gerannt*	to run
riechen	riecht	roch	gerochen	to smell
rufen	ruft	rief	gerufen	to call
schaffen	schafft	schuf	geschaffen	to manage
scheiden	scheidet	schied	geschieden*	to separate
scheinen	scheint	schien	geschienen	to shine
schlafen	schläft	schlief	geschlafen	to sleep
schlagen	schlägt	schlug	geschlagen	to hit
schließen	schließt	schloss	geschlossen	to shut
schneiden	schneidet	schnitt	geschnitten	to cut
schreiben	schreibt	schrieb	geschrieben	to write
schreien	schreit	schrie	geschrien	to cry
sehen	sieht	sah	gesehen	to see
sein	ist	war	gewesen*	to be
senden	sendet	sandte	gesandt	to send
singen	singt	sang	gesungen	to sing
sitzen	sitzt	saß	gesessen	to sit
sollen	soll	sollte	gesollt	ought to
sprechen	spricht	sprach	gesprochen	to speak
stehen	steht	stand	gestanden	to stand
stehlen	stiehlt	stahl	gestohlen	to steal
steigen	steigt	stieg	gestiegen*	to climb
sterben	stirbt	starb	gestorben*	to die

Verb tables

infinitive	present	imperfect	perfect	English
stoßen	stößt	stieß	gestoßen	to push
streichen	streicht	strich	gestrichen	to paint
tragen	trägt	trug	getragen	to carry
treffen	trifft	traf	getroffen	to meet
treiben	treibt	trieb	getrieben	to do
treten	tritt	trat	getreten	to step
trinken	trinkt	trank	getrunken	to drink
tun	tut	tat	getan	to do
überwinden	überwindet	überwand	überwunden	to overcome
vergessen	vergisst	vergaß	vergessen	to forget
verlieren	verliert	verlor	verloren	to lose
verschwinden	verschwindet	verschwand	verschwunden*	to disappear
verzeihen	verzeiht	verzieh	verziehen	to pardon
wachsen	wächst	wuchs	gewachsen*	to grow
waschen	wäscht	wusch	gewaschen	to wash
weisen	weist	wies	gewiesen	to show
wenden	wendet	wandte / wendete	gewandt / gewendet	to turn
werben	wirbt	warb	geworben	to advertise
werden	wird	wurde	geworden*	to become
werfen	wirft	warf	geworfen	to throw
wiegen	wiegt	wog	gewogen	to weigh
wissen	weiß	wusste	gewusst	to know
wollen	will	wollte	gewollt	to want to
ziehen	zieht	zog	gezogen	to pull

*Verbs which take *sein* in the perfect and pluperfect tenses.

Glossary

ab from (time)
ab und zu now and again
abends in the evening
Abendschule (f) evening/night school
Abenteuer (nt) adventure
abenteuerlustig adventurous
aber but
Abitur (nt) school leaving exams, A level equivalent
Abonnent (m), Abonnentin (f) subscriber
achten auf to pay attention to
Actionfilm (m) action film
Adresse (f) address
ärgern to irritate, to annoy
Ahnung (f) idea
aktiv active
Aktivität (f) activity
albern silly
Algerien Algeria
Alkohol (m) alcohol
allein alone
alles everything
Alltag (m) daily routine, everyday life
Alpen (pl) the Alps
Alptraum (m) nightmare
alt old
älter als older than
Altstadt (f) old town
sich amüsieren to enjoy oneself
am Ende at the end
am ersten Mal the first time
am liebsten best of all
Amerika America
Amt (nt) post, position
an der frischen Luft in the open air
andere other
ändern to change
anders different
Änderung (f) change
Anfang (m) start
anfangen to start, to begin
Anfänger (m) beginner
Angst (f) fear
Angst machen to frighten
ankommen to arrive
anrufen to phone, to ring

anschauen to watch
sich anschließen to join
Apartment (nt) flat, appartment
Apfel (m) apple
App (f or nt) app
April April
arabisch Arabic
Arbeit (f) work
arbeiten to work
Arbeitgeber (m) employer
Arbeitslosigkeit (f) unemployment
Arbeitsplatz (m) workplace, place of work
ärgerlich annoying
Arktis (f) Arctic
arm poor
Arm (m) arm
Armut (f) poverty
Art (f) type, kind
Artikel (m) article
Arzt (m), Ärztin (f) doctor
Aspekt (m) aspect
Atmosphäre (f) atmosphere
auch also
auch nicht … not … either
auf dem Land in the countryside
Aufenthalt (m) stay
Aufgabe (f) task
aufgeben to give up
aufnehmen to take (photos), to record (videos), to pick up
aufpassen (auf) to pay attention (to), to take care (of)
aufsetzen to put on
sich aufstehen to get up
sich aussehen to look like
aufwachsen to grow up
Augen (pl) eye
August August
aus from, out of
Ausbildung (f) training, education, development
Ausflug (m) excursion, trip
ausgeben to spend
ausgehen to go out
auskommen mit to get on with

Ausland (nt) foreign countries, abroad
ausprobieren to try out
ausreichend satisfactory
Ausrüstung (f) equipment
ausschlafen to sleep in, to have a lie-in
außerdem in addition, furthermore
Ausstellung (f) exhibition
Auto (nt) car
Autogramm (nt) autograph
Automobilrennfahrer (m), Automobilrennfahrerin (f) racing driver
Autor (m), Autorin (f) author
Bad (nt) bath, bathroom
Bahnhof (m) train station
bald soon
Balkon (m) balcony
Ball (m) ball
Banane (f) banana
Band (f) band, group (music)
Bärenpark (m) bear park
Bart (m) beard
Basketball (m) basketball
bauen to build
Bauer (m), Bäuerin (f) farmer
Baum (m) tree
beeindrückend impressive
befriedigend fair
beginnen to begin
Begleitung (f) accompaniment
bei at the house of, with
bei uns with us, at our house
beide both
Bein (nt) leg
bekannt known, famous
bekommen to receive, to get
beliebt beloved
benutzen to use
bequem comfortable
Berg (m) mountain
Beruf (m) job, career
berühmt famous
sich beschäftigen (mit) to be busy (with), to be dealing (with)
beschreiben to describe
besitzen to possess, to own
besondere special

besser better
Bestandteil (m) component part, element
Beste (nt) (the) best
bestellen to order
bestimmt certain, definite, certainly, definitely
besuchen to visit, to go to
beten to pray
betrunken drunk
Bett (nt) bed
Bevölkerung (f) population
Bewegung (f) movement
bewundern to admire
bezahlen to pay
Beziehung (f) relationship
Bibliothek (f) library
Bier (nt) beer
bieten to offer
Bild (nt) picture
billig cheap
Biologie (f) biology
bis until, up to
bis bald bye for now, see you soon
bisher until now, up to now, yet
bitten to request
Blatt (nt) sheet, leaf
blau blue
bleiben to stay
Blick (m) view
blöd silly
Blume (f) flower
Boden (m) ground, floor, bottom
Bootsfahrt (f) boat trip
böse bad, mad, naughty, angry
Böse (nt) evil
brauchen to need
braun brown
brechen to break
brennen to burn
Brief (m) letter (mail)
Brille (f) glasses
Brot (nt) bread
Brücke (f) bridge
Bruder (m) brother
Buch (nt) book
Bühne (f) stage

Glossary

Bundesrepublik, BRD (f) Federal Republic (of Germany)
Bungeesprigen (nt) bungee jumping
bunt colourful, multicoloured
Büro (nt) office
Busfahrer (m), Busfahrerin (f) bus driver
Café (nt) café
Campingplatz (m) campsite
Chance (f) chance, opportunity
Charakter (m) character
chatten to chat
Chef (m) boss
chinesisch Chinese
Chor (m) choid
Club (m) club
Cola (f) cola
Computer (m) computer
cool cool
Cousin (m), Cousine (f) cousin
damals then, at that time
danach afterwards, after
danken to thank
dann then
darstellen to portray
das erste Mal the first time
das macht nichts that doesn't matter
dass that
Daten (pl) data
dauern to last
davon of it, of them
dekorieren to decorate
denken to think
denn because
der Vorteil (m) advantage
deshalb therefore
Deutsch (nt) German
Deutsche Demokratische Republic (DDR) (f) German Democratic Republic
Deutschland Germany
Dezember December
dich you, yourself (familiar singular, direct object pronoun)
dick fat
die Dokumentarsendung (f) documentary programme
die Schweiz Switzerland

die Sportsendung (f) sports programme
dienstags on Tuesdays
dies-(er, e, es) this, that
digital digital
direkt direct, directly
diszipliniert disciplined
doch however, but
dominieren to dominate
donnerstags on Thursdays
doof stupid
Doppelstunde (f) double lesson
Dorf (nt) village
dort there
dorthin to there
Drache (m) dragon
draußen outside
dreimal three times, thrice
Droge (f) drug
Druckpresse (f) printing press
dunkel dark
durch through
dürfen (to) be allowed to, may
sich duschen to shower
Effekt (m) effect
egoistisch selfish
Ehe (f) marriage
ehemalig former
ehrlich honest
Ei (nt) egg
eifersüchtig jealous, envious
eigen own
Eigenschaft (f) quality
eigentich actual, real, actually, really
ein bisschen a bit
ein paar a few
einander each other
eines Tages one day
einfach simple, simply
Einfluss (m) influence
Einheit (f) unity
einige a few, some
einkaufen to shop
einladen to invite
einmalig unique
einpacken to wrap (up)
einsam lonely
sich einsetzen für to fight for
Eintrittskarte (f) entrance ticket

Einwohner (m) inhabitant
Einzelkind (nt) only child
einzig only, single
Eis (nt) ice, ice cream
elektronisch electronic
Eltern (pl) parents
E-Mail (f) email
empfehlen to recommend
endlich finally
Energie (f) energy
sich engagieren für to be committed to
Englisch (nt) English
entdecken to discover
Entdecker (m), Entdeckerin (f) discoverer
entfernt distant, away
sich entscheiden to decide
sich entspannen to relax
entspannend relaxing
enttäuschend disappointing
Enttäuschung (f) disappointment
entweder ... oder ... either ... or ...
sich entwickeln to develop
Entwicklung (f) development
Erde (f) Earth, ground, soil
Erdkunde (f) geography
Erfahrung (f) experience
erfinden to invent
Erfinder (m), Erfinderin (f) inventor
Erfolg (m) success
erfolgreich successful
erforschen to research
Erforscher (m), Erforscherin (f) researcher
sich erinnern to remember
erklären to explain
erlauben to allow
erlaubt allowed
erleben to experience
ermüdend tiring
sich ernähren to feed yourself
Ernährung (f) food, diet
ernst serious, seriously
ernst nehmen to take seriously
erreichen to reach, to achieve
erstens, zweitens, drittens first(ly), second(ly), third(ly)
Erwachsene (m or f) adult

erzählen to tell, to narrate
es gefällt mir I like, it pleases me
es gibt there is, there are
es schneit it's snowing
essen to eat
Essen (nt) food, meal
etwa about, approximately
etwas something
etwas Gutes something good
etwas Positives something positive
euch you, yourself (familiar plural, direct object pronoun)
Europa Europe
experimentieren to experiment
explodieren to explode
Fabrik (f) factory
Fach (nt) subject
Fähigkeit (f) ability
fahren to go, to drive
Fahrrad (nt) bike, bicycle
Fall (m) case
fallen to fall
Familie (f) family
Fan (m) fan, supporter
Fanatiker (m) fanatic, endie Aktithusiast
Fantasiefilm (m) fantasy film
fantastisch fantastic
Farbe (f) colour
fast almost
Fastfood (nt) fast food
faszinierend fascinating
faul lazy
faulenzen to laze about
Februar February
feiern to celebrate
Feiertag (m) holiday, celebration day
Feld (nt) field
Fenster (nt) window
Ferien (pl) holidays, school break
fernsehen to watch TV
fertig ready, finished
fest fixed
Fest (nt) festival, celebration
Feuer (nt) fire
Feuerwerk (nt) firework
Figur (f) figure
Film (m) film

Glossary

finden to find
Firma (f) firm
Fisch (m) fish
Fitness-Studio (nt) gym
Flasche (f) bottle
Fleisch (nt) meat
fleißig hardworking, diligent
fliegen to fly
fließend fluent, fluently
Flüchtling (m) refugee
Flug (m) flight
Flughafen (m) airport
Fluss (m) river
Folge (f) consequence
fördern to promote
Fortschritt (m) progress
Foto (nt) photo, photograph
Fotograf (m), Fotografin (f) photographer
Frage (f) question
Französisch (nt) French
Frau (f) woman, wife
frei free
Freiheit (f) freedom
Freitag Friday
freitags on Fridays
Freiwasserschwimmen (nt) wild swimming
Freizeit (f) free time
Fremdsprachen (pl) foreign languages
Freund (m) friend, boyfriend
Freund*in (nt), Freund*innen (pl) friend, friends (gender neutral)
sich freuen auf to look forward to
Freundin (f) friend, girlfriend
freundlich friendly
Freundschaft (f) friendship
frisch fresh
früher earlier
sich fühlen to feel
Frühling (m) Spring
Frühstück (nt) breakfast
führen to lead
fünfzehn fifteen
funktionieren to function, to work
für for
furchtbar terrible
Fußball (m) football
Fußball spielen to play football

Gans (f) goose
ganz whole, all the, quite
gar nicht not at all
Garten (m) garden
Gast (m) guest
Gebäude (nt) building, buildings
geben to give
geboren born
Geburtstag (m) birthday
Gedicht (nt) poem
geduldig patient, patiently
Gefahr (f) danger, risk
gefährlich dangerous
gefallen to please
Gefühl (nt) feeling
gegen against
gegenüber opposite
gehen to go
gehören zu to belong to
Geige (f) violin
gelb yellow
Geld (nt) money
Gelegenheit (f) opportunity
gemein mean
gemeinsam in common
Gemüse (nt) vegetables
genannt called
genau exact, exactly
Generation (f) generation
genießen to enjoy
genug enough
gern(e) gladly, (with a verb) like to
gesamt whole, entire
Gesamtschule (f) comprehensive school
Geschäft (nt) business, shop
Geschenk (nt) present
Geschichte (f) story, history
geschieden divorced
Geschwindigkeit (f) speed
Geschwister (pl) siblings, brothers and sisters
Gesellschaft (f) society
Gesicht (nt) face
Gespräch (nt) conversation
gestern yesterday
gesund healthy
Gesundheit (f) health
getrennt separated
Gewalt (f) violence, force

gewinnen to win
glänzen to shine, to glitter
Glas (m) glas
glauben to believe
Gleichberechtigung (f) equal rights
Gleitflieger (m), Gleitfliegerin (f) glider pilot
globalisiert globalised
Glück (nt) luck, good fortune, happiness
glücklich happy
Grad (nt) degree (temperature)
grau grey
griechisch Greek
groß big, tall
großzügig generous
grün green
Grund (m) reason
Grundschule (f) primary school
Gruppe (f) group
gruselig gruesome
Grüß dich! Greetings! Hello!
gucken to look, to watch
Gummibärchen (nt) gummy bear
günstig cheap, favourable
gut good, well
gut bezahlt well paid
gute / schlechte Laune haben (to) be in a good / bad mood | being in a good / bad mood
gute Laune machen to put in a good mood
Gymnasium (nt) grammar school
Gymnastik (f) gymnastics
Haare (pl) hair
hacken to hack
Hähnchen (nt) chicken
halb half
halten to stop, to hold
Hand (f) hand
handeln von to be about
Händewaschen (nt) handwashing
Handy (nt) mobile phone
hart hard
Hauptschule (f) secondary school
Hauptstadt (f) capital city
Haus (nt) house

Hausaufgaben (pl) homework
Haushalt (m) household
Haustier (nt) pet
heilig holy
Heimat (f) home, native country
heiraten to marry
heißen to be called
helfen to help
Helm (m) helmet
Herausforderung (f) challenge
Herbst autumn
Herz (nt) heart
heute today
heute Morgen this morning
heutig current
Hexe (f) witch
hier here
Hilfe (f) help
hilfsbereit helpful
himmlisch heavenly
hinter behind
Hintergrund (m) background
historisch historic
Hobby (nt) hobby
hoch high
hochladen to upload
Hochzeit (f) wedding
hoffen to hope
hoffentlich hopefully
hold dear, sweet, fair
Honig (m) honey
hören to hear, to listen to
Horrorfilm (m) horror film
Hotel (nt) hotel
hübsch pretty
Hintergrund (m) background
ich möchte I would like
ideal ideal
Idee (f) idea
im Freien in the open air
im Moment at the moment
im Vergleich zu in comparison to
Imbiss (m) snack, snack bar
immer always
immer mehr more and more
immer noch still
in den 80er Jahren in the eighties
in der Nähe near, in the vicinity
in der Nähe von near to

hundertdreiundachtzig

Glossary

in Form bleiben to keep fit
in letzter Zeit recently
in Ordnung in order, all right
Indien India
Industrie (f) industry
Informatiker (m), Informatikerin (f) computer scientist
Information (f) information
informieren to inform
Insel (f) island
insgesamt in all, altogether, in total
intelligent intelligent
Intensität (f) intensity
interessant interesting
Interesse (f) interest
sich interessieren für to be interested in
international international
Internet (nt) internet
inzwischen in the meantime
Italien Italy
Jahr (nt) year
.. Jahre alt ... years old
Januar January
japanisch Japanese
je nach depending on
jeden Tag every day
jeder everyone
jedes Wochenende every weekend
jedoch however
jemand someone
jetzt now
Job (m) job
joggen to jog
Joghurt (m or n) yoghurt
Journalismus (m) journalism
Journalist (m), Journalistin (f) journalist
Jugendliche (f) young person, adolescent
Juli July
jung young
Junge (m) boy
jünger als younger than
Juni June
Jura (m) law
Kaffee (m) coffee
Kaffeefilter (m) coffee filter
Kalender (m) calander
kalt cold

Kamera (f) camera
kämpfen to fight
Kanal (m) channel (TV), canal
Kantine (f) canteen
Kanzler (m), Kanzlerin (f) chancellor
Kapitän (m) captain
kaputt broken, ruined
Karneval (m) Carnival
Karriere (f) career
Karte (f) ticket, card
Kartoffeln (pl) potatoes
Käse (m) cheese
Käsebrot (nt) bread and cheese
Katze (f) cat
kaufen to buy
Kaugummi (m or nt) chewing gum
kaum hardly
kein no, not any
Keks (m) biscuit
Keller (m) cellar
Kellner (m), Kellnerin (f) waiter, waitress
kennen to know (people)
kennenlernen to get to know
Kenntnis (f) knowledge
Kilo (nt) kilo
Kilometer (m) kilometre
Kind (nt) child
kindisch childish
Kino (nt) cinema
Kirche (f) church
Klasse (f) class
klassisch classical
Klavier piano
Kleidung (f) clothes, clothing
klein small, short
Kleinigkeit (f) minor thing, trivial matter
klettern to climb
Klettern (nt) climbing
Klima (nt) climate
Klimawandel (m) climate change
klingen to sound
Knabe (m) boy
kochen to cook
Kollege (m), Kollegin (f) colleague
komisch funny
kommunizieren to communicate

Komödie (f) comedy
können can, to be able to
Kontakt (m) contact
Kontaktlinse (f) contact lens
Konzentration (f) concentration
Konzert (nt) concert
kosten to cost
Kostüm (nt) costume
Kraft (f) strength, power
krank ill
Krankenhaus (nt) hospital
kreativ creative
Krieg (m) war
Krimi (m) crime drama, thriller
Kritik (f) criticism, review
Küche (f) kitchen
Kuchen (m) cake
Kultur (f) culture
kulturell cultural
sich kümmern um to take care of, to concern ourselves about
Kunde (m), Kundin (f) customer
Kunst (f) art
Künstler (m), Künstlerin (f) artist
Kurs (m) course
kurz short
kurz vor shortly before
Küste (f) coast
Kutur (f) culture
lachen to laugh
Land (nt) country, countryside
Landschaft (f) landscape
lang long
langfristig long-term
langsam slow, slowly
langweilig boring
Laptop (m) laptop
Lärm (m) noise
laufen to run
laut loud, noisy
leben to live
Leben (nt) life
Lebensmittel (pl) food, foodstuffs, groceries
Lebenspartnerschaft (f), zivile Partnerschaft (f) civil partnership
Lebensstil (m) lifestyle
Lebensweise (f) way of life
lecker delicious

ledig single
Lehrer (m), Lehrerin (f) teacher
leicht light, easy, easily
leiden to suffer, to stand, to bear
leider unfortunately
leisten to perform, to achieve
sich leisten to perform, to achieve
Leistung (f) achievement
lernen to learn
lesen to read
Lesen (nt) reading
letzte Woche last week
Licht (nt) light
lieb kind
lieben to love
lieber more gladly, rather
Liebesfilm (m) romance film
lieblings- favourite
Lieblingsfach (nt) favourite subject
Lied (nt) song
Lied (nt) song
liegen to lie
lila purple
Linie (f) line, route (e.g. bus)
links left, on the left
Liste (f) list
Liter (m or nt) litre
Liter (m) litre
lockig curly
Lokal (nt) inn, restautant, bar, meeting place
lösen to solve, to loosen
Lösung (f) solution
Luft (f) air
Luftballon (m) balloon
Lust (f) desire
lustig fun, funny, enjoyable
machen to make, to do
Mädchen (nt) girl
Mahlzeit (f) meal
Mai May
malen to paint
manchmal sometimes
mangelhaft poor
Mann (m) man, husband
Mannschaft (f) team
Manuskript (nt) manuscript
Marke (f) brand
Markplatz (m) market square

Glossary

März March
Maschine (f) machine
Mathe (f) maths
Medaille (f) medal
Medien (pl) (the) media
Meer (nt) sea, ocean
mehr more
Mehrheit (f) majority
mehrsprachig multilingual
Mehrsprachigkeit (f) multilingualism
mein my
meinen to mean
meiner Meinung nach in my opinion
Meinung (f) opinion
meiste most
meistens mostly
Meisterschaft (f) championship
meistgesprochen most spoken
Melodie (f) melody
Mensch (m) person, human being
mental mental
Meteorologie (f) meteorology
Meter (m) metre
Methode (f) method
mich me, myself (direct object pronoun)
Migrant (m), Migrantin (f) migrant
Migration (f) migration
Milch (f) milk
mindestens at least
Minute (f) minute
mir to me, me (indirect obj)
mir ist schlecht I feel sick
mit with
mit dem Auto by car
mit dem Bus by bus
mit dem Flugzeug by plane
mit dem Zug by train
mit der Straßenbahn by tram
mit der U-Bahn by underground
mit wem with whom
miteinander with each other
miterleben to experience, to live through
Mitglied (nt) member
mitkommen to come with
mitmachen to join in
mitsingen to sing along

mittags at midday
Mittagspause (f) lunch break
Mitte (f) middle
mittel (mittlere) medium
Mitternacht (f) midnight
mittwochs on Wednesdays
Mobbing (nt) bullying
modern modern
mögen to like
möglich possible
Möglichkeit (f) possibility
Monat (m) month
Mond (m) moon
montags on Mondays
morgen tomorrow
Morgen (m) morning
morgens in the morning
Moschee (f) mosque
müde tired
Müll (m) rubbish, waste
Museum (nt) museum
Musik (f) music
musikalisch musical
müssen must, to have to
mutig courageous
Mutter (f) mother
Mutti (f) Mum, Mummy
Mütze (f) hat
nach Hause gehen to go home
Nachbar (m), Nachbarin (f) neighbour
Nachmittag (m) afternoon
nachmittags in the afternoons
Nachricht (f) news, message
nächst- next
nächstes Jahr next year
Nacht (f) night
Nachteil (m) disadvantage
Nachtisch (m) pudding, dessert
nahe close to
Nähe (f) vicinity
Name (m) name
national national
Natur (f) nature
natürlich natural, naturally, of course
Naturwissenschaften (pl) natural sciences
neben next to
Nebenjob (m) extra job, side job

nerven to annoy, to irritate
nervös nervous
nett nice
Netz (nt) net, network
neu new
Neujahr (nt) New Year
neulich recently
neunzehn nineteen
nicht der Fall not the case
nicht weit von not far from
nichts nothing
nichts Besonderes nothing special, nothing particular
nie never
nieder down,
niedlich cute
niemand no one
noch still, yet
normalerweise normally, usually
Note (f) mark, grade
Noten (pl) marks/grades
nötig necessary
November November
nur only
Nuss (f) nut
nutzen to use
nützlich useful
Oberschule (f) grammar school
Obst (nt) fruit
obwohl although
öffentlich public, publicly
öffentliche Verkehrsmittel (nt) public transport
(in der) Öffentlichkeit (f) (in) public
oft often
ohne without
Oktober October
Oktoberfest (nt) Munich beer festival
Olympiade (f) Olympics
Oma (f) grandma
Onkel (m) uncle
Opa (m) grandpa
Orchester (nt) orchestra
Organisation (f) organisation
organisieren to organise
Ort (m) place, town, location
Österreich Austria
österreichisch Austrian
Paar (nt) pair, couple

Paket (nt) package
Pandemie (f) pandemic
Papier (nt) paper
Park (m) park
Partei (f) (political) party
Partner (m), Partnerin (f) partner
Partnerschaft (f) partnership
Party (f) party
Pause (f) break
Pension (f) guest house
perfekt perfect
Person (f) person
persönlich personal, personally
Pfarrer (m), Pfarrerin (f) vicar
Pfleger (m), Pflegerin (f) carer, keeper
Philosoph (m) philosopher
Physik (f) physics
Physiker (m), Physikerin (f) physicist
Pizza (f) pizza
Plastik (nt) plastic
Platz (m) space, room, square
plötzlich suddenly
Politik (f) politics
Politiker (m), Politikerin (f) politician
Polizei (fl police
Polizist (m), Polizistin (f) police officer
polnisch Polish
Pommes (pl) chips, fries
Popmusik (f) pop music
populär popular
Portion (f) portion
positiv positive
Post (f) post, mail, post office
Potenzial (nt) potential
Preis (m) price, prize
privat private
Privatleben (nt) private life
Privatleben (nt) private life
pro per
Problem (nt) problem
produzieren to produce
Profi- professional
profitabel profitable
Programm (nt) program (IT), channel (TV)
Projekt (nt) project
Prüfung (f) exam

hundertfünfundachtzig

Glossary

Publikum (nt) audience, the public
Pullover (m) pullover
Pulver (nt) powder
pünktlich punctual, in/on time
Puppe (f) doll
putzen to clean
Pyramide (f) pyramid
Qualität (f) quality
Rad fahren to cycle, to go by bike
Radio (nt) radio
Rap (m) rap (music)
Rassismus (m) racism
Rauchen (nt) smoking
realistisch realistic, realistically
Realität (f) reality
Rechnung (f) bill
Recht (nt) right, law
rechts right, on the right
recyceln to recycle
reden to talk
Regel (f) rule
regelmäßig regular, regularly
Region (f) region
Regisseur (m), Regisseurin (f) director
regnen to rain
reich rich
Reis (m) rice
Reise (f) journey, trip
Reisebüro (nt) travel agency
Religion (f) relignion, religious studies
Restaurant (nt) restaurant
retten to save, to rescue
Revolution (f) revolution
Rezeption (f) reception
richtig right, correct
riskant risky
Rock (m) skirt, rock music
Rolle (f) role
Rollstuhl (m) wheelchair
Roman (m) novel
Romanze (f) romance
rot red
Rotkohl (m) red cabbage
Ruhe (f) peace, calm
ruhig calm, quiet
Ruhm (m) fame
rumänisch Romanian
russisch Russian

Sache (f) thing, matter
sagen to say
Salat (m) salad
sammeln to collect
samstags on Saturdays
sanft gentle
Sänger (m), Sängerin (f) singer
sauber clean
Sauerstoff (m) oxygen
schade a shame
schaffen to create
scharf spicy, sharp, hot
Schauspieler (m), Schauspielerin (f) actor
scheinen to shine, to seem
schenken to give as a present
schicken to send
schießen to shoot
Schiff (nt) ship, boat
Schiffahrt (f) boat trip
Schlaf (m) sleep
schlafen to sleep
schlank slim, thin
schlecht bad
schließlich finally, eventually
schlimm terrible
Schlimmste (nt) (the) worst
Schloss (nt) castle
Schlüssel (m) key
schmecken to taste
schmutzig dirty
Schnee (m) snow
schneien to snow
schnell fast, quick, quickly
Schock (nt) shock
Schokolade (f) chocolate
Schokolade (f) chocolate
schon already
schön beautiful
schrecklich terrible
schreiben to write
Schritt (m) step
Schularbeit (f) schoolwork
Schuld (f) blame, fault
Schule (f) school
schulen to school, to train, to educate
Schüler (m), Schülerin (f) student, pupil
Schulgebäude (nt) school building

Schulgelände (nt) school grounds
Schultag (m) school day
Schutz (m) protection
schützen to protect
schwarz black
Schwarzwald (m) Black Forest
Schwester (f) sister
schwierig difficult
Schwimmbad (nt) swimming baths
schwimmen to swim
Schwimmen (nt) swimming
sechzehn sixteen
See (m or f) sea if feminine, lake if masculine
sehen to see
Sehenswürdigkeit (f) sights, things worth seeing
sehr very
Seifenoper (f) soap opera
sein to be
seit since, for
seit … Jahren for … years
seitdem since then, since
Sekunde (f) second
selten rare, rarely
Sendung (f) programme
September September
sich himself / herself / yourself (formal) / themselves (direct object pronoun)
sicher safe, secure, certain, sure
Sicherheit (f) safety, security
siebzehn seventeen
Sieg (m) victory
Silvester (m or nt) New Year's Eve
simsen to text
singen to sing
sitzen to sit
Skateboarden (nt) skateboarding
Snowboarden (nt) snowboarding
sofort immediately, straight away
sogar even
Sohn (m) son
solange as long as
Soldat (m) soldier
sollen should
Sommer (m) summer

sondern (but) rather
Sonne (f) sun
Sonnenenergie (f) solar power
sonnig sunny
sonntags on Sundays
sonst otherwise, else
Sorge (f) worry, care
Soundtrack (m) soundtrack
sowohl both … and
sozial social
Spanien Spain
spannend exciting
Spannung (f) tension
sparen to save
Spaß machen to be fun
spät late
später later
spazieren gehen to go for a walk
Speisekarte (f) menu
Spektakel (nt) spectacle
spenden to donate
Spezialeffekt (m) special effects
Spiel (nt) game, match
spielen to play
Spieler (m), Spielerin (f) player
Sport (m) sport, PE
Sportler (m), Sportlerin (f) sportsperson
sportlich sporty
Sprache (f) language
sprechen to speak
springen to jump
Stadion (nt) stadium
Stadt (f) town
Stadtmitte (f) town centre
Staffel (f) season, series
stammen aus to come from
stark strong, strongly
statt instead of
stattfinden to take place
Stau (m) traffic jam
stehen to stand
stehlen to steal
steigen to rise, to increase, to climb
Stelle (f) place, job
stellen to place, to put
sterben to die
Stern (m) star
stief- step-

Glossary

Stiefel (m) boot
stimmen to be correct
stören to disturb
Strand (m) beach
Straße (f) street
streamen to stream
Streit (m) argument, fight
streiten to quarrel, to argue
streng strict
Stress (m) stress
stressig stressful
studieren to study
Studium (nt) study, studies
Stuhl (m) chair
Stunde (f) hour, lesson
stundenlang for hours
Stundenplan (m) timetable
suchen to seek, to look for
süchtig addicted
Supermarkt (m) supermarket
surfen to surf
süß sweet
Süßigkeit (f) sweet
sympathisch kind
Synagoge (f) synagogue
Syrien Syria
System (nt) system
Tablet (nt) tablet (computer)
Tag (m) day
Tagung (f) conference, session
talentiert talented
talentiert talented
Tante (f) aunt
tanzen to dance
Tasche (f) pocket, bag
Tasse (f) cup
tauchen to dive
tausend a thousand
Team (nt) team
Technik (f) technology, technique
Technologie (f) technology
Tee (m) tea
teilen to share
teilnehmen to take part
Teilnehmer (m), Teilnehmerin (f) participant
Temperatur (f) temperature
Tennis (nt) tennis
teuer expensive
Text (m) text, lyric

Theater (nt) theatre
Thema (nt) theme
tief deep
Tieftauchen (nt) deep diving
Tier (nt) animal
Tierheim (nt) animal refuge
Tiernährnung (f) animal feed
Tisch (m) table
Titel (m) title
Toastbrot (nt) toast
Tochter (f) daughter
Toilette (f) toilet
toll great
Ton (m) sound, tone
Tor (nt) gate, gateway, goal
total total, totally, completely
Tourismus (m) tourism
Tradition (f) tradition
traditionell traditional, traditionally
tragen to wear
Trainer (m) trainer
trainieren to train
Training (nt) training
Trainingslager (nt) training camp
Traum (m) dream
traurig sad
treffen to meet
treiben to do (e.g. sport), to drive, to pursue
Treppe (f) flight of stairs
trinken to drink
trotz despite
Tschüß! Bye!
tun to do
Tür (f) door
türkisch Turkish
Tüte (f) bag
üben to practise
über about, above, over
überglücklich delighted, beyond happy
überlegen to consider
übernachten to spend the night
übernehmen to take over
überraschen to surprise
überwinden to overcome
überzeugend convincing
um ... Uhr at ... o'clock
um ... zu ... in order to ...

um sich herum around themselves
Umschlag (m) envelope
umsteigen to change (transport)
Umwelt (f) environment
umweltfreundlich environmentally friendly
umziehen to move (house, location)
Umzug (m) procession, parade
unbedingt absolutely
und and
Unfall (m) accident
ungeduldig impatient
ungefähr about, approximately
ungenügend inadequate, unsatisfactory
Ungerechtigkeit (f) injustice
unglaublich unbelievable, unbelievably
Uni (f) uni, university
Universität (f) university
unmöglich impossible
uns us, ourselves (direct object pronoun)
unterhalten to entertain
Unternehmen (nt) company
Unterricht (m) lessons, classes, teaching
unterrichten to teach
Unterschied (m) difference
unterwegs on the way
unvergesslich unforgettable
Urlaub (m) holiday
Valentinstag (m) Valentine's Day
Vater (m) father
Vati (m) Dad, Daddy
Vegetarier (m), Vegetarierin (f) vegetarian
verändern to change
Veranstaltung (f) event
verantwortlich responsible
Verantwortung (f) responsibility
Verband (m) association
verbessern to improve
verbringen to spend (time)
verdienen to earn
Verein (m) association, club
Vergangenheit (f) past
vergessen to forget

verheiratet married
Verkehr (m) traffic
sich verkleiden to dress up, to wear fancy dress
verlassen to leave
verletzen to injure
verlieren to lose
verlobt engaged
Verlobte (m or f) fiancé(e)
vermeiden to avoid
veröffentlichen to publish, to release
verrückt mad
verschmutzen to pollute
Verschmutzung (f) pollution
verschwenden to waste
verschwinden to disappear
Verspätung (f) delay
versprechen to promise
verstehen to understand
sich verstehen mit to get on with
versuchen to try
verursachen to cause
Video (nt) video
viel a lot
viele a lot, many
Vielfalt (f) variety
vielleicht perhaps
Viertel (nt) quarter
vierzig forty
virtuell virtual
Vogel (m) bird
vollzeit full time
vollziehen to complete
vor in front of
vor einem Jahr a year ago
vorbereiten to prepare
Vorbild (nt) role model
vorsichtig careful
sich vorstellen to imagine
Vorstellungsgespräch (nt) job interview
Vorteil (m) advantage
wachen to wake
während during
Wahrheit (f) truth
wahrscheinlich probable, probably
Wald (m) forest, wood
Wand (m) wall

Glossary

wandern to go for a walk, to hike
wann when
warm warm
warten auf to wait for
warum why
was what
sich waschen to wash (oneself)
Wasser (nt) water
Wasserfall (m) waterfall
Wasserpark (m) water park
Weg (m) path, way
wegen beause of, due to
wegwerfen to throw away
Weihnachten (nt) Christmas
weihnachtlich festive
Weihnachtsmarkt (m) Christmas market
weil because
weit far
weiter further
weiterhin furthermore, on top of that
Welt (f) world
wenig little
weniger als less than
wenn if, when, whenever
wer who
werden to become
Wettbewerb (m) competition
Wetter (nt) weather
wichtig important
wie how
wieder again
Wiedervereinigung (f) reunification
willkommen welcome
Wirkung (f) effect
Wirtschaft (f) economics, economy
wissen to know
Wissenschaftler (m), Wissenschaftlerin (f) scientist
witzig funny
WLAN (nt) wifi
wo where
Woche (f) week
Wochenende (nt) weekend
wohnen to live
Wohnung (f) flat, appartment
Wohnzimmer (nt) living room
Wolke (f) cloud

wollen to want
Wort (nt) word
wunderbar wonderful
Wurst (f) sausage
Wüste (f) desert
Zeichentrickfilm (m) cartoon
zeigen to show
Zeit (f) time
Zeitung (f) newspaper
Zentrum (nt) centre
zerstören to destroy
ziehen to move, to pull
ziehen nach to move to
Ziel (nt) goal
ziemlich quite
Zimmer (nt) room
zu Ende finished, at the end
zu Fuß gehen to go on foot, to walk
zu Hause at home
zuerst first of all
zufrieden happy, content
Zufriedenheit (f) contentment
zugänglich available
Zukunft (f) future
zuletzt in the end
zum Beispiel for example
(jdn) zum Lachen bringen to make (sb) laugh
zurück back
zurück back
zurücktreten to resign, to step back
zusammen together
zuschauen to watch
Zuschauer (m) viewer, spectator
Zusteller (m), Zustellerin (f) delivery agent
Zutaten (pl) ingredients
Zweck (m) purpose
zweimal two times, twice
zweistündig two-hour
Zwillinge (pl) twins
zwischen between
zwölf twelve